Football Grounds in Britain and Europe – Part One

By: Steve Wilson

ISBN: 978-1-291-82796-5

First Footing Volume 01
Steve Wilson

First Footing
Volume One
By: Steve Wilson

1970, wearing the tangerine polo-neck jumper that nearly led to trouble at places like Swindon

Introduction

Although never a great player of any particular game, I have been a "sports' spectator" for the majority of my life, with football being my major interest. From a very early beginning as an 'armchair' supporter to endless days on the terraces around Europe I have followed 'my teams', whether the competition be the World Cup, European Cup or just a meaningless pre-season friendly played in front of a handful of spectators. In my early days I would go and watch any game I could, including Charity matches at Stanley Park Arena, and local-league Cup finals played at Bloomfield. Not all of the experiences have been good ones - the most tragic, of course, being on a warm May evening in 1985 in Brussels when thirty-nine football supporters died as a result of the riot preceding the Liverpool versus Juventus European Cup final. That experience affected me deeply, and made me keep away from the game I used to worship for several years.

The intention of this book is to report on when I went to see a home game involving each of the club sides at all levels that I have visited, incorporating a copy of the match programme for the particular game along with any other memorabilia. Some clubs are included more than once because they have changed grounds and I have visited both locations. For other clubs, such as Port Vale, Sheffield Wednesday and Skelmersdale, I visited the ground to watch a neutral match, such as a cup semi-final, before I saw the host team in action there. Both the neutral match and the eventual visit to see the club's own home game are included in the records. My visit to see some teams, such as Kirkham and Wesham, ended up with my producing my own 'match programme', as they didn't have a publication for the game I went to, but in those instances an actual match programme from another of their home games is included.

Where possible I have taken photographs of the grounds, or included a match ticket or lottery ticket for the club, but I owe thanks to Rob Frowen for the loan of some of the tickets and match programmes that I have scanned in to add a touch of completeness to some of the clubs, to those clubs and individuals who have kindly emailed programme images to me to use in the same way (such as the 1923 Glentoran Supporters Committee, who produce the Glentoran programme), and finally to web-site editors such as Stewart Walker (www.footballgrounds.freeserve.co.uk) and Craig Patton (www.footballgroundswebsite.co.uk) for kindly giving me permission to use some of their photographs of stadia.

After visiting each of the ninety-two English and forty-two Scottish League grounds, I was featured on Duncan Adams' Internet Football Ground Guide website in the 'Done the Lot' section, at wysiwyg//main.2/http:/dspace.dial.pipex.com/town/park/yth45/done92.htm

Introduction

© Copyright Duncan Adams 1998-2001

This section is dedicated to those Football Fans who have visited all the grounds in their particular League. So if you have visited all 92 Premier & Football League grounds in England & Wales, all 42 in Scotland, or all of the Football Conference, League of Wales etc... then this is the place where you can in some way celebrate your achievement.

Plus it gives others who are contemplating visiting all of the grounds and those that are already on their way to completing them, some inspiration and practical advice. Therefore if you have recently completed the 92 or any of the other Leagues, or are about to and you would like to also be featured in this section, then please e-mail me.

Steve Wilson recently completed the 92 Premier & Football League grounds in England & Wales & the 42 in Scotland and you can read about his experiences below. To read about other fans who have previously featured in this section (all of whom have done the 92) then just click on their name below;

Daniel Musson from Luton
Richard Wells from Leicester
Steve Curwood from Blackpool
Barry Sear from London
David Denton from Chesterfield
Peter Holdridge from Leicester
Duncan Adams (author of this site) from Birmingham.
Eric Van Dorp from the Netherlands.
Mark Osborne from Swindon.

Name: **Steve Wilson**

Age: **48**

Team Supported: **Blackpool, although I did have a fifteen year spell following Liverpool in the 70's and 80's**

First League Ground Visited & When:

Bloomfield Road, Blackpool v Tottenham, September 8th 1962

Last Ground Visited to complete the 92:

St James Park Exeter, Exeter v Blackpool

Date Completed: **March 31st 2001**

How Long Has It Taken You To Visit All 92?

Over 30 years, but I only decided to complete the 'set' just over two years ago when I realised I had been to some 50 English grounds. I also decided at that time to include

Introduction

Scottish teams as well, and completed my visits there on Saturday May 5th when I saw Dundee play Kilmarnock.

Best Ground visited (& why).

In England, probably Pride Park at Derby, which was one of the first of the 'new' grounds I went to. Even though there were only 20,000 there for a Worthington Cup tie against Swansea, there was an excellent atmosphere. In Scotland, Hampden, Ibrox and Parkhead are all totally different but equally impressive, and despite the modernisation at Ibrox and Parkhead you still get that impression of tradition at the grounds.

Poorest Ground Visited:

Probably Macclesfield's Moss Rose ground, though since I visited it in 1998 I believe a new stand has been built.

Best experience on your travels:

Probably way back in April 1970 when Blackpool won 3-0 at Preston to clinch promotion to the old first division and at the same time relegate Preston. There were well over 30,000 in Deepdale, and
Blackpool filled all four sides of the ground. It's a pity we couldn't hold on to those fans.

Steve At Exeter:

Worst experience on your travels:

Although most away games in the trouble-filled 70's and 80's were bad, nothing compares to what I witnessed at the Heysel in 1985. I didn't go to another game anywhere for five years after that.

Funniest experience on your travels:

Not funny at the time, but driving to London last September to see Romford play Hemel Hempstead in an FA Cup qualifying match. I had been interested in Romford for some reason since I was at school, so I checked on the Ryman League web site and chose that match to see them. When I got to the ground twenty minutes before scheduled kick-off it was empty - I found out that the game had been switched to Hemel and was being played on the Monday night! I had no alternative but to drive the 200 miles back home again.

Most Goals Seen In One Match:

Excluding testimonial matches, 11 - Liverpool 11 Stromgodset 0 in the Cup Winners Cup in

1974, and Liverpool 10 Oulu Palloseura 1 in the European Cup in 1980. I did see 13 in one day, though, going to Liverpool 4 Chelsea 3 in the morning and then getting back to Blackpool in time for their 3-3 draw with Torquay (May 1985).

Best Goal Seen:

A Kenny Dalglish goal for Liverpool at Birmingham in the 1980-81 season was stunning, from Ray Clemence to the back of the net in five seconds and four first time passes, ending with a superb volley from Kenny

Best Match Attended:

Difficult to choose as I've seen close to 1,200 now. Probably a tie between two games played in 1970 - my first game at Anfield, when Liverpool beat Everton 3-2 after being 0-2 down, and an FA Cup tie at Blackpool when we beat Arsenal 3-2, again after being 0-2 down.

Stupidest Chant Heard:

During the fuel crisis I went to see Oldham play at the magnificent Madejski stadium in Reading. There were about 50 Oldham fans there, and they chanted "Sh*t ground, no fans". But Reading had the perfect response when they scored twice in the first five minutes, and chanted "What a waste of petrol" at the Oldham fans.

Any tips for those attending to visit the 92?

Pre-season fixtures can be ideal for getting to a lot of grounds in a short time. Last July, I spent 12 days in North-East Scotland and saw 13 games. Also, don't always believe what you see on the Internet. I checked on the Cheltenham web site before going to see their Sunday lunchtime game against Swansea in February 2000. The site had a page for all-ticket matches, which I checked, and there was no mention of this game being all-ticket. When I got to the ground, I was told it WAS all-ticket and no tickets were available on the day. Fortunately, I was able to convince officials that I wasn't a trouble maker and was able to get in. So if in doubt ring the club beforehand.

Top Of Page

Return To The Main Menu

Contents – Volume I

1. **Blackpool** v Tottenham Hotspur

Played at **Bloomfield Road** on 8th September 1962

Football League Division One

Blackpool (1)1 [Green]
Tottenham (0)2 [Allen, Norman]

Attendance 31,773

8

1 Blackpool – Bloomfield Road

The first time I remember taking an interest in football at all was when the 1961 FA Cup Final, between Tottenham Hotspur and Leicester City, was on television. My mother wanted Tottenham to win and become the first side this century to complete the League and FA Cup double, and she was very keen on their captain, Northern Ireland international Danny Blanchflower. Her enthusiasm must have transferred itself to me as I watched the televised game avidly. Spurs won the game 2-0, with Smith and Dyson scoring in the second half. I remember Spurs had a goal disallowed for offside while the match was still goalless. My mother showed that she didn't really know much about the rules of football by saying that it shouldn't have been disallowed if the Leicester player was too slow to be able to get back to make the attackers on-side!

That started me off supporting Tottenham, as they featured on many occasions on the television over the next few years. I relished reading all about them in the football book that I received for Christmas 1961, and rejoiced as they retained the FA Cup a year later when they defeated Burnley 3-1 at Wembley, with Jimmy Greaves amongst the goalscorers. That season they were also covered on television with highlights of their European Cup ties, culminating in a valiant bid to overcome Benfica in the European Cup semi-final at White Hart Lane, winning 2-1 on the night but losing 4-3 on aggregate. That evening brought the famous Spurs song of "Glory, Glory Alleluia, As The Spurs Go Marching On" into the homes of millions.

I went to my first 'live' football matches with Robert Frowen (who became Blackpool's 'Cable Cat' mascot more than thirty years later) and his father. The games were a couple of schools' matches at Bloomfield Road, Blackpool losing 2-1 to Bristol (after being 1-0 ahead) and then losing 7-1 to Liverpool. I wanted to move on to the 'real' thing, though, so when the fixtures for the 1962-63 season were published, I decided that I would try to go and see Tottenham play at Blackpool. It was also a very appropriate first live match, for as well as Spurs being the side I first saw on television, when I was less than two months old I had apparently 'listened' in my pram as Blackpool beat Bolton 4-3 to win the 1953 'Matthews' FA Cup Final, with Stan Mortensen scoring a hat trick and Bill Perry netting the winning goal in the last minute. Moreover, the day after I was born in Blackpool, the home team beat Tottenham 2-0 at Bloomfield Road in a First Division match, Mudie and Perry scoring in front of almost 27,000 spectators.

The Blackpool versus Tottenham game was scheduled for September 1962. I somehow persuaded my parents to let me go to this game with my sister Patricia (she was fifteen, I was nine and a half). Like all children, the wait to me seemed more like years than just a couple of months, but eventually the big day, Saturday September 8th 1962, arrived, and off we went to the game. We went in the East Paddock, and were part of a crowd of 31,773 - quite a normal attendance for Blackpool home games at the time - and waited for kick-off time to arrive. As the crowd grew, the terracing became more and more congested, and I cried as I realised I couldn't see anything. Pat tried to help, but eventually one of the men in the crowd put me on the shoulders to watch and my happiness was restored. The game itself was very exciting, with Blackpool 1-0 ahead at half-time through what I believed was a Johnny Green goal, which he rolled in from the edge of the box – the official match report, though, credited Ray Charnley with the goal. Tottenham, challenging at the top of the table, fought back and seemed certain to equalise when they were given a late penalty. Blanchflower took it, but Tony Waiters saved the shot, and he also saved the rebound, but at the cost of a kick to the head that left him dazed. Tottenham took full advantage of this, with Les Allen in the eighty-fourth minute and Maurice Norman in the eighty-sixth scoring the goals which gave them a slightly lucky win, and sent me home extremely happy.

Blackpool had been in the First Division since just before the Second World War, and were leading the league with three wins out of three when war on Germany was declared. Due to the fact that many servicemen were stationed at the seaside during the conflict, Blackpool became a force in war-time football as they were able to call on players of the calibre of Stanley Matthews and Jock Dodds. In 1943, they won the Northern War Cup by defeating Sheffield Wednesday 4-3 on aggregate, setting up an all-England champions eliminator against Arsenal at Chelsea. Despite being the underdogs, Blackpool came back from two goals down to lift the title with a 4-2 triumph. They managed to continue this vein of achievement when normality resumed after 1945, regularly finishing in the top half of the First Division, their best achievement being runners-up to Manchester United in 1955-56. Although they eventually finished eleven points behind United, they were still title contenders when they visited Old Trafford with three games to go. Dave Durie, later to become my Sunday School teacher, put 'Pool ahead, but United came back to win 2-1 and clinch the title. Had Blackpool held on to their lead, it's possible that the Seasiders would have become England's first representatives in the European Cup instead of Busby's side. It was Wembley, though, that most people thought of when the name Blackpool was mentioned, and after defeats in 1948 and 1951, they at last lifted the trophy in that 1953 final.

Blackpool's record victory came during the war year, with a 15-3 triumph over Tranmere Rovers, Dodds scoring seven of the goals. A week later, the record winning margin was recorded as Burnley were trounced 13-0. In peacetime football, Charlton were defeated 8-4 in a First Division game in 1952, but the record margin of victory came with a 7-0 First Division hammering of Sunderland in 1957. The record attendance of 38,098 against Wolverhampton was set in 1955, and Blackpool featured in the first ever Football League game to be televised 'live', against Bolton in 1960. In the 1990's, Blackpool made four consecutive appearances in the Lancashire Cup Final, winning the first three – with the 1-0 defeat of Manchester United the highlight of this run.

With the abolition of the maximum wage, Blackpool found competing with the spending ability of the big city clubs an impossibility, and after a League Cup semi-final appearance in 1962, when they lost to Norwich by that familiar 4-3 aggregate score, they gradually slid out of the top flight of football clubs. They did, though, manage one more day of glory when in 1971 they won the Anglo-Italian Cup by defeating Bologna 2-1 on their own ground, John Craven and Mickey Burns scoring the goals that brought the silverware back to the seaside. Other than this moment of triumph, Blackpool rarely again made the domestic headlines during the rest of the century, although they began the new millennium by winning the LDV Vans final at Cardiff's Millennium Stadium in 2002 and 2004 and in 2010 they once again – if only briefly – reached the top flight.

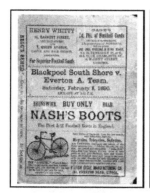

Everton'A' v Blackpool A
South Shore, 1890

England v Ireland 1932 –
souvenir

England v Ireland 1932

Football League v Irish League
1960

UEFA European Women's
Championships 2005 – group
stages at Blackpool

England U-21 v Northern
Ireland U-21 2012

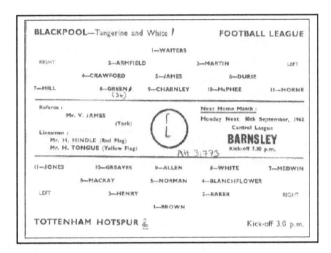

Centre pages from the match programme, Blackpool 'Club Call' card and a 'Golden Gamble' ticket

The match as reported in the Blackpool v Bradford City programme, February 22nd 2005 – with the Blackpool scorer given as Charnley.

A MATCH TO REMEMBER · 1962

Tottenham Hotspur were known as the "£350,000 team of professional footballers" when they visited Blackpool for the first match of the Illuminations period on 8 September 1962. And the tag was justified because for the first time for many a long day all tickets for the game were sold out in advance.

A match to remember.

The few remaining tickets on the day of the game had been sold early on the Saturday morning to Spurs' fans who had travelled overnight and who had formed a long queue outside the ticket office from nine o'clock in the morning.

Spurs had started the season well and had lost only one of five games with the other four being won, scoring 18 goals and conceding only seven in the process. And the London team were favourites to continue their run as they had not lost a game at Bloomfield Road for five years and had won five times at the ground since the War.

There were eight internationals in the Tottenham line-up that was Brown, Baker, Henry, Blanchflower, Norman, Mackay, Medwin, White, Allen, Greaves and Jones. Blackpool had to play its fourth successive game without regular centre half Roy Gratrix for whom the young Glyn James continued to replace in a side that was Waiters, Armfield, Martin, Crawford, James, Durie, Hill, Green, Charnley, McPhee and House.

The crowd swarmed into the ground and the terrace packers were informed by loudspeaker as to how best to accommodate spectators also, on a gloriously sunny afternoon, numbered 31,777.

Danny Blanchflower won the toss and Blackpool defended the Spion Kop goal in the full glare of the sun. But it was the south goal that was under pressure in the opening minutes as, within 60 seconds of the kick-off, Roy Charnley steered a long pass out to Horne whose centre cannoned back off Henry to the waiting Barrie Martin. The full back crossed the ball high for Green and Charnley laid in

attempt to head it goalwards but getting in each other's way, neither connected and the danger passed. A second raid immediately followed and this was only brought to a half when Henry upended Horne to concede a free kick that, unfortunately for Blackpool, came to nothing.

Blackpool continued to press and McPhee curled a shot just over the bar and then Crawford hit a shot wide from a pass rolled back to him by Green. And then, after fully six minutes, the Tottenham forwards made inroads into the Blackpool half. But on two occasions White found himself in a shooting position only to hit the ball firstly too high and then too wide. The next few minutes were then in the Spurs possession just as the opening had been in Blackpool's possession. Greaves, ever the goalpoacher, next ran on to a White pass only to shoot it wide of Waiters but also wide of the post. And he repeated the dose a minute later when he sidled into position almost unnoticed but sent his shot once again wide of the goal. Martin then beat a couple of players before losing control of the ball which fell kindly to Charnley but the centre forward shot wide and after 15 minutes the game was fairly even. Waiters than made a couple of mistakes that went unpunished. Firstly he punched out a shot which he should have caught and the ball was eventually scrambled behind for a corner and then he lost the ball in its flight, palmed it weakly out before Armfield came to the rescue by heading it clear from almost under the bar.

Blackpool then conceded two free kicks, one when Crawford sent Jones sprawling and another when McPhee halted Mackay which resulted in the Blackpool player going into referee Mr James' book. Both free kicks came to naught before Brown was forced into a full length save by a low shot from McPhee. And then, after 33 minutes, Blackpool took the lead. James cleared a Tottenham corner to McPhee who quickly switched the ball to his left wing partner Des Horne. The South African showed Baker a clean pair of heels and raced to the edge of the penalty box from where he had scored a magnificent goal against Nottingham Forest on the previous Monday evening. But this time he sliced his shot and it skidded across the goal where Charnley, almost tobogganing in, knocked it past the diving Brown's right hand as he was falling (pictured).

The crowd was in an uproar and almost missed Spurs' immediate counter-attack that ended with Mackay firing a fast shot straight at Waiters from 30 yards out. The half ended with the score unchanged but Blackpool having had to survive some fierce pressure from the Tottenham forwards for the final 10 minutes. This had, at least, given Glyn James the opportunity to show his mettle and he had played the best half he had played to that time in the First Division. Both sides could have scored in the opening minutes of the second half. Jones headed a cross down and towards goal but Waiters held the ball safely and then Horne crashed a shot into the side netting only to find the whistle had blown for off-side against him. The action thereafter was fast and furious and end-to-end; Henry hit a rising shot that Waiters held confidently, James cleared under pressure and then a White header sent Waiters falling on his knees to parry the ball and clear it.

At the other end Charnley raced clear only for his cross to be headed out for a corner and then a Crawford shot was beaten away by a diving Brown. And then it was Spurs who had a shot by Medwin cannon off Martin for a corner that was headed inches wide by centre half Norman with Waiters struggling to get to the ball. Fifteen minutes into the half and Blackpool had a remarkable escape when White's shot rebounded out from an unsuspecting defender and then his second shot beat Waiters only to hit another defender on the line with the ball eventually bouncing to safety. Two minutes later and Blackpool very nearly put the game beyond the reach of Spurs. Hill, seeming at first to dally too long on the ball, then found himself

some space and hit a stinging drive which glanced the cross bar as it flew high into the Kop. So fast and furious was the action that James had to go off for running repairs, as did Jones who returned with a bandage around his right foot.

And with 20 minutes remaining it was still a game to be won by either side; Waiters punched out a rising shot by Allen, Mackay beat Waiters with a scorching low drive only for Martin on the line to save the day for Blackpool. And then it was Blackpool's turn again as a low cross from Horne was just about to be stroked home by Charnley when Norman made a desperate challenge that diverted the ball wide. Then came more drama with just 15 minutes remaining. Spurs raided down the centre and Waiters, hesitating, dashed out and went sprawling as he palmed the ball away just inside the penalty area. The ball ran loose and Mackay took aim with Waiters still out of his goal. His fast, rising shot was destined for the net when out went Barrie Martin's arm to deflect the ball over the bar. It was an unquestionable penalty much to the jubilation of the Spurs players. Their excitement was, however, short-lived for Waiters saved Blanchflower's penalty kick as he dived low to his right. He could not hold the ball and it rolled out to White who was about to shoot it back in when Waiters threw himself at the forward's feet and beat the ball away.

Then six minutes from time Blackpool disappointingly gave away a simple goal. There was no imminent danger when Martin settled on the ball; he had all the time in the world to clear the ball but he preferred to pass it back to Waiters. Unfortunately the pass was nowhere near the goalkeeper and Waiters never had a chance to reach it and he was left stranded as Allen chased the loose ball and stroked it into the empty net. This unsettled Blackpool and two minutes later they conceded what was to prove the winning goal. Medwin chased a pass down to the corner flag and his cross was met by the marauding centre half Norman who rose unmarked and nodded into the net at the far post. There was no time for Blackpool to get back into the game and the only consolation from a 2-1 defeat was the encouraging performances from James and McPhee.

Gerry Wolstenholme

1 Blackpool – Bloomfield Road

14

Tranmere (h) 1942 – record score 15-3

Burnley (h) 1942, record margin of victory – 13-0

Blackpool v Chelsea ticket from 1996

1961 FA Cup Final Ticket, Tottenham v Leicester

Blackpool Draw ticket

Wolves (h) 1939 – league leaders the day before War broke out

1953 FA Cup Final Ticket, Blackpool v Bolton

Tottenham (h) when I was one day old – 7.3.53

Sheffield Wednesday (a) War
Cup North Final 1943

Arsenal – War Cup Final 1943
at Chelsea

Sheffield Wednesday (h) War
Cup North Final 1943

Sheffield Wednesday (a) FA
Cup Third Round 1953

Huddersfield Town (h) FA Cup
Fourth Round 1953

Southampton (h) FA Cup Fifth
Round 1953

Southampton (a) FA Cup Fifth
Round Replay 1953

Arsenal (a) FA Cup Sixth Round
1953

Tottenham at Villa Park, FA
Cup Semi-Final 1953

Pirate programme from 1953 FA Cup Final

Bolton at Wembley 1953 FA Cup Final

Song-sheet from 1953 FA Cup Final

Manchester United (a) – 'title decider' 1955-56

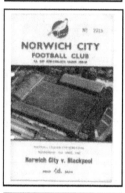

Norwich City (a) FL Cup Semi-Final 1962

Norwich City (h) FL Cup Semi-Final 1962

Bologna (a) 1971 Anglo-Italian Cup Final

Tottenham v Leicester 1961 FA Cup Final

Arsenal (a), 1953 FA Charity Shield

Sheffield Wednesday (h), LDV North Final 2004

Poster for Roma (a), Anglo-Italian Final 1972

Bolton Wanderers (h), Sherpa Van Final North 1989

Preston 0 Blackpool 7, May 1948

Blackpool 8 Charlton 4, September 1952

Wolverhampton Wanderers (h), September 1955 – record 38,098 attendance

Blackpool 7 Sunderland 0, October 1957

Bolton Wanderers (h), First Live televised game, September 1960

Manchester United (h), Marsden Lancashire Cup Final 1993

PRICE **6d**

PRESTON North End

FOOTBALL CLUB LTD

OFFICIAL PROGRAMME

(including "THE FOOTBALL LEAGUE REVIEW")

No. 1   SATURDAY, AUGUST 19th, 1967

too good to miss!

Lion Ale

The Best Beer in the North West

MATTHEW BROWN & CO. LTD.

LION BREWERY
BLACKBURN

---

2. Preston North End v Blackpool

Played at **Deepdale** on 19th August 1967

Football League Division Two

Preston North End 0
Blackpool (1)2 [Ingram, Charnley]

Attendance 21,499

2 Preston North End - Deepdale

I didn't go to my first away game until I had been watching matches for almost five years, by which time Blackpool had been relegated to the Division Two. I had seen almost a hundred games at Bloomfield Road during this period.

Blackpool's first spell in the Second Division since the war began with a derby fixture at Deepdale against Preston, which is why I chose this game to be my first away match. I went by train on the short journey to Preston. As local as the game was, this was just about the first time I had ever been to the town, and I had lived in Blackpool all of my fourteen and a half years. Preston had a famous footballing past, having been League Champions in 1889 and 1890, and FA Cup winners in 1889 and 1938. Indeed, they won the first ever league title without losing a game and the cup in the same season without conceding a goal to become the first side to win the 'double'. In 1941, they defeated Arsenal to win the Football league War Cup to add to their stature as one of the nation's leading sides. With the removal of the maximum wage limit, the future of the smaller town clubs such as Blackpool, Preston, Bolton and Blackburn was called into doubt, and the pendulum swung towards the big city giants from Merseyside and Manchester. Following relegation in 1961, Preston had almost won their way back into Division One in 1964, finishing just outside the promotion places behind Leeds and Sunderland. They had also reached the FA Cup final, twice leading against West Ham before an injury to goalkeeper Alan Kelly ultimately proved crucial as they lost in the final minute 3-2. That was as good as it got for North End, as the rest of the century became a long hard struggle. Even three years later in 1967, Preston were no longer one of the sides favoured for being involved in the promotion race. In the League Cup, they reached the Fourth Round twice in the sixties, only to suffer heavy defeats at Aston Villa in 1963 (2-6) and Grimsby in 1966 (0-4). They also reached the same stage in 1972 and 1981.

There was, not surprisingly, a large Blackpool following in the 21,499 crowd, all congregated on the Town End. I had a 'lucky' rabbit's foot with me, and I decided to 'call' it after the first Blackpool player to score. Blackpool's leading goalscorer was Ray Charnley, but at the time he was not one of my favourite players, and I hoped he wouldn't be that first scorer. Fortunately for me, after about an hour Gerry Ingram marked his full league debut with the opening goal, and my rabbit's foot became known as Gerry from then on. Shortly afterwards, Charnley *did* score, to give us a comfortable 2-0 victory and a nice start to the campaign. Kevin Thomas kept his first clean sheet as Blackpool's goalkeeper, but gave me a fright as he belted the ball into his own net as the final whistle blew. This was a slightly dangerous thing to do, as it wasn't unknown for a whistle to sound from the crowd, and referees had in the past allowed goals or awarded penalties after players had acted rashly, thinking that play had been stopped.

Ray Charnley left Blackpool not long after this game, joining Preston, and he opened the scoring for them in the return game at Bloomfield Road before Christmas. By that time I had begun to appreciate what a fine player he was, and I think the entire crowd enjoyed that goal – especially as Blackpool went on to win the game 4-1 and complete the double over their Lancashire rivals.

Huddersfield Town at Wembley
1938 FA Cup Final

Arsenal at Wembley 1941 War
Cup Final

Servette Geneva (h), Preston
Guild 1952

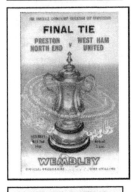

West Ham United at Wembley
1964 FA Cup Final

Aston Villa (a) FL Cup Fourth
Round 1963

Manchester United (h) FA Cup
quarterfinal 1966

Preston v Blackpool ticket and
cup voucher

Manchester United (a) FA Cup
quarterfinal 1966

Arsenal, 1941 Football League
War Cup Final

BOLTON WANDERERS
FOOTBALL CLUB

BURNDEN PARK, BOLTON

Directors :
J. BATTERSBY, Esq. (Chairman).
H. T. TYLDESLEY, Esq. (Vice-Chairman).
C. N. BANKS, Esq.
Ald. J. ENTWISTLE, J.P.
W. HAYWARD, Esq.
E. GERRARD, Esq., J.P.
Major J. GREENHALGH.

Hon. Medical Adviser :
Dr. J. B. WRIGHT.
Hon. Orthopædic Surgeon :
Mr. C. H. CULLEN, F.R.C.S.
Hon. Consultant Surgeon :
Mr. M. LENTIN, F.R.C.S.

Manager-Secretary : W. RIDDING

Tel. Bolton 21101
Telegrams " Wanderers," Bolton

OFFICIAL
PROGRAMME
6D.

SEASON 1967-68 — LEAGUE—SECOND DIVISION

SATURDAY, SEPTEMBER 30th, 1967

BOLTON WANDERERS v.

BLACKPOOL

---

3. Bolton Wanderers v Blackpool

Played at **Burnden Park** on 30th September 1967

Football League Division Two

Bolton Wanderers (1)1 [Phillips]
Blackpool (1)2 [Oates, Green]

Attendance 16,452

3 Bolton Wanderers – Burnden Park

On Saturday, September 30th 1967, I went to my second away game, at Bolton. Wanderers were another team who had suffered as a result of the removal of the wage limit, and they had dropped out of the First Division in 1964. Their glorious past included three memorable FA Cup victories in 1923, 1926 and 1929, the most famous of all being the "White Horse" Final of 1923 when some 200,000 people watched their victory over West Ham. In more recent times, they had defeated Manchester United 2-0 in the 1958 final, Nat Lofthouse scoring both goals, including one with a charge on the goalkeeper that was legal at the time but would not have been allowed thirty years later. But this result was not the one the nation wanted to see as sympathies were with a United team still suffering from the trauma of the Munich air disaster three months earlier, when so many of their players died. Consequently, many Bolton fans still feel as if their achievement was undermined, and much ill feeling still exists towards the men from Old Trafford. Wanderers did receive Wembley acclaim, though, after a thrilling 4-3 play-off victory over Reading in 1995, coming back from two goals down in a manner reminiscent of Blackpool's comeback *against* Bolton in 1953. This was their second Wembley visit of 1995, having lost 2-1 to Liverpool in the League Cup final just months earlier.

I should have been going with Mick Webb to Blackpool's match at Burnden Park, but he cried off at the last minute, so I decided to go on my own. On the train I met up with Mick 'Dazz' Daly and went with him to the game. Bolton had just knocked Liverpool out of the League Cup in mid week, Francis Lee being the star of the 3-2 victory, but fortunately for us he was absent from the team for our game, as he was about to move to First Division Manchester City. The game was a very entertaining affair, with Graham Oates hitting the post with a 'rocket' shot before putting Blackpool ahead. Bolton came back to level matters before the interval through Phillips, but Blackpool had the final word when Tony Green finally scored his first goal for the club - a moment well worth waiting for.

On the way back to the station there was a bit of a scuffle between a couple of Bolton fans and a Blackpool fan, but it was nothing very serious. It did, though, signal the beginning of a new sinister side of attending football matches, and within a few short months hooliganism swept the country.

In view of the fact that this was my first real experience of any 'bother' at all at a game, it was chilling to realise in later years that the first murder at a soccer game would come in another Blackpool v Bolton game. This took place at Bloomfield Road in August 1974 when a young Blackpool fan (Kevin Ollson) was stabbed through the heart by a Bolton fan at the tea bar at the back of the Kop. This wasn't the first time that tragedy had struck at a Bolton game, for in 1946 thirty-three people were killed at the Bolton v Stoke FA Cup tie when a barrier collapsed – the first such tragedy at an English ground.

West Ham United at Wembley
1923 FA Cup Final

Manchester City at Wembley
1926 FA Cup Final

Portsmouth at Wembley 1929
FA Cup Final

Stoke City (h) FA Cup 1946

Manchester United at Wembley
1958 FA Cup Final

Blackpool (a) 1974

Ancona (h) Anglo-Italian Cup
1994

Reading at Wembley, First
Division Play-Off Final 1995

Match ticket from 1979

4. Everton v Tranmere Rovers

Played at **Goodison Park** on 9th March 1968

FA Cup Round Five

Everton (2)2 [Royle, Morrissey]
Tranmere Rovers 0

Attendance 61,982

4 Everton – Goodison Park

Three days after my fifteenth birthday, I saw my first game that didn't involve Blackpool. It was a fifth round FA Cup tie between Everton and Tranmere Rovers, played at Goodison Park in front of 61,982, the biggest crowd I had been in at that time. I had an affinity with all of the Merseyside clubs after finding the people very helpful and friendly during my visits to the area train spotting as a boy, although I was supporting Rovers in this match. I had taken an interest in them over the previous few seasons as they struggled to survive in Division Four, and I had been looking forward to this game ever since Tranmere had defeated First Division Coventry in the previous round.

In contrast to the position Tranmere were in, Everton were one of the glamour clubs of the land, and had won the cup as recently as 1966, when they came back from 0-2 down to defeat Sheffield Wednesday 3-2. Mike Trebilcock, a late replacement for international striker Fred Pickering, had scored the first two goals and Derek Temple netted the winner. A major force in English football with six league titles and FA Cup victories in 1906 and 1933 prior to this recent triumph, the Goodison club were to experience some miserable times before seeing real glory again. After lifting the league title for a seventh time in 1970, they had a barren period throughout the rest of the seventies and the early eighties until a three-year run of success saw them lift the championship twice, the FA Cup once, and continental success was achieved with a 3-1 victory in Rotterdam against Rapide Vienna as the Cup Winners Cup was captured. This flurry of silverware proved to be a false dawn, as the rest of the century resulted in only one additional trophy in the Goodison cabinet, following a 1995 FA Cup victory over Manchester United.

Before the Everton v Tranmere game, I saw a large group of Rovers fans walking round the ground singing the praises of goalkeeper Jimmy Cumbes to the tune of 'Jennifer Juniper' by 'The Hollies'. The song went something like "Jimmy Cumbes, Saves a Penalty, Jimmy Cumbes, Saves a Penalty, Will He Save It, Yes I Think So, Will he Miss It, I Don't Think So" etc. - how banal it all seems now! As well as being an accomplished goalkeeper, Cumbes was also a County Cricketer for Lancashire.

The game was all-ticket except for the 'Boys Pen' at the top of the Gwladys Street End, and I paid to go in there, crouching low so as not to appear my true age of 15. Everton won the game 2-0, Royle and Morrissey scoring first half goals. Tranmere's task was made much harder through the absence of their striking partners George Yardley (out injured) and George Hudson (injured in the opening minutes of the game), but it was a tremendous achievement for them to reach this far in the competition.

A lot of interest was shown in the half time and full-time scores, mainly those involving Liverpool at Tottenham (another cup tie which finished 1-1) and (for me anyway) Blackpool in their league game at Plymouth. Blackpool led 2-0 at half-time, and listening to a radio on the bus while going back to the city centre to catch my coach home, I thought I heard the reporter say Blackpool get four at Plymouth. My delight soon turned to despair, though, as I realised that he'd said Blackpool *draw* at Plymouth.

Manchester City at Wembley,
1933 FA Cup Final

Sheffield Wednesday at
Wembley, 1966 FA Cup Final

Manchester United at Wembley,
1995 FA Cup Final

Rapid Wien, 1985 European
Cup Winners Cup Final

Inter Milan (h) European Cup
1963

Panathinaikos (h) European
Cup quarterfinal 1971

Bayern Munich (a), 1985 Cup
Winners Cup Semi-Final

Match ticket v Tranmere

Bayern Munich (h), 1985 Cup
Winners Cup Semi-Final

SEASON 1967-68   LEAGUE DIVISION TWO
BLACKPOOL
SATURDAY 23 MARCH 1968   K.O. 3.15 PM

1/-

OFFICIAL PROGRAMME

5. Queens Park Rangers v Blackpool

Played at **Loftus Road** on 23rd March 1968

Football League Division Two

Queens Park Rangers (1)2 [Clarke, I. Morgan]
Blackpool 0

Attendance 18,498

5 Queens Park Rangers – Loftus Road

On Saturday, March 23rd 1968, I travelled by train to London to see the crucial match in the promotion run-in to the end of season, Queens Park Rangers v Blackpool. On the journey, I met up with some members of the supporters' club, led by Ron Turner (who organised travel at this time) and his daughter Valerie, and went round with them for the rest of the day. We had lunch in a West London café, and I somehow managed to leave without paying for it, as I thought Ron had sorted out the bill for all of us. At the ground, I bought myself a 'Rangers' plaque commemorating their 'League Cup Final victory and Third Division Promotion' double of a year earlier, as a belated 15th birthday present. 1966-67 had been the best season in the history of the London club, winning the Third Division in a canter and then lifting the League Cup in the first final to be played at Wembley. Facing First Division West Bromwich Albion, they found themselves two goals behind, but Roger Morgan, Marsh and Lazarus scored the goals to send West London delirious. They were to reach the final again in 1986, only to lose to Oxford, and in 1982 they played two FA Cup finals against Tottenham, being somewhat unfortunate to lose the replay to a Glenn Hoddle penalty. They were also a quarter of an hour from being League Champions in 1976 until Liverpool struck with devastating effect at Wolverhampton.

Rangers' old ground in 1968 was still only up to Third Division standard, and it was packed to capacity with 18,498 inside. Unfortunately, there was some trouble too. We started out on one end of the ground, but as it was difficult to see we walked round to the Rangers end. We hadn't been there long before some Rangers 'supporters' started pushing and generally making things uncomfortable for us (although as we had a young boy with us, they held off from anything too rough, and even warned each other to be careful about the boy).

The ground was so packed that I struggled to see the action on the pitch, and I don't think I saw either of the goals. A fine run by Green saw him produce a low cross that Milne touched back to McPhee, but the finish saw the ball fly wide. After ten minutes, McPhee fouled Marsh, and Hazell took the free kick, putting in a cross that Ian Morgan met with his head and directed past Taylor from eight yards out. Springett saved easily from a Milne shot, and Alcock headed a Green corner just over as Blackpool looked for the equaliser. Roger Morgan hit a twenty-five yard effort just wide as Rangers sought the comfort margin a second goal would bring, but Green's centres were troubling the home defence, Armfield forcing a save out of Springett following one good cross.

In the second half, Taylor dived to turn an Allen effort from twenty yards for a corner. Craven was a foot too high from equalising from a similar distance, before Rangers took a two-goal lead twenty minutes into the second half. Allen crossed the ball to Clarke, who chested the ball down and shot past Taylor. With eight minutes to go, Clement headed a White effort off the line with Springett beaten. Rangers held on and won the game 2-0, which obviously pleased the home fans. The result meant Rangers had completed the double over Blackpool, and it was to have a big impact on the promotion race at the end of the season.

There was further trouble back at Euston station, with Alan Shepherd of the supporters' club getting his glasses broken in a scuffle, but eventually we were back on the train and we were happy to see that the Blackpool team were on it as well. Some members of our party were very scathing about John Craven, singing songs such as 'The sun shines out of Craven's a**e, Show us your a**e John Craven' as he walked through our carriage on his way to and from the buffet car. John was, in truth, an excellent servant for the club, and in later years he totally won round the fans, becoming club captain (and scoring in the Anglo-Italian Cup final victory in Bologna) before moving on to Crystal Palace and Coventry. Tragically, he died suddenly at the young age of 49 a week before Christmas in 1996.

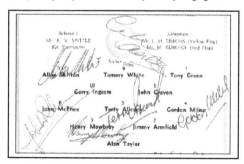

Blackpool autographs on the team line-up page of the programme

Birmingham City (a) LC Semi-Final 1967

Birmingham City (h) LC Semi-Final 1967

West Bromwich Albion at Wembley, LC Final 1967

West Bromwich Albion, FA Cup Semi-Final 1982

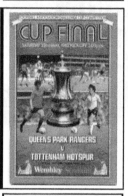

Tottenham Hotspur at Wembley, FA Cup Final 1982

Tottenham Hotspur 1982 at Wembley, FA Cup Final replay

AEK Athens (h) EUFA Cup 1977

Queens Park Rangers v Blackpool ticket, 1969

Reykjavic (a) EUFA Cup 1984

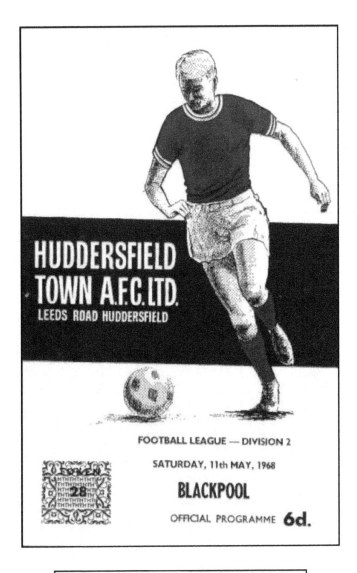

FOOTBALL LEAGUE — DIVISION 2

SATURDAY, 11th MAY, 1968

BLACKPOOL

OFFICIAL PROGRAMME **6d.**

---

6. Huddersfield Town v Blackpool

Played at Leeds Road on 11th May 1968

Football League Division Two

Huddersfield Town (1)1 [Legg]
Blackpool (0)3 [Suddick, McGill own goal, Skirton]

Attendance 11,603

As the season reached its climax, the fight from promotion from the Second Division had now come down to just three teams. Ipswich (with the best goal average) were now on 58 points, two ahead of Queens Park Rangers and Blackpool. Ipswich had a simple-looking home game against Blackburn to finish with. I desperately wanted both Blackpool and Queens Park Rangers to be promoted, but the only way my 'dream' promotion could occur now was for Ipswich to lose to Blackburn, Rangers to win at Aston Villa and Blackpool to win by at least 5-0 at Huddersfield. Eventually I accepted that this was all extremely unlikely, and I finally realised that it was between Blackpool and QPR for the final spot. Once I had accepted this, all my admiration of, and support for, QPR disappeared for this final day of the season.

Huddersfield were a side whose great days were long behind them. They were the first team to win the League Championship three seasons in a row, between 1924 and 1926, the first two of them under the leadership of the legendary Herbert Chapman, who went on to lead Arsenal to a similar treble. They also lifted the FA Cup in 1922, the year before the final moved to Wembley, and they were runners up in 1920 at Stamford Bridge (after a 2-1 semi-final victory over Bristol City, also at Stamford Bridge) and at Wembley in 1928, 1930 and 1938. But since then, they had achieved very little, although signs of a revival were there as they reached the semi-final of this season's League Cup before succumbing to Arsenal – the same side who beat them in the 1930 FA Cup Final appearance, and then emulated their three-in-a-row championship feat. They did make a return visit to Wembley in 1995, defeating Bristol Rovers in a Second Division play-off final.

I went to Huddersfield on the Blackpool special train. As we passed through Manchester Victoria station, we taunted United fans who were awaiting the arrival of Sunderland supporters. It was to be a sad day for United, as Sunderland shocked them by winning 2-1, and with Manchester City winning 4-3 at Newcastle, the title went across to Maine Road. Yet just a few short weeks earlier, United had seemed certainties for the title, until they had three home games against the other three title challengers (City, Liverpool and Leeds) and proceeded to lose them all by the same 2-1 scoreline.

When we arrived in Huddersfield, it seemed impossible that the game could take place, as the rain was absolutely torrential and we heard that the pitch was waterlogged. I walked around the sodden streets for an hour or two, trying in vain to eat my chips without the streams of water getting in the way. On entering the ground eventually, all we could see of the 'pitch' was a mass of mud. I believe that the sole reason the game went ahead was because of its overall importance, and to postpone it could have given Blackpool a distinct advantage when it was eventually played as they would know exactly what was required to win promotion. There were also well over 5,000 Blackpool fans at the ground, and the Yorkshire police must have been worried about what the reaction would be if the game were postponed.

As it was, there was a considerable amount of trouble between the two sets of fans and they fought repeatedly on the Huddersfield end, as Blackpool fans attempted successfully to 'take' the 'Cowshed'. There was even the ludicrous sight of Blackpool fans fighting amongst themselves until the home supporters came into the ground. There were still sporadic outbreaks of fighting throughout the game, although Blackpool had taken overall control.

Suddick 'scored' from a fifth minute free kick, awarded after Hutchison was fouled, but Oldfield left the ball as he knew the award was indirect and nobody had got a touch to Suddick's shot. Oldfield saved another Suddick free kick four minutes later, while Taylor saved easily from Dobson in Huddersfield's first attack. Shaw's effort just cleared Taylor's goal after a mistake by the 'Pool 'keeper who saw the ball slip out of his hands, and on nineteen minutes Suddick put a close-range header over the bar. Five minutes later, Craven's back pass stuck in the mud and Taylor only just got to it ahead of Worthington, diving at the striker's feet to claim the ball. Five minutes before half time, with the game delicately poised, Taylor conceded a free kick for taking too many steps while holding the ball. Dobson rolled the ball across to Legg, who smashed home the opening goal. That was still the score when the half-time whistle blew, and we went into the break trailing in a game we couldn't afford to lose.

During the interval, we began to move around the ground towards the open end, which Blackpool would be attacking for the remainder of the game. It was far too wet to leave our cover, so we stood in the Paddock staring at the half-time scoreboard, waiting for the score from Villa Park to appear. The Blackpool fans were chanting, 'Aston Villa, Aston Villa, We'll support you once this year'. The first sets of scores that were posted were of little interest to us, but then they posted the set containing the

QPR match. Letter 'l' was what we were interested in, and the score went up - Aston Villa 1 .... Queens Park Rangers 0 ... 1 ... 2 ... 3 ... 4 ... 5 ... 6 ... 0 (clearly some sadistic comedian was operating the scoreboard). As it finally settled on the '0', the ground erupted (the fact that we were also losing was irrelevant, as we knew *we* were going to win).

The second half was one-way traffic towards the Huddersfield goal amidst a rising crescendo of noise. Green was wide with a good effort, but Blackpool's equaliser came after Mowbray had been fouled out on the left. Hutchison's free kick led to a half-hit James shot, and the rebound fell to Suddick on the edge of the area, who drove home a superb equaliser, prompting the first pitch invasion of the afternoon by exuberant Blackpool fans. Blackpool took the lead a few minutes later with a bizarre own goal. Skirton flicked the ball on in an attempt to find White, but full back McGill reached the ball first. He turned it back to his goalkeeper, but the 'keeper slipped in the mud and the ball went beyond Oldfield and in, causing a second pitch invasion by the 'Pool fans. Almost immediately, 'score flashes' were received, and the main body of Blackpool fans still behind the opposite goal began singing "Villa 2, Rangers 0, Alleluia" - followed a few minutes later by "Villa 3, Rangers 0, Alleluia". The sad individual who had started this rumour must have been delighted with his work, as we were soon to realise. The group I was with ignored the torrents of rain and moved onto the open end behind the goal we were attacking. With a few minutes to go, we moved towards the players' entrance to greet our conquering heroes as they left the pitch. Five minutes from time, Green was fouled and McPhee took the free kick. White flicked his cross on and Skirton shot past Oldfield from close range for the third goal. The Blackpool fans were in full voice, singing the promotion songs as Skirton beat the 'keeper with another attempt only to see the ball stop in the thick mud on the goal line.

Then we had our first doubts of the afternoon. A lad who I'd seen at the cricket at Blackpool the previous summer had a radio with him, and he told us that it was 1-1 at Villa Park. Even so, this was still good enough to see Blackpool promoted, and as the final whistle blew at Huddersfield we invaded the pitch to cheer off the players, standing in the pouring rain and calling for Morty. Then the voice of doom sounded. Keith Bradley had put through his own goal eight minutes from time and QPR had won 2-1 - the goal was completely against the run of play to make matters worse. Blackpool had missed out on promotion by 0.2 of a goal on goal average, despite obtaining 58 points, the highest number of points **ever** for a side who didn't get promoted - when we did win promotion two years later, it was achieved with five fewer points. The seven match winning run to end the season had come to naught in the end, and our only other remote hope of promotion disappeared when the score came through that Ipswich had drawn 1-1 with Blackburn Rovers. That point was enough to give Ipswich the second division title by a point from QPR.

It was a silent party that trudged its way back to the railway station. On the platform, I heard on the radio the outcome of the Rugby League Cup Final at Wembley. Leeds had defeated Wakefield Trinity 11-10 on another rain-soaked pitch because of a missed conversion from directly in front of the posts by Don Fox of Wakefield with the final kick of the game, one of the most famous incidents in Rugby League history. As Wakefield were the team I followed in that sport, my day of misery was almost complete now. On the Monday evening, Fox was interviewed on the television, and as part of the article he nonchalantly kicked conversions from the spot where he had missed to demonstrate how easy it all *should* have been.

The remainder of our train journey home was a mixture of numbness and misery, as the fact that we were still a Second Division side began to sink in. Nearly thirty years later, I could sympathise with my eldest son Iain's feelings after Blackpool's promotion play-off defeat by Bradford City when he too was fifteen. My final memory of the day is of getting off the train at South Station and walking to the bus stop with the freezing rain lashing into my forehead - the weather was perfect for the way the day had turned out. May 11th 1968 will long remain as one of the most disappointing days of my life.

Aston Villa v Queens Park
Rangers, Division Two, 11.5.68

Ipswich v Blackburn, Division
Two, 11.5.68

Rugby League Cup Final from
Wembley, 11.5.68

Bristol City, 1920 FA Cup Semi-
Final

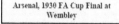

Arsenal, 1930 FA Cup Final at
Wembley

Preston North End, 1922 FA
Cup Final

Arsenal (a) 1968 League Cup
Semi-Final

Arsenal (h) 1968 League Cup
Semi-Final

Bristol Rovers at Wembley, 1995
Division Two Play-Off Final

Huddersfield v Blackpool ticket from 1994 – the last game at Leeds Road

THE END OF AN ERA
Huddersfield Town AFC
v
Blackpool FC
Saturday 30th April 1994
Kick off 3:00pm
Adult £8.50 Concessionary £5.00
Endsleigh Insurance League Division Two

VISITORS STAND

| TURNSTILE | ROW | SEAT |
| 10 | M | 20 |

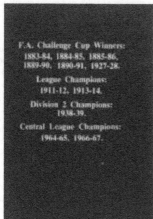

F.A. Challenge Cup Winners:
1883-84, 1884-85, 1885-86,
1889-90, 1890-91, 1927-28.

League Champions:
1911-12, 1913-14.

Division 2 Champions:
1938-39.

Central League Champions:
1964-65, 1966-67.

BLACKBURN ROVERS F.C.

Directors:
C. R. Davies (Chairman), A. L. Fryars
(Vice-Chairman), D. Hull, A. Duckett,
J.P., G. N. Forbes, J. Wilkinson,
W. H. Bancroft, W. I. Hubert

Secretary:
D. Grimshaw

Manager:
E. Quigley

Wednesday, August 28th

BLACKPOOL

season 1968/69

official programme 1/-

---

7. Blackburn Rovers v Blackpool

Played at **Ewood Park** on 28th August 1968

Football League Division Two

Blackburn Rovers (0)1 [Craven own goal]
Blackpool (1)1 [White]

Attendance 21,062

40

7 Blackburn Rovers – Ewood Park

I was working at Blackpool Pleasure Beach during the summer of 1968, and took time off for the mid-week evening game at Ewood Park against Blackburn Rovers.

Like Huddersfield, Blackburn's best years were long behind them. They won the FA Cup five times, including a hat-trick between 1884 and 1886, and the League Championship twice – all before the First World War broke out. Apart from another FA Cup victory in 1928, though, they had won nothing since. They were to remain in the doldrums until the 1990's, when the benevolent Jack Walker became chairman and used his millions to make Rovers a force in the game again, as they gained promotion via the play-offs in 1992, won the Premiership in 1995 and the Worthington Cup in 2002, defeating Tottenham 2-1 in the Cardiff final.

Blackpool were still undefeated in 1968-69, and including the games at the end of the previous season they were looking to equal the club record of a dozen league matches without defeat. James headed a Skirton cross on, and Tom White hooked a great shot into the roof of the net to give Blackpool an interval lead. Six minutes into the second half, Darling's twenty yard effort seemed to be covered by Taylor until it hit John Craven and deflected past the 'keeper for an own goal, ensuring a share of the points as the game finished 1-1. I don't remember much more about the game, but I do remember an incident on my way to the ground as I walked from the railway station. I almost found myself sandwiched between a bus and a car as I crossed the road, not noticing the road works on the bus' side. As I gratefully reached the pavement, a couple of Blackburn supporters said "Do that again, we missed it!" - had they been aware that I was a Blackpool fan, then they may have made sure I did it again!

Blackburn v Southampton ticket from 2002

41

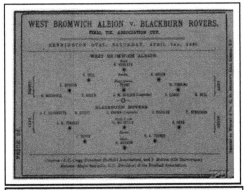

West Bromwich Albion at Kennington Oval, 1886 FA Cup Final

Huddersfield Town, 1928 FA
Cup Final at Wembley

Leicester City at Wembley,
Division Two Play-Off final 1992

Tottenham at Millennium
Stadium, 2002 LC Final

Spartak Moscow (h),
Champions League 1995

Newcastle United, 1952 FA Cup
Semi-Final

Bolton Wanderers, 1958 FA Cup
Semi-Final

Sheffield Wednesday, 1960 FA
Cup Semi-Final

43

8. Wrexham v Blackpool

Played at **The Racecourse Ground** on 4th September 1968

Football League Cup Round Two

Wrexham (0)1 [Ingle]
Blackpool (0)1 [White]

Attendance 15,102

8 Wrexham – The Racecourse Ground

My first visit to the Wrexham ground was during the mid-sixties, at a time when I and a group of fellow fans used to go train-spotting on Saturdays when Blackpool were away. On one such Saturday, we went to Crewe, and decided to carry on to Wrexham to visit the railway sheds there. As we walked from the station to the sheds, we passed a lot of people walking in the opposite direction, and when we talked to them, we found out that they were Wrexham fans, but that their game had just been postponed. We carried on until we reached the ground, and got talking to an official there. When he found out we were Blackpool supporters visiting the town, he gave us a large bundle of that season's Wrexham programmes to share out amongst ourselves! Wrexham were one of the littler sides as far as league status went, but that act showed how they were a big club as far as looking after the supporters went. Their main area of success came in the Welsh Cup, with a record number of twenty-three victories in the tournament, and another record twenty-two appearances as a losing finalist. Subsequent European forays were a reward for their success, but they also came close to FA Cup glory in 1978, with a quarterfinal tie at home to Arsenal. Sadly, that was where their cup run came to an end at the feet of the side who would end up beaten finalists. Strangely enough, they also reached the quarterfinal of the League Cup that same season, going out to Liverpool, who were also destined to lose the final of that competition by a single goal. The quarterfinal stage of the FA Cup was also reached in 1974 and 1997, and of the League Cup in 1961.

My first visit to see a game came a week after Blackpool's league match at Blackburn in 1968. On paper, Blackpool had an easy-looking League Cup tie away to their Fourth Division opponents. I went on the supporters' club coach for the first time to this match, and was part of a huge crowd of over 15,000.

The Wrexham team included ex-Pool favourites Ray Charnley (whose stay at Preston hadn't lasted very long), Ian Moir and Tony Beanland, along with a lad called Alan Bermingham. He had become nationally famous in 1967, when little Skelmersdale United had reached the FA Amateur Cup final at Wembley. They had played Enfield, one of the giants of amateur football, and were level at 0-0 in the last minute of extra time when 'Skem' were awarded a penalty. Bermingham took it but failed to score, and the miss cost Skelmersdale the trophy as Enfield won the replay 3-0 at Maine Road.

Blackpool were in the middle of a long unbeaten run, currently at fourteen games, but Wrexham caused 'Pool plenty of problems. Charnley missed a low cross at the far post on sixteen minutes and Beanland, saw his second half shot hit a defender and deflect over the bar. Armfield scrambled a Kinsey shot off the line as the Fourth Division outfit looked the likelier winners. Ingle and Moir played well up front for Wrexham, and it was Ingle who opened the scoring with ten minutes to go. That looked like winning the tie for the Welshmen until White stabbed home Blackpool's last minute equaliser after a Suddick free kick had run loose. The final whistle went just fifteen seconds later to break the hearts of the brave Welshmen.

Blackpool won the replay fairly comfortably, despite a tricky opening half, by a scoreline of 3-0, but even then Wrexham had their share of ill fortune as Bermingham once again missed a crucial penalty in a cup-tie.

Merthyr Tydfil (a) Welsh Cup
Semi-Final 1995

Cardiff City (a), 1965 Welsh
Cup Final

Cardiff City (a) Welsh Cup
Final 1972

Swansea Town, Welsh Cup
Final 1957

Roma (h) European Cup
Winners Cup 1984

Manchester United (a) 1990
European Cup Winners Cup

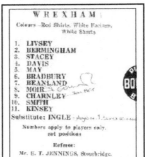

FC Magdeburg (a) European
Cup Winners Cup

Autographed line-up for
Wrexham v Blackpool 1968

Ticket for Arsenal game, FA
Cup quarterfinal 1978

Arsenal (h) FA Cup quarterfinal 1978

Cardiff City (a), Welsh Cup Final 1975

Liverpool (h) FL Cup quarterfinal 1978

Manchester United (h), Cup Winners Cup 1990

Peterborough (h), promotion special 1978

Anderlecht (h), European Cup Winners Cup quarterfinal 1976

Anderlecht (a), European Cup Winners Cup quarterfinal 1976

MILLWALL
FOOTBALL
CLUB

official
programme
one shilling
(Incorporating Football League Review)

FOOTBALL LEAGUE DIVISION TWO
SATURDAY SEPTEMBER 14th 1968   KICK OFF 3.00 p.m.

BLACKPOOL (autographed)

---

9. Millwall v Blackpool

Played at **The Den** on 14th September 1968

Football League Division Two

Millwall (0)1 [Jones]
Blackpool (0)2 [White, Suddick]

Attendance 13,198

9 Millwall – The Den

Saturday, September 14th brought my second game in London, against a Millwall side who were challenging Blackpool at the top of the table. I went down by train with Robert Frowen and another lad, but I left them at Euston as they were trying to get on the tube without paying. I went to get my ticket as it seemed a pointless risk to take to me and I went the rest of the way on my own, eventually arriving at the Den just before kick-off time. I also experienced the seedier side of London life, when I turned down the 'offer' from one pervert to go with him to one of the empty platforms!

As it was raining torrentially, I didn't bother to look whereabouts I was, but just entered the ground at the first entrance I came to - which happened to be the notorious Millwall end, home of the worst hooligan following in the country. However, things weren't too bad for me there, and I didn't feel inhibited at all during the game.

Millwall were rampant during the opening twenty minutes, but fine goalkeeping by Taylor and some resolute Blackpool defending kept them at bay. Blackpool did hit the post as well as creating the best chance of the game before Suddick met a Skirton cross to score with a fine header three minutes before half-time. In the second half, Kitchener hit the post with an excellent shot, and Blackpool broke immediately to the other end, where White scored the second goal. Jones reduced the arrears for Millwall on eighty-eight minutes to set up a tense finish, but Blackpool deservedly held on to sentence Millwall to their first home defeat in almost a year. It was at this game that I first heard fans singing to the tune of 'Hey Jude' by The Beatles - 'Na, na na na, na na na na, na na na na, Mill-wall' (it sounded a lot better than it looks in print!).

On the way back to Euston I heard some more good news as Rangers had won 4-2 at Celtic to continue their own good start to the season. At the station I saw the Blackpool team in the Euston bar and collected some autographs to round off a fine day out.

Millwall had always been a lower-league club, with their biggest claim to fame being that they were the first Third Division side to reach the FA Cup Semi-Finals, way back in 1937, when they were narrowly defeated by Sunderland. This was their third appearance at that stage, having reached the semi-finals in 1900 and 1903, on each occasion going down by three goals to the side who would lose to Bury in the final. In 1988, however, they won the Second Division title and reached the top flight for the first time in their history, going on to lead the First Division for a while in the 1988-89 season. after a subsequent drop through the divisions once more, they reached Wembley in 1999, going down 1-0 to Wigan in the Auto Windscreen Final. This wasn't Millwall's first appearance at the stadium, as they lost 2-0 to Chelsea in a War Cup South final more than fifty years earlier. In the League Cup, they were beaten at the quarterfinal stage three times, in 1974, 1977 and 1995. Finally, in 2004, they reached an FA Cup Final, although this one was played in Cardiff instead of at Wembley. Unfortunately for the 'Lions', they froze on the big day and lost 3-0 to Manchester United.

They also had a formidable reputation at the Den, going *fifty-nine* league matches without defeat there between 1964 and 1967, and also establishing a Football League record by being undefeated at home throughout a season in four separate divisions – Division Three South in 1927-28, Division Four in 1964-65, Division Three in 1965-66 and Division Two in 1971-72. Unfortunately, when they did eventually lose at home in 1967, against Plymouth, the game was marred by serious rioting – a plague that was to haunt Millwall throughout the decades, especially following an FA Cup quarterfinal defeat at Luton in 1985 and a play-off Semi-Final defeat to Birmingham in 2002.

Bus, tube and rail tickets used to reach The Den

Birmingham City (h) FA Cup
Fifth Round 1957

Luton Town (a), FA Cup
quarterfinal 1985

Manchester United (a), Division
One, 1988-89

Swindon Town (a), Football
League Cup quarterfinal 1994-95

Steward's ribbon for 1903 FA
Cup Semi-Final v Derby County

Aston Villa (a), Football League
Cup quarterfinal 1976-77

Chelsea 1945 War Cup Final South

Derby (h) 1937 FA Cup Round Five – Record Gate 48,672

Plymouth (h) 1967 – End of unbeaten home run of 59 games

Ipswich (h) FA Cup Quarterfinal 1978

Wigan at Wembley, Auto Windscreen Shield Final 1999

Derby (a) First Division Play-Off Semi-Final 1994

Millwall v Blackpool ticket from 1969

Blackpool team photograph as autographed at Euston

10. Sheffield United v Blackpool

Played at Bramall Lane on 28th September 1968

Football League Division Two

Sheffield United (1)2 [Reece, Addison]
Blackpool (1)1 [Green]

Attendance 15,947

10 Sheffield United – Bramall Lane

Sheffield United were another side with a glorious past but a dismal present. They were league champions in 1898, and won the FA Cup four times before 1925 was out, including a 3-0 defeat of Chelsea at Old Trafford in 1915 and a victory over Cardiff at Wembley in 1925, but since then there had been little for their fans to shout about. Their last FA Cup Final appearance was a defeat against Arsenal in 1936, although they did reach two semi-finals in the 1990's, the first of which was an all-Sheffield affair at Wembley against rivals Wednesday in 1993. Unfortunately for the red half of Sheffield, the Owls emerged triumphant in the end. In the League Cup, they hadn't progressed beyond the quarterfinal stage, a point they reached in 1962, 1967 and 1972, until 2003. That 2002-2003 season saw United reach the semi-finals of both the FA Cup and the League Cup, only to lose narrowly on both occasions. They did, though, reach the Millennium Stadium that same season in the First Division play-off final against Wolverhampton, only to lose the match 3-0.

Blackpool's unbeaten run stood at twenty-three matches in all competitions, including pre-season friendly games, stretching back to an April defeat at Ewood Park. This had generated a tremendous interest in the town, and it was as part of a large Blackpool following that I went by train to the league game at Sheffield United, hoping to extend that run to twenty-four. Our chants of "We're Undefeated" were sadly soon to be silenced. The journey involved a change of stations at Manchester, for we arrived at Victoria but had to cross the city to Piccadilly to catch the connection to Sheffield. This wasn't as straightforward as it sounded, for the reputation of Manchester football fans was such that you didn't want to be in the city if you supported another side, but after a few worrying moments we managed to complete the transfer across the city.

Even though the game brought an end to Blackpool's unbeaten run, 'Pool still had the men of the match in Green and Suddick. When the game began, Powell for United beat three men and shot over in the opening minutes. Little else happened in a first half of indescribable boredom until six minutes before half time, and against the run of play, when Woodward curled in a corner and Reece headed the opening goal. Four minutes later, Hutchison was fouled, took the free kick himself, and passed to Green, whose ferocious shot brought the equaliser. Play until half time continued at this new level of excitement, but the whistle for the interval brought an end to the afternoon's entertainment.

The second half was even worse than the first, even though Blackpool took total control, with White missing from three yards and skimming the bar with a volley. However, with twenty minutes remaining Powell flicked the ball to Addison and Sheffield were back in front. One Green run in the second half took him past five Sheffield defenders before he put over a perfect cross, but White couldn't tuck the ball away. Blackpool were still not finished, but when Suddick had a drive parried by Hodgkinson and White missed the rebound, everybody knew it just wasn't going to be our afternoon. The local newspaper headline proclaimed that Blackpool were 'temporarily off the top of Division Two' - it was to be several years, in fact, before we did reach those lofty heights again. The journey home was uneventful, with even the cross-Manchester transfer holding no terrors on this occasion.

Bristol City (h), 1988 Play-Off
Semi-Final

Bristol City (a), 1988 Play-Off
Semi-Final

Leeds United (a), 1968 FA Cup
quarterfinal

Chelsea, 1915 FA Cup Final at Old Trafford

Cardiff City, 1925 FA Cup Final at Wembley

Arsenal, 1936 FA Cup Final at Wembley

Southampton, 1902 FA Cup Final

Derby County, 1899 FA Cup Final

Newcastle United, 1998 FA Cup Semi-Final

Arsenal, 2003 FA Cup Semi-Final

Liverpool (a) 2003 League Cup Semi-Final

River Plate (h), 1978

Liverpool (h), 2003 League Cup
Semi-Final

Liverpool (h) ticket, 2003 League Cup Semi-Final

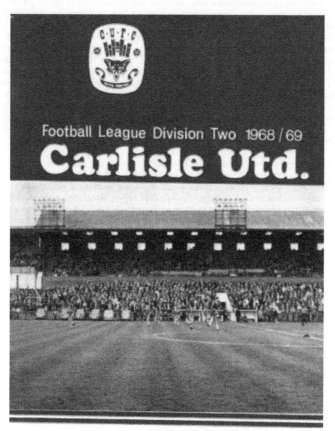

11. Carlisle United v Blackpool

Played at **Brunton Park** on 19th October 1968

Football League Division Two

Carlisle United (1)1 [Murray]
Blackpool 0

Attendance 10,519

Blackpool were now in the middle of a long run where they couldn't win in the league, although they had made good progress in the League Cup, knocking out First Division sides Manchester City and Wolverhampton. Three days after the victory over Wolves we had the chance to get back to winning ways in the league at Carlisle. United were one of the league's little clubs, with very little along the way to get excited about, although they did come close to Wembley in 1970, only to lose their two-legged semi-final to West Bromwich Albion. That same season they reached the FA Cup Fifth Round, losing 2-1 to Middlesbrough. Six years earlier, they had lost 1-0 to eventual finalist Preston at the same stage, and in 1975 they progressed to the quarterfinals of the competition during their single season as a top-flight club. Although relegated back to the Second Division at the end of that season, they did for a while sit on top of the table after victories in their opening three fixtures. Carlisle eventually achieved some success on the cup front in the late 1990's, first by reaching the Auto Windscreen final only to lose 1-0 to Birmingham in 1995, then by triumphing in the competition two years later when Colchester were defeated 4-3 in a penalty shootout following a goalless drawn game.

I went on the supporters' club coach with Pete Badley, who I had met while working during the summer at the Pleasure Beach. Pete was really an Evertonian, but he came along to a few Blackpool matches with me. Carlisle's Brunton Park ground struck me as being a very isolated place, most notably when we ate our lunchtime sandwiches in a field outside the ground, surrounded by a herd of cows! The desolation obviously affected the team on the pitch too, and Carlisle won by the only goal of the game, scored by Murray in the fifteenth minute, when he took an inside pass from Barton and turned to shoot past Taylor in a single fluid movement. It was Carlisle's first home win of the season, although Blackpool had the chances to extend the home sides winless run. Suddick missed with a header and had a fine shot saved, and Milne shot wide from a Hutchison cross. Late on, Green set up a simple chance for Marsden, but the man who had scored his first senior goal against Wolves fired over and the chance had gone. It wasn't all Blackpool, though, and Barton blazed over on *five* separate occasions, while Balderstone missed an open goal ten minutes from the end.

The trip turned out to be a nightmare for me, as I first became aware that I suffered from travel sickness, most notably as we went over Shap Fell, and I was extremely relieved to get back on to firm ground again in Blackpool.

Golden Gamble Ticket from 2001

Colchester United at Wembley, 1997 Auto Windscreens Final

West Bromwich Albion (a) 1970 League Cup Semi-Final

Preston (a) FA Cup Fifth Round 1964

Liverpool (h), First Division 1974-75

Middlesbrough (h), FA Cup Fifth Round 1970

Fulham (h), FA Cup quarterfinal 1975

Carlisle v Blackpool ticket from 1996

West Bromwich Albion (h) 1970 League Cup Semi-Final

12. Coventry City v Blackpool

Played at **Highfield Road** on 4th January 1969

FA Cup Round Three

Coventry City (0)3 [Machin, Curtis, Shepherd]
Blackpool (0)1 [Brown]

Attendance 28,537

12 Coventry City – Highfield Road

The first Saturday of 1969 was reserved for the Third Round of the FA Cup competition, and Blackpool were drawn away to Coventry City, a team I 'supported' even though I had never seen them play. I went on the football special from Blackpool South along with Mick and Ollie O'Brien, and we were full of dreams of a trip to Wembley in May. With Coventry in the First Division, Blackpool were the underdogs, yet they acquitted themselves well. Martin screwed a first minute shot wide for the home team, and Blackpool responded when Brown headed a Green cross wide seven minutes later. Thomson had to dive across goal to save an excellent header from Hateley just before the half hour, only for the action to once again return to the other end, where Glazier saved a fierce Green effort. As Blackpool continued to press forwards, a Brown cross was almost turned into his own goal by Curtis, with the ball just going outside the post. Four minutes before the break, Hateley headed through to Hunt, who put the ball under Thomas, only to find out he was offside. Blackpool could be more than satisfied with their first half performance.

In the first minute of the second half, Thomas saved brilliantly from a twenty-five yard Carr drive, and eight minutes later the 'keeper again made an excellent stop to thwart Coop. But Blackpool soon settled down again, and on sixty-six minutes Green put Brown through on goal. The small inside forward beat Curtis before shooting past Glazier to put us ahead. Those Wembley dreams didn't seem far-fetched at all now, and at the normal finishing time of 4:45 we still held that 1-0 lead. Unfortunately, Coventry games kicked-off a quarter of an hour later than most other matches, and in the final eight minutes leading up to 5 o'clock, City dashed any hopes we had of making further progress in the competition. Machin equalised, which still gave us the chance of a Bloomfield Road replay, then Curtis and Shepherd added further goals to dash even that hope and leave us sorry 3-1 losers. Rowe did have a chance to restore our lead immediately following City's equaliser, but it went begging and Coventry proved that you only get one chance at this level by taking the ball to the other end of the pitch and scoring the second goal themselves.

I was still wearing my new Blackpool peaked cap (bought especially for the anticipated cup run) as our group walked forlornly back to the railway station after the game. Some other Blackpool fans warned us to hide our colours and get back as quickly as we could, for Coventry fans were on the streets searching for Blackpool supporters. We learned later that their ploy was to go up to people, ask them if they knew where 'King Richard Street' was, and if the 'victims' didn't know, they would set on them -it appeared that they were actually on King Richard Street when the attacks were made. We, from the Second Division, were not used to such organised bouts of hooliganism as appeared to be the case in the top league.

The FA Cup was to provide Coventry with their only real moment of glory, although the fact that they managed to avoid relegation from the top flight for more than thirty years was an achievement in itself. Their promotion in 1967 was achieved with a final game victory over nearest challengers Wolverhampton, a game that attracted a record attendance of 51,457 to Highfield Road. City almost reached Wembley in the League Cup in 1981, only to suffer a heavy defeat at West Ham in the semi-final. They went down at the same stage of the competition nine years later. In 1987, though, they took on Tottenham at Wembley in the FA Cup Final, and despite going behind they fought back to win 3-2, in the process ending Tottenham's 100% record in FA Cup Final appearances. Keith Houchen, who two years earlier had scored the last minute penalty winner that saw York knock Arsenal out of the cup in the Fourth Round, continued his assault on North London with a fine, headed goal. My only regret about this performance was the fact that I missed it, as Barbara's cousin Maureen was getting married that afternoon and I was amongst the guests instead of being sat in front of the television set!

Rail ticket from a subsequent visit to Coventry

Tottenham at Wembley, FA Cup
Final 1987

West Ham (h) League Cup
Semi-Final 1981

West Ham (a) League Cup
Semi-Final 1981

Coventry in Europe, Fairs Cup
1970

Coventry v Bayern Munich,
Fairs Cup ticket 1970

Coventry v Wolverhampton,
Record Crowd 1967

Nottingham Forest (h) 1990
League Cup Semi-Final

Nottingham Forest (a) 1990
League Cup Semi-Final

Leeds United, 1987 FA Cup
Semi-Final

13. Middlesbrough v Blackpool

Played at Ayresome Park on 22nd February 1969

Football League Division Two

Middlesbrough (1)2 [Hickton penalty, Webb]
Blackpool (1)1 [Craven]

Attendance 18,672

13 Middlesbrough – Ayresome Park

Going to away matches was now becoming a nerve-wracking affair, and the game I went to at Middlesbrough towards the end of February 1969 was one of the most frightening experiences I have had at a football game. I had again travelled on the supporters' club coach, and we had been dropped off some way from the ground, having been given instructions as to where to meet the coach after the game.

The game didn't go well for us. Blackpool fell behind to a dubious tenth minute penalty, converted by Hickton, but Craven levelled the scores with a well-taken goal midway through the first half. In the third minute of injury time, with a draw seeming certain, Rook met the ball first time and hooked it against the upright. Webb was quickest to react, and his header brought the winning goal. The Blackpool team were incensed at where all of the extra time came from, but the goal stood. Taylor had made some superb saves to keep Blackpool in the game, otherwise they would have been beaten well before that controversial final minute.

We expected that with Middlesbrough scoring the winner so late, at least it would mean that their supporters were happy, and would not be looking for trouble. Robert Frowen and I waited for the coach outside the ground, and we saw hundreds of Teesside hooligans facing us across the road. The tension was unbearable, as there were no police anywhere around, and there was absolutely nowhere for us to go to get away from the threat, but incredibly nothing happened to us. Even so, by the time our coach arrived to 'rescue' us, I was a nervous wreck. Even when we were on the coach, things didn't improve, and the police (when they finally arrived) had to ask the Blackpool fans to keep quiet to avoid antagonising the Middlesbrough crowd who were still waiting outside. This was my first experience of Middlesbrough, and, sad to say, subsequent visits there were hardly any more pleasant.

Middlesbrough were one of the great non-achievers in football, for after early initial success when they won the FA Amateur Cup in 1895 and 1898, success eluded the Teessiders. They had to wait until 1976 before they won their first trophy, and that was only the Anglo-Scottish Cup. Things changed, though, in the late 1990's, when Wembley was reached in the League Cup finals of 1997 and 1998, with an FA Cup Final appearance also in 1997. Sadly for Boro fans, they were to lose all three finals, two of them to Chelsea. By a strange coincidence, Chelsea had also been the opposition when Boro' contested the minor Zenith Data Systems Cup in 1990 and the play-off final of 1988.

| Chelsea, FA Cup Final 1997 | Leicester City, Football League Cup Final 1997 | Chelsea, Football League Cup Final 1998 |

| Chelsea (h) Play-Off Final 1988 | Chelsea (a) Play-Off Final 1988 | Chelsea Zenith Data Systems Final 1990 |

| Roma (h), Anglo-Italian Cup 1970 | Liverpool (a) League Cup Semi-Final 1998 | Liverpool (h) League Cup Semi-Final 1998 |

Manchester City (h) 1976 League Cup Semi-Final	Middlesbrough – Liverpool ticket from 1975	Manchester City (a) 1976 League Cup Semi-Final

Manchester United (a), FA Cup quarterfinal replay 1970	Manchester United (h), FA Cup quarterfinal 1970	Liverpool (a), FA Cup quarterfinal 1977

Leicester City (h), FA Cup Fifth Round 1965	Aberdeen (h), Anglo-Scottish Cup 1975

BOOTHFERRY PARK HULL

FOOTBALL LEAGUE DIV 2

versus

BLACKPOOL

SATURDAY
1st MARCH, 1969
Kick-off 3.0 p.m.

Official Programme 1'-

---

14. Hull City v Blackpool

Played at **Boothferry Park** on 1st March 1969

Football League Division Two

Hull City (2)2 [Lord, Butler]
Blackpool (0)2 [Craven, Alcock]

Attendance 10,896

The experience at Middlesbrough didn't put me off travelling to away matches, and a week later I was again on the supporters' club coach for the long journey to Hull. The 'Tigers' had to play second fiddle in Hull to the city's two rugby league clubs, Hull FC and Hull Kingston Rovers, their biggest claim to fame being an FA Cup semi-final appearance in 1930, when it took a replay before Arsenal conquered them. Their record attendance of 55,019 was set in 1949, for an FA Cup quarterfinal tie against Manchester United, but apart from another quarterfinal against Stoke in 1971 and a pre-season Watney Cup Final appearance against Stoke in 1973, there had been little to cheer since then. In the League Cup, their best performance was in reaching the Fourth Round in 1974, 1976 and 1978.

The coach journey to Yorkshire turned out to be one of the worst trips of my life, for I began to feel sick as soon as we reached the Pennines, and by the time we arrived at the ground I felt terrible. Our usual practice was to wait outside the players' entrance for any free stand tickets from the likes of Jimmy Armfield, although I never actually remember getting one myself - people like trip-organisers Alan Shepherd and Ossie McDonald always took the few that were available. Because I felt so awful, I decided to buy a stand ticket instead of going on the terracing, but before I could get one I was sick right outside the ticket office. I felt a little better after this, although I was still dreading the return trip, and I also found I had plenty of room round what had previously been a busy ticket office!

Once the game started, Hull soon had me feeling ill again, as they took a 2-0 lead before half time. Wagstaff set up Hull's opening goal with a neat flick and Lord finished low past Taylor. The second goal came from a Butler cross that Taylor misjudged, the ball drifting over him and going in. Just as it seemed we were heading for another away defeat, we finally started to play with twenty minutes remaining. We levelled the scores with a few minutes to go, and I was even hopeful that we might snatch a win, but the players seemed satisfied with the point and settled for an undeserved 2-2 draw. Armfield had a hand in both Blackpool's goals. For the first, Green sent him down the wing and Craven headed home his cross, and then the skipper was also involved in Alcock's goal.

The result meant that I could at least face the return trip across the Pennines in a slightly happier mood, and it proved to be an easier journey home than I had feared.

14 Hull City – Boothferry Park

Boothferry Park after Hull moved to their new stadium

Stoke City, Watney Cup Final
1973

Stoke City (h), FA Cup
quarterfinal 1971

Chelsea (a) FA Cup quarterfinal
1966

Manchester City (a), Full
Members Cup Final (N) 1985

Manchester United (h), FA Cup
quarterfinal 1949

Manchester United, Watney
Cup Semi-final 1970

Chelsea (h) FA Cup quarterfinal
Replay 1966

Hull v Blackpool ticket, 1969

Liverpool (h), FA Cup Fifth
Round 1989

15. Bury v Blackpool

Played at **Gigg Lane** on 26th March 1969

Football League Division Two

Bury (2)2 [Jones, Collins]
Blackpool 0

Attendance 6,675

15 Bury – Gigg Lane

I had thought of going to see Bury play Fulham just after Christmas, but had decided against it as the weather was bad and I thought the game might be postponed. It *wasn't*, and I missed a 5-1 home victory! My initial visit was only supposed to be delayed for a few weeks, with Blackpool due there in February, but this game *was* called off due to the weather. Consequently, it was late March before I made my way to Gigg Lane for the first time.

Blackpool were still stuttering, especially away from home, and what had started off as a probable promotion season was becoming a mediocre battle to remain in the top half of the table. Back in November, Blackpool had thrashed Bury 6-0 at Bloomfield Road, makeshift striker Graham Rowe netting a hat trick, and with the Manchester side destined to be relegated at the end of the season, the return game promised a victory on the road for a change. I again went on the supporters' club coach, using the ticket from the original date of the game, in February.

Unfortunately, football is never that simple, and Blackpool lost 2-0 to a Bobby Collins-inspired team. Collins sent a ball over the Blackpool defence on the quarter hour and Jones took it superbly before hitting his shot into the net, and Collins made it 2-0 from Kerr's partially-cleared cross after twenty-four minutes. Thomas made two great saves to keep Jones efforts out, with Blackpool's only chance of scoring coming when Forrest snatched the ball off Suddick's toes late on in the game. Three days later, Blackpool went to Burnden Park, thrashed Bolton 4-1 in the best performance of the season – and the board promptly sacked popular manager Stan Mortenson for non-football related matters!

Bury, meanwhile, were one of the most famous names in football, although their success was all a long way in the past. They had won the FA Cup in 1900 and 1903, defeating Southampton 4-0 and Derby by a record 6-0 scoreline. They finished fourth in the league table in 1925-26, but since then had done very little, apart from losing on aggregate to Birmingham City in the 1963 League Cup Semi-Final. They reached Wembley in the Third Division play-off final in 1995, only to lose to Chesterfield.

Bury v Fulham 1968

Bury v Arsenal ticket from 1959, v Shrewsbury ticket 1994
and coach ticket from Blackpool 1969

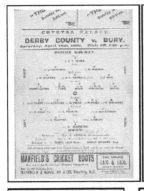

Derby County, FA Cup Final
1903

Birmingham City (a) League
Cup Semi-Final 1963

Birmingham City (h) League
Cup Semi-Final 1963

Liverpool (a), FA Cup Fifth
Round 1980

Manchester United (h), Football
League Cup Fourth Round 1987

Derby County (h), FA Cup
Fourth Round 1950

Birmingham City (h) FLC Semi-
Final 1963 - postponed

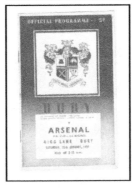

Arsenal (h) FA Cup Third
Round 1959

Blackpool (a), Lancashire Cup
Final 1994

16. **Fulham** v Blackpool

Played at **Craven Cottage** on 12th April 1969

Football League Division Two

Fulham 0
Blackpool 0

Attendance 7,154

16 Fulham – Craven Cottage

Our play didn't improve for our last away match, at relegated Fulham in April. I went by train as usual for trips to London, again with Robert Frowen, but my travel sickness was now affecting me on train journeys and I felt ill throughout the day. The boat race had taken place a week earlier, Cambridge defeating Oxford on the Thames and passing right by the Craven Cottage ground. This afternoon, though, was extremely windy, and neither side were able to master the conditions. Blackpool failed to be lifted at all by the West-end scene, and an abysmal goalless draw resulted. Green and Armfield performed well for Blackpool, as did Byrne and Conway for Fulham. Armfield headed one goalbound effort from Fulham's ex-Tottenham star Cliff Jones off the line. With just under a quarter of an hour to go, Suddick blasted a shot over the Fulham bar, and Blackpool's best chance of the game had gone. Taylor was the busier of the two goalkeepers, making a superb one-handed save to keep a Lloyd volley out. Lloyd did get the ball in the net, but the 'goal' was disallowed for offside, and the same player also put a shot well wide early in the second half. To complete a bad day, I still felt ill on the train journey home, and didn't even enjoy the fact that once again the players were on the same train.

Fulham reached the FA Cup Semi-Finals in 1958 and 1962, losing on each occasion after a replay to the eventual beaten finalists, Manchester United and Burnley respectively. Added to two Semi-Final defeats in 1908 and 1936, luck didn't seem to favour the Cottagers, but in 1975 they finally reached Wembley – although again their Semi-Final with Birmingham went to a replay. In the all-London final, they lost 2-0 to two Alan Sealey goals in a minute for West Ham. Their next taste of glory came in 2002, when another Semi-Final defeat was registered against Chelsea but victory in the Inter-Toto Cup guaranteed them EUFA Cup football for the 2002-2003 season. In the League Cup, they didn't have as much success, with quarterfinal appearances in 1968, 1971 and 2000 their best performances.

Under the chairmanship of Harrod's owner El Fayyad, Fulham rose from the Third Division to the Premiership around the turn of the Millennium, and they also achieved national success with their women's football side at the same time, taking over from Doncaster and Arsenal as the dominant force in ladies' football. For much of this period Fulham were without a permanent home, sharing Queens Park Rangers' ground whilst awaiting redevelopment of the listed Craven Cottage buildings, finally returning to their spiritual home for the 2004-05 season.

Blackpool autographs on the match programme

West Ham United at Wembley, FA Cup Final 1975

Manchester United, FA Cup Semi-Final 1958

Manchester United, FA Cup Semi-Final replay 1958

Burnley, FA Cup Semi-Final 1962

Birmingham City, FA Cup Semi-Final 1975

Burnley, FA Cup Semi-Final replay 1962

Birmingham City, FA Cup Semi-Final replay 1975

Chelsea FA Cup Semi-Final 2002

Huddersfield Town (h) League Cup quarterfinal 1968

Blackpool (h), FA Cup quarterfinal 1948

Leicester City (h) 2002 – last game at the 'old' Craven Cottage

Arsenal (h) – last 'home' game at Loftus Road, 2004

Hertha Berlin (a) EUFA Cup 2002

Fulham v Blackpool ticket 1997

Hajduk Split (h) EUFA Cup 2002

FC Haka (h), Inter Toto Cup 2002

Charlton Athletic, FA Women's Cup Final 2003

Watford (h), the return to Craven Cottage 2004

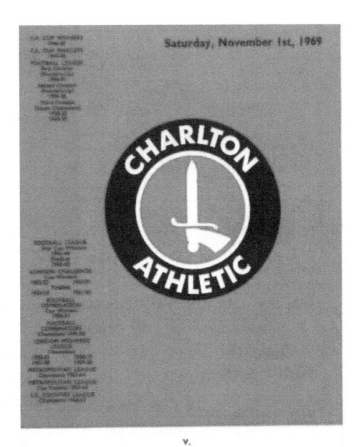

17 Charlton Athletic – The Valley

Blackpool made a poor start to the 1969-70 season and were languishing towards the bottom of the table in the early weeks, but they gradually began to climb the table with a series of away victories. After three in a row, at Middlesbrough, Millwall and Sheffield United, our next match was away to Charlton. I had seen all of our league games bar the one at Norwich, and was intent on getting to as many as possible in the season. For this game I went to London by train with my regular travelling companions of Mick O'Brien and Rob Frowen, meeting up with Ian Carden (who was at University in London) when we arrived in the capital. We went to get some fish and chips before the game, and I almost choked when I realised that the fashion in London was to leave the backbone in with the fish! It was not one of the best meals I ever had!

London fans in particular were notorious for causing trouble, and as we entered the ground a group of Charlton youths approached us. They were all rough looking, and we expected the worst, but instead they took us into the Charlton supporters club and bought us all a drink, looking after us in the way that all true supporters should treat opposition fans. The leader, a leather-jacketed lad called 'Ygor' told us about some of the trouble that they had been involved in during the season, at places like Bolton, yet we didn't feel under any threat at all. There was also a small skinhead, who stood out as he was wearing a suit, which was unheard of at the time. We left them just before kick-off to take our places in the paddock, for a game that appeared to be destined for a goalless draw until Blackpool scored twice in the closing minutes. First of all Moore was tackled as he attempted to dribble clear, and McPhee thumped the ball into the net. In celebration, Rob charged up and down the terraces like a complete and utter lunatic, bringing puzzled looks from the local supporters around us. Charlton threw everything forward in an attempt to get the equaliser, but on the break 'Pool went 2-0 in front. Brown found himself free down the wing, and his cross fell for Craven to score past Wright. Gregory did put the ball into the net for Charlton, but the 'goal' was disallowed for a foul on Thomson, and Blackpool ended with a thoroughly deserved victory.

We were still expecting some trouble from Charlton supporters after the game, so I bought a Charlton rosette and Rob a Charlton hat, which we wore on the tube in an attempt to pass ourselves off as home fans. Unfortunately, as we stopped off at one station, hordes of Arsenal fans, returning from a 5-1 victory at Crystal Palace boarded the train. At every subsequent stop, they all charged off, then all charged back on again, and we sat there as unobtrusively as possible, hiding our recently purchased Charlton favours. A few stations down the line, a mob of Tottenham fans waited on the platform following their home match, and how a full-scale riot didn't occur is still a mystery to me now, but somehow we found ourselves back at Euston unscathed.

On the train home, we once again travelled with the Blackpool players, and went up to them for their autographs. Jimmy Armfield was interested in where we had got the Charlton colours, but as we tried to explain the reasoning behind the purchase and the subsequent nightmare tube journey, he looked at us as if we were mentally retarded. I'm sure he thought we had stolen the colours from some poor Charlton fans!

Charlton achieved their place in the football record books during a three-year spell in the mid 1930's. They were Third Division South champions in 1934-35, promoted from the Second Division as runners-up in 1935-36, and First Division runners-up in the 1936-37 season. During the war they played Chelsea at Wembley in a War Cup final, and their run of form continued after the war when they contested the first two FA Cup finals, losing 4-1 to Derby in 1946, and defeating Burnley 1-0 in 1947. Both marches went to extra-time, and remarkably both also featured the ball bursting! Athletic also made further Wembley appearances towards the end of the century, taking on Blackburn Rovers in the Full Members Final of 1987, and winning promotion in 1998 following a penalty shoot-out against Sunderland after a thrilling 4-4 draw in the play-off final. They had also emerged victorious in the play-offs before they were played at Wembley, and when they consisted of teams trying to go up and one side attempting to stay up, Leeds being the unlucky side in this two-legged affair. In the League Cup, they only managed three appearances in the Fourth Round, in 1963, 1965 and 1979. Perhaps their greatest claim to fame, though, comes with their involvement in the record score for a league match. Four days before Christmas 1957, they entertained Bill Shankly's Huddersfield Town, and at one point were trailing 1-5, as well as being a man down due to injury. Winger Johnny Summers, who was sadly to die of cancer at the early age of 33, chose this game to be his eternal memorial, scoring five times and making the other two goals as Charlton overturned the deficit to triumph 7-6!

1944 War Cup Final (South) at
Wembley v Chelsea

1947 FA Cup Final at Wembley
v Burnley

1998 First Division Play-Off
Final at Wembley v Sunderland

Leeds United (a) First Division
Play-Off Final 1987

Leeds (at Birmingham) Division
One Play-Off Final Replay 1987

Leeds United (h) First Division
Play-Off Final 1987

Blackburn Rovers 1987 Full
Members Cup Final, Wembley

Arsenal, 1943 War Cup South
Final at Wembley

A.S.O. Ostende (h), 1966

Manchester United (a), FA Cup
quarterfinal 1994

Leyton Orient (a), League Cup
Fourth Round 1962-63

Manchester United (h), FA
Youth Cup Semi-Final 2003

Bolton (h) FA Cup quarterfinal
2000

Autographs of Blackpool in 1969

Huddersfield (h), 7-6 game from
1957

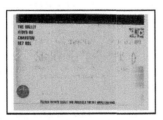

Charlton v Blackpool FA Cup ticket from 2002
and rail ticket from 1969

87

FOOTBALL LEAGUE – Division 2

NEWS and RECORD

Aston Villa
(Claret Shirts, Blue Shorts)

1 John PHILLIPS
2 Michael WRIGHT
3 Charlie AITKEN
4 Barrie HOLE
5 Lew CHATTERLEY
6 Fred TURNBULL
7 Emment KAPENGWE
8 Brian GODFREY
9 Lionel MARTIN
10 Bruce RIOCH
11 Willie ANDERSON
12

Blackpool
(White Shirts, Tangerine Shorts)

1 Harry THOMSON
2 Jimmy ARMFIELD
3 Henry MOWBRAY
4 John McPHEE
5 Glyn JAMES
6 David HATTON
7 Ron BROWN
8 John CRAVEN
9 Fred PICKERING
10 Alan SUDDICK
11 Tom HUTCHISON
12

Saturday, 15th NOVEMBER, 1969

ONE SHILLING

---

18. Aston Villa v Blackpool

Played at **Villa Park** on 15th November 1969

Football League Division Two

Aston Villa 0
Blackpool 0

Attendance 24,942

After the run of victories away from home had been brought to an end with a derby defeat at Blackburn, Blackpool had a chance to get back to winning ways with a visit to struggling Aston Villa, who were under the management of Tommy Docherty. As our coach pulled on to the car park, hundreds of skinhead Villa fans were staring at us, as if they were noting our faces for later. The game turned out to be an atrocious goalless draw, memorable only for the appearance for Villa of the first Zambian footballers to make it into the Football League, Emment Kapengwe and Freddie Mwila. Suddick was only just off target twice with snapshots, and a Pickering volley also missed narrowly, as Blackpool looked the likelier scorers, but for Villa the Zambians looked too slow for this standard of football.

One half time score of interest to both sets of fans was Preston 4 Birmingham 0 (which was also the score after ninety minutes). This provided some mixed fortunes for Villa fans, who cheered because the hated Birmingham rivals were losing, but as Preston were down at the bottom of the league along with Villa, they could really have done with Preston losing.

Our trip back to the coach park was worrying, with Villa troublemakers lining the route looking for Blackpool fans, and once again I breathed a huge sigh of relief when we reached the safety of the coach - going to away games was certainly an experience!

Aston Villa were one of the most famous names in football, even though they were going through a tough patch when I first visited them. League Champions six times by 1910, they had to wait until 1981 to collect their seventh title. They also had seven FA Cup victories to their name, although again they had a long interval of non-achievement between the sixth success in 1920 and the seventh in 1957, if you discount the War Cup Final victory over Blackpool in 1944. In 1897, they had won the Football League and FA Cup double, emulating Preston's achievement of eight years earlier. Villa won the inaugural Football League Cup competition in 1961, and went on to have further success in the competition in 1975, 1977, 1994 and 1996, but their greatest achievement came in 1982, when a Peter Withe goal saw them defeat Bayern Munich 1-0 to lift the European Cup. They also triumphed in Europe in 2001, albeit in the more sedate Inter Toto Cup.

Ticket for Leicester v Liverpool FA Cup Semi-Final replay 1974

Villa v Liverpool ticket 1982

Ticket for Liverpool v West Ham United League Cup Final replay 1981

Aston Villa v Barcelona ticket from the European Super Cup, 1982, and Villa v Santos programme, 1972

Bayern Munich in Rotterdam,
1982 European Cup Final

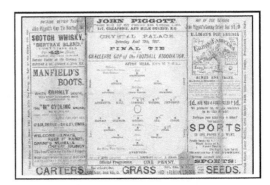

Everton, 1897 FA Cup Final

Barcelona (h) 1982 European
Super Cup

Penarol, 1982 World Clubs' Cup
in Tokyo

Basel (h) 2001 Inter-Toto Cup
Final

1892 FA Cup Final v West
Bromwich Albion

1913 FA Cup Final v
Sunderland

1920 FA Cup Final v
Huddersfield

Blackpool (a) 1944 War Cup
North Final

Blackpool (h) 1944 War Cup
North Final

1957 FA Cup Final v
Manchester United

1975 League Cup Final v
Norwich City

1994 League Cup Final v
Manchester United

1996 League Cup Final v Leeds
United

1977 League Cup Final v
Everton

1977 League Cup Final Replay v
Everton

1977 League Cup Final Second
Replay v Everton

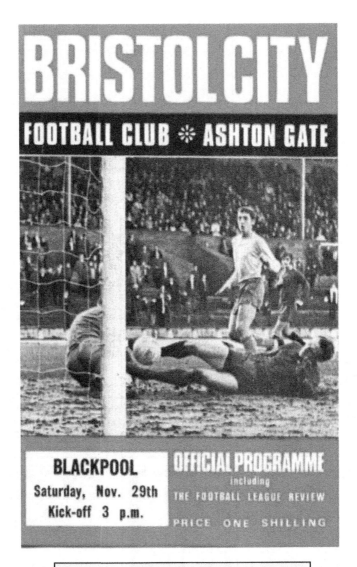

19. Bristol City v Blackpool

Played at Ashton Gate on 29th November 1969

Football League Division Two

Bristol City (1)2 [Rooks, Sharpe]
Blackpool (0)1 [Hutchison]

Attendance 14,818

19 Bristol City – Ashton Gate

Blackpool made it three away games without a win when they were beaten 2-1 at Bristol City at the end of November. I again travelled on the supporters' club coach, and after we entered the ground, a group of about a dozen of us decided to 'take' the Bristol end. We stood there in the middle of it in complete control - that is until the main force of Bristol fans arrived just a few minutes before kick-off. We looked likely candidates for a kicking, but managed to escape to watch the game from the far left-hand corner of their Kop.

In a game played on a frozen pitch, City went into the lead when Rooks scored from a corner. It should have been 2-0 when Bush clipped a simple effort wide at the far post, and Blackpool's sole response was a Suddick attempt from twelve yards. City went 2-0 in front when Sharpe turned in Garland's sliced shot, and it took until three minutes from time before Tommy Hutchison pulled a goal back for us. He then hit the bar directly from a corner to almost snatch a draw, but anything other than a 2-1 defeat would have been unjust judging by our performance on the afternoon. After the promising October had brought thoughts of a surge up the league table, prospects looked bleak again for Blackpool now November had finished, though results of our main contenders did allow some hope for optimism.

Bristol City were yet another club whose days of greatness lay in the distant past. They had finished as runners-up in the league in the 1906-07 season and were FA Cup runners-up in 1909. They won the Welsh Cup in 1934 and reached the semi-final of the Football League Cup in 1971 and 1989, losing to the eventual winners on each occasion. The Robins tasted Wembley success by defeating Bolton 3-0 in the 1986 Freight Rover Trophy, and won the competition again at the Millennium Stadium in 2003 with a 2-0 success over Carlisle, but for a city as large as Bristol this was a woefully poor return for their loyal supporters.

Bristol City v Liverpool ticket, FA Cup quarterfinal 1974

Bolton Wanderers, Freight Rover Final 1986

Carlisle United, LDV Vans Trophy Final 2003

Liverpool (h), FA Cup quarterfinal 1974

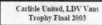

Tottenham Hotspur (h) Football League Cup Semi-Final 1970-71

Tottenham Hotspur (a) Football League Cup Semi-Final 1970-71

Nottingham Forest (h) Football League Cup Semi-Final 1989

Nottingham Forest (a) Football League Cup Semi-Final 1989

Walsall (h) Third Division Play-Off Final 1988

Walsall (a) Third Division Play-Off Final 1988

20. Birmingham City v Blackpool

Played at St Andrews 26th December 1969

Football League Division Two

Birmingham City (1)2 [James own goal, Hateley]
Blackpool (0)3 [Hutchison, James, Suddick]

Attendance 29,540

20 Birmingham City – St Andrews

The postponement of the game at Swindon just before Christmas meant that we didn't play away from home after the Bristol City defeat for almost a month. On Boxing Day we again headed for Birmingham for the game at St Andrews against Birmingham City.

For all that they came from England's second largest city, Birmingham had achieved practically no success at all in their history. In complete contrast to their neighbours Aston Villa, the side formerly known as Small Heath had never won the league, and had only made two appearances in the FA Cup Final, losing to another neighbour, West Bromwich, in 1931, and to Manchester City in the "Bert Trautman broken neck" final of 1956. They achieved as much in Europe as they did domestically, reaching the final of the Inter Cities Fairs Cup in both 1960 and 1961, when Barcelona and Roma proved too strong for the Blues. Their one moment of cup glory came in 1963, when they defeated arch-rivals Villa over two legs to win the Football League Cup, and they also contested the first match to be played at Cardiff's Millennium Stadium after Wembley was no longer available, losing an epic 2001 League Cup Final against Liverpool on penalties.

Birmingham returned to Cardiff the following year and defeated Norwich on penalties to win the First Division play-off final, and with Wembley victories over Tranmere in 1991 and Carlisle in 1995 in the Leyland Daf / Auto Windscreens Cup, they finally managed to achieve the level of success that their size warranted.

On arrival at the ground, we went into their club shop, and bought a few souvenirs depicting their ex-striker Fred Pickering, including one large poster that I later got autographed by 'our' Fred (but sadly, the autograph faded as I'd only given him a felt-tipped pen to write it with).

We stood behind the goal in a packed stadium, and in a good first half Birmingham took a 1-0 lead when Glyn James put through his own goal after nine minutes, steering a low cross from Thomson into the net. Pickering battled without support against his old club as Blackpool struggled to make an impact before half time. Les Shannon must have had strong words with the team during the interval, for they came out for the second half in an attacking frame of mind, and it was no surprise when Tommy Hutchison equalised early in the half. The mob of Birmingham supporters who had been standing alongside Blackpool fans behind the nets launched a furious assault on us as we celebrated the goal, scattering Blackpool fans into groups of no more than three or four people. Further goals by James and Suddick in the next quarter of an hour were greeted with total silence by the away support as we desperately tried to avoid any more trouble.

Rob, Mick, Ian and I left to go back to the coach with a few minutes to go and Blackpool comfortably in front by 3-1 (we missed a late second goal by City's Hateley which reduced the final victory margin to 3-2). We had hoped to avoid any trouble this way, but we soon realised that we had made a mistake. Hundreds of City hooligans were running towards the road where our coaches were parked, and we found ourselves right in the middle of them having to run down the road with them. We joined in singing the "So let's fight" songs, terrified of what would happen if anyone noted our accents, but as we rounded a corner we saw police waiting, and thankfully they cleared the mob away. Ian, though, was not so lucky, for he was a longhaired Blackpool fan in the middle of a mob of skinheads. On the pretext that he didn't know the words to the song, they had kicked him to the ground inflicting a terrible beating on him. We later saw another Blackpool longhaired fan who had also been beaten up, and other people said that they saw the mob behind Ian pointing him out to the rest of the gang just before the attack began. His face was covered in lumps and smeared in black boot polish, and our excellent victory was soon forgotten as we started a miserable journey home.

The following day, we all felt a sense of immense satisfaction when we heard that Queens Park Rangers hooligans had stoned the Birmingham fans' coaches after their game in London. We felt no sympathy at all for them when we heard how they had to travel home for a hundred miles in freezing weather with the wind roaring in through the broken windows.

Aston Villa (h) Football League
Cup Final 1963

Barcelona (h) Inter Cities Fairs
Cup Final 1960

Aston Villa (a) Football League
Cup Final 1963

Barcelona (a) Inter Cities Fairs
Cup Final 1960

Manchester City, 1956 FA Cup
Final

Liverpool, Football League Cup
Final 2001

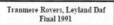

Tranmere Rovers, Leyland Daf
Final 1991

Carlisle United, Auto
Windscreens Shield Final 1995

Norwich City, First Division
Play-Off Final 2002

Blackpool, 1951 FA Cup Semi-Final

Derby County, 1946 FA Cup Semi-Final Replay

Chelsea (h), 1968 FA Cup quarterfinal

St Andrews Opening 1906

Small Heath v Wolverhampton 1896

Genoa (h), 1995 Anglo-Italian Cup

Small Heath v Preston from 1905

Birmingham v Liverpool ticket 1982

WATFORD
FOOTBALL
CLUB

SEASON 1969-70

(Graphic Photo)

Saturday, 10th January, 1970

FOOTBALL LEAGUE DIVISION TWO

BLACKPOOL

Kick-off 3.00 p.m.

OFFICIAL PROGRAMME   ONE SHILLING

---

21. Watford v Blackpool

Played at **Vicarage Road** on 10th January 1970

Football League Division Two

Watford 0
Blackpool (1)1 [Pickering]

Attendance 12,052

The first game I went to in 1970 was at Watford, a week after Blackpool had drawn their FA Cup Third Round match against Arsenal at Highbury. The Vicarage Road pitch was covered in snow, but a group of Blackpool fans who had travelled down and arrived early in the morning helped to clear it away so that the match could take place. Their work was rewarded when a Fred Pickering goal gave us a 1-0 victory in a game that I remember more for our stand seat than for the actual match. We were at the far right of the stand, next to a window that was so filthy it was almost impossible to see through, and any play in the near corner of the ground was hidden from my view. Although the ticket did indicate that the view was partially obscured, I was expecting to be sat behind a stanchion, where I would be able to move my head to see round the obstruction.

Watford did most of the attacking, looking to complete the double after their 3-0 victory at the seaside earlier in the season. In the second half Endean hit the bar with a tremendous shot, but by then Blackpool were already in front. Blackpool's goal came in the first half when Hutchison put a measured pass through to Suddick, whose cross was met by Pickering's head. In the second half, Walley nearly beat Thomson with a low snap shot and Green forced Thomson to make a save. At the other end, Walker had to go full length to save from Craven.

On our journey home from Watford, we stopped at a motorway service station and met a coach-load of Arsenal fans returning from their 2-1 defeat at Old Trafford, where Peter Marinello had put the 'Gunners' ahead on his debut. It looked like an ugly scene would develop, as they told us what would happen to us (both on and off the pitch) when the FA Cup replay took place, but fortunately nothing more serious developed. After stopping at the motorway services, we continued on our journey home, stopping for a drink at the Birmingham City supporters club. Strangely enough, although they didn't make us welcome on our Boxing Day visit, the people of Birmingham showed plenty of hospitality on this occasion and we had a very enjoyable evening.

The remainder of the journey home was passed in a fairly drunken haze. Rob Frowen was extremely inebriated and totally unaware of where he was, after a few renderings of the Watford song in praise of their striker - 'Na na na na, na na na na, Hey Ey, Barry Endean', to the tune of "Steam's" "Goodbye". Consequently, his equally drunk girlfriend Shirley seemed more interested in me than in the drunken Rob.

Watford went on to knock Liverpool out of the FA Cup in the quarterfinal, precipitating the break-up of Bill Shankly's team of the 60's, only to lose 5-1 to Chelsea in the semi-final. Nothing much happened at Vicarage Road until Elton John became chairman and Graham Taylor was appointed manager. Taylor had taken Lincoln to the Fourth Division with a record points total, and the young manager took Watford from that same Fourth Division in 1978 to runners-up in the First Division by 1983, and the following year they faced Everton at Wembley in the FA Cup Final. Had they taken the chances that came their way, Watford would have been celebrating an astounding cup victory. Taylor's side also reached the League Cup semi-final in 1979, bowing out to eventual winners and European Champions Nottingham Forest, but they had Wembley success when defeating Bolton Wanderers 2-0 in the 1999 First Division play-off final. They reached the Semi-Final of the FA Cup again in 2003, losing by the odd goal to Southampton.

Watford v Blackpool ticket 1970

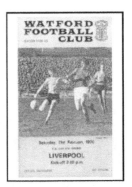

Everton, 1984 FA Cup Final

Bolton, 1999 First Division Play-Off Final

Liverpool (h), FA Cup quarterfinal 1970

Chelsea, FA Cup Semi-Final 1970

Nottingham Forest (a) 1979 Football League Cup Semi-Final

Nottingham Forest (h) 1979 Football League Cup Semi-Final

Sparta (a) EUFA Cup 1983

Kaiserslautern (h) 1983 EUFA Cup

Southampton, 2003 FA Cup Semi-Final

SATURDAY, 31st JANUARY, 1970
VERSUS
BLACKPOOL
KICK-OFF 3 p.m.

BLUEBIRDS

1/-

JOURNAL

22. Cardiff City v Blackpool

Played at **Ninian Park** on 31st January 1970

Football League Division Two

Cardiff City (1)2 [Toshack 2]
Blackpool (1)2 [Burns, Suddick]

Attendance 24,717

Blackpool defeated Arsenal 3-2 in a memorable FA Cup Third Round replay, coming from 0-2 down at half time and getting the winning goal in the last minute. True to form, though, they then proceeded to lose at home to lowly Mansfield in the fourth round. That defeat left promotion as our only target, and the run in commenced with a difficult game in South Wales a week later at Cardiff.

John Toshack put City ahead in the first half, beating fellow Welsh international James to a header and planting it past Thomson. Blackpool equalised almost immediately through Mickey Burns, allowing our small band of supporters in the seats behind the goal to turn the taunts back on to the home fans who had just been mocking us. Bell had tripped Burns on the edge of the area, and Suddick's free kick reached the Blackpool striker, who shot past Davies in the home goal. In the second half, Toshack again beat James in the air to restore City's lead, but again Blackpool equalised immediately, this time when Hutchison's run put Suddick through to stroke the ball past Davies.

Blackpool had conceded seven goals to Cardiff over the last two seasons, and John Toshack had scored them all, but Harry Thomson was on top form, preventing City from scoring a third goal. In fact, Blackpool almost stole a win right on the final whistle, as Armfield put Hutchison clear for a run in on the Cardiff goal, but with only the goalkeeper standing between him and the winning goal, the referee blew the final whistle to leave the game drawn at 2-2. We again stopped off in the Midlands on the way home, this time calling at the Walsall Supporters' Club.

Cardiff had made history back in the 1920's when they became the first side to take the FA Cup out of England after defeating Arsenal 1-0 in 1927. Two years earlier, they had lost 1-0 to Sheffield United in the final. Most of City's triumphs, though, came via the Welsh Cup, with victories in the competition in 1912, 1920, 1922, 1923, 1927, 1928, 1930, 1956, 1959, 1964, 1965, 1967, 1968, 1969, 1970, 1971, 1973, 1974, 1976, 1988, 1992 and 1993. Through these successes they competed in the European Cup Winners Cup with some success, reaching the semi-final against Hamburg in 1968. The story could have been even better, for they drew the first leg away from home and were level in the second leg until a late goalkeeping error gifted Hamburg the victory. The irony of it all was that Cardiff's victory over Arsenal came about due to an error made by the Arsenal goalkeeper. Cardiff reached the quarterfinal of the Cup Winners Cup three years later, winning 1-0 at home against Real Madrid before losing the second leg at the Bernabeu 2-0. City were also defeated at the penultimate level in the 1965-66 League Cup competition, losing on aggregate 10-3 to West Ham United after two five-goal defeats. In 2003, they won promotion to the First Division after a 1-0 play-off final victory over Queens Park Rangers at the city's own Millennium Stadium.

Cardiff v Blackpool ticket, 1999

Aston Villa – opening of Ninian Park 1910 (left) and Wrexham (a), Welsh Cup Final replay 1960 (right)

1927 FA Cup Final v Arsenal

Hamburg (h) 1968 European
Cup Winners Cup Semi-Final

Hamburg (a) 1968 European
Cup Winners Cup Semi-Final

West Ham United (a) Football
League Cup Semi-Final 1965-66

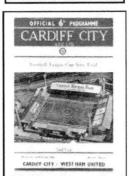

West Ham United (h) Football
League Cup Semi-Final 1965-66

Queens Park Rangers, 2003
Second Division Play-Off Final

Hednesford Town, 1992 Welsh
Cup Final

Barry Town, 1994 Welsh Cup
Final

Wrexham, FAW Cup Final 2000

Wrexham, Welsh Cup Final 1988

Hereford United (a) 1968 Welsh Cup Final

Hereford United (h) 1976 Welsh Cup Final

Swansea Town (a) 1969 Welsh Cup Final

Stourbridge (a) 1974 Welsh Cup Final

Wrexham (h) Welsh Cup Final 1971

Chester (h) Welsh Cup Final 1970

Wrexham (a) 1971 Welsh Cup Final

Wrexham (a) 1967 Welsh Cup Final

| Wrexham (a) 1965 Welsh Cup Final | Wrexham (h) 1967 Welsh Cup Final | Wrexham (h) 1965 Welsh Cup Final Replay |

| Real Zaragoza (h) 1965 Cup Winners Cup quarterfinal | Swansea Town (h), 1969 Welsh Cup Final | Real Madrid (h), 1971 Cup Winners Cup quarterfinal |

| Lovell's Athletic, Welsh Cup Final 1959 | Stourbridge (h), Welsh Cup Final 1974 | New South Wales in Sydney, 1968 |

FOOTBALL LEAGUE DIVISION 2 TUESDAY 31st MARCH 7.30 p.m.

---

23. Leicester City v Blackpool

Played at **Filbert Street** on 31st March 1970

Football League Division Two

Leicester City 0
Blackpool 0

Attendance 32,784

23 Leicester City – Filbert Street

Easter 1970 was good for Blackpool, for home victories over Aston Villa and promotion rivals Sheffield United brought four points out of four. The next evening saw the toughest match of the three, away to one of our other rivals for promotion in Leicester City. This game proved to be one of the most memorable of the season, but for strange reasons.

Leicester had gained a reputation as the 'nearly' men since the war, beaten in four FA Cup Finals between 1949 and 1969. They did win the League Cup in 1964, but in the competition's pre-Wembley days. Even the play-off finals proved elusive, with Wembley defeats in 1992 and 1993 before the Wembley bogey was laid with play-off victories over Derby in 1994 and Crystal palace in 1996. The League Cup was won again in 1997 – although it took a non-Wembley replay before Leicester could lift the trophy, and they had to wait until the last year of Wembley finals, in 2000, before they won a major Wembley final, defeating Tranmere Rovers 2-1 in the League Cup.

The weather on the journey down was atrocious, with rain similar to that we experienced in Huddersfield in May 1968. We went into a pub in Leicester as soon as we arrived in the city and I needed one drink to rid me of the 'nightmare' memory of one old woman we had passed on the way into Leicester. She had a hideous purple face - I still shudder when I remember it all these years later. Just before it was time for us to leave the pub for the ground, we found that it was surrounded by Leicester hooligans, one of whom charged in and tried to get Blackpool fans to come out and fight. We stayed in as late as possible, then left just before kick-off expecting the mob to be still there, but fortunately the streets were deserted.

We went straight to the ground, where inside there were more than 32,000 people, but the pitch resembled a lake. Shortly before the scheduled kick-off time, referee Jim Finney called the game off. An announcement over the loudspeakers asked everybody to wait for further instructions. I was thinking how I wouldn't be able to afford another trip down here, and was feeling thoroughly miserable, when Finney came back out on to the pitch. A few minutes later, he announced that the game would go ahead after all, seemingly changing his mind because of the numbers of fans who were in the ground.

We fully expected the game to be a joke, and doubted if it would continue beyond half time, with our tricky winger Tommy Hutchison's "dainty" style being totally ineffective. Instead, an excellent 0-0 draw resulted, with Hutchison one of the stars of the evening and the pitch gradually getting better as the game went on. James blocked three Fern efforts early in the game, and in the second half both Matthews and Fern had attempts blocked on the line. Glover hit a shot wide, and although Blackpool were mainly pushed back on the defensive, they had strong appeals for penalties turned down when Hutchison and Murray went down under challenges in the area and Pickering capitalised when a backpass stuck in the mud, only to hit the side-netting with his shot. Even so, we left thinking that this was definitely a case of a point won rather than one dropped.

Manchester United at Wembley,
1963 FA Cup Final

Stoke City (a) 1964 Football
League Cup Final

Stoke City (h) 1964 Football
League Cup Final

Middlesbrough, 1997 Football
League Cup Final replay

Derby County, 1994 Division
One Play-Off Final

Crystal Palace, 1996 Division
One Play-Off Final

Athletico Madrid (h), European
Cup Winners Cup 1961-62

Leicester v Nottingham Forest
ticket from 1995

Red Star (a), EUFA Cup 2000

24. Swindon Town v Blackpool

Played at **The County Ground** on 7th April 1970

Football League Division Two

Swindon Town (1)1 [Horsfield]
Blackpool (1)1 [Burns]

Attendance 28,520

Swindon now seemed to be the only side that could prevent Blackpool from gaining promotion. Although we only had three games left, they were all away from home, at Swindon where we were making our third attempt to play the match, our local derby at Preston and finally the second re-arranged game at Oxford, Swindon's local derby opponents. We needed three points to be sure of promotion, provided that we didn't lose at Swindon. Rumours were rife that if we needed a win or a draw at Oxford, United would 'throw' the game as promotion for Swindon could have crippled Oxford financially, but hopefully we would already have secured the necessary points by the time we went to the Manor Ground.

Swindon had won the League Cup in 1969 by defeating Arsenal at Wembley 3-1 after extra time – Roger Smart gave them the lead, Bobby Gould equalised very late on for Arsenal, but in extra time two Don Rogers goals sent the trophy to the West Country. They had almost failed to reach Wembley at the final stage, losing at home in the semi-final to First Division Burnley but winning the away leg, and eventually coming from behind to win the replay. As promotion from the Third Division was also achieved, Swindon emulated Queens Park Rangers' feat of two years earlier. The run of success continued with a 3-0 win in Napoli to win the Anglo-Italian Cup in 1970, as well as an FA Cup quarterfinal appearance the same season, before a period in the doldrums. Swindon thought they had reached the top flight in 1990 after defeating Sunderland at Wembley in the Second Division play-off final, only to be refused their place following financial irregularities at the County Ground. Not to be beaten, Swindon were back in the play-offs again three years later, defeating Leicester 4-3 in a thriller to reach the Premier League for the first time. Once there, though, they couldn't consolidate and were soon battling it out in the lower divisions of the Football League once again. Town were also FA Cup semi-finalists in 1910 and 1912.

The supporters' club ran two coaches to Swindon, and it was noticeable that most attention was centred on the additional coach, as it had a lot of 'bigwigs' on it. Photographs of some of these 'once-a-year' supporters even appeared in the Gazette, whilst the regulars who had travelled across the country all season were shunned. We arrived in Swindon quite early and walked around the inside of the ground before the gates were closed in readiness for the arrival of the evening's crowd. The local fish and chip shop ranked alongside the one we had visited at Charlton earlier in the season as the worst I'd ever had the misfortune to visit. I suppose the one thing in its favour was that this one sold a fish that didn't include its backbone, unlike the one I had bought in all innocence when we went to the Valley.

We weren't expecting any trouble from the home fans, as they had been voted the league's best supporters in the previous season, beating Liverpool into second place. As soon as the gates were officially opened, we entered the ground on the Swindon end, but we soon had to move as the home fans hurled eggs at us! They even turned the standard chant of 'Aggro' into 'Eggro'. We went to the other end of the ground, to find another mob of Swindon supporters, undoubtedly intent on causing trouble, but we eventually managed to get ourselves in place behind the goal.

It was obvious that this game was going to be a 28,000 sell-out, so when I had bought a 'match-the-crowd' ticket before the game and saw it printed a crowd of just over 20,000 I knew that I had no chance of winning. It also said that if the attendance exceeded 23,000 or so, then that ticket would be the winning ticket, so whoever bought that ticket would know they had won as soon as they opened it. The official attendance was 28,520, but the game failed to live up to the high expectations of this enormous West Country gathering. Swindon took the lead through Horsfield after just three minutes, when he followed up to score after Butler's snap-shot had been blocked. Thomson then saved a close range effort from Don Rogers, and in reply Pickering put an angled shot across goal after twenty minutes. Blackpool equalised ten minutes before half time when Mickey Burns headed a lobbed Suddick pass over Downsborough. Blackpool now began to get on top, and the Swindon defence were forced to make some desperate saving clearances.

In the second half, Rogers had one solo run which earned the home team a fruitless corner, Noble had an effort disallowed quarter of an hour before the end, and on eighty-two minutes the same player missed a sitter, shooting wide from twelve yards out. Swindon fans were not happy with Blackpool's robust tackling, claiming that we were far too dirty. They were probably justified in their claims, as we had abandoned our normal flowing football that had been used to such good effect in away matches, settling instead for a 'must-not-lose' approach. There were no further goals, and Blackpool left the pitch knowing that one win would clinch promotion, whereas Swindon realised that their chances had all but disappeared now. After the game, the streets were full of Swindon fans looking for Blackpool supporters who they could take their revenge on. Mick and I had to stand in a local bus queue at one stage, and I had to cover my tangerine polo-neck shirt with a white handkerchief as we tried to avoid any trouble, and even then I heard one of them shout, "They're hiding in that bus queue". Swindon may have won the award for the best-behaved supporters, but that night the town became a place I was exceedingly glad to get away safely from.

Arsenal, 1969 Football League
Cup Final

Napoli (a) 1970 Anglo-Italian
Cup Final

A.S. Roma (h) 1969 Anglo-Italian
League Cup Winners Cup Final

Golden Goal Ticket

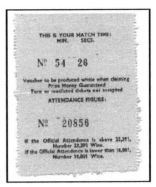

Swindon v Blackpool ticket 1995

Leicester City, 1993 First
Division Play-Off Final

Wolverhampton (h) 1980
Football League Cup Semi-Final

Bolton (h) 1995 Football League
Cup Semi-Final

Crystal Palace (h) First Division
Play-Off Semi-Final 1989

Burnley (a) 1969 Football
League Cup Semi-Final

Burnley 1969 Football League
Cup Semi-Final Replay

Burnley (h) 1969 Football League Cup Semi-Final

Leeds United (h), FA Cup
quarterfinal 1970

119

**FOOTBALL LEAGUE
2nd DIVISION**

UNITED v BLACKPOOL

SATURDAY, 18 APRIL, 1970. Kick-off 3 p.m.

25. Oxford United v Blackpool

Played at **The Manor Ground** on 18th April 1970

Football League Division Two

Oxford United (0)2 [Clayton, Hatch]
Blackpool 0

Attendance 9,190

I had taken an interest in Oxford, formerly known as Headington, ever since they had knocked First Division leaders Blackburn out of the FA Cup in the Fifth Round of 1964 whilst still a Fourth Division side. They only joined the league in 1962, replacing Accrington, amazed everybody by reaching the Second Division in 1968, and continued to surprise many people by reaching the First Division in the 1980's. With stars such as John Aldridge and Ray Houghton in their side, they went to Wembley and won the League Cup in 1986, trouncing Queens Park Rangers 3-0. This was the undoubted high point of their career, and within fifteen years they had plummeted back to the bottom division.

Blackpool had just clinched promotion to the First Division with a 3-0 victory at Preston, Fred Pickering scoring all three goals. Inevitably, the last game at Oxford was an anti-climax, and we were well-beaten 2-0 by second half goals from Clayton and Hatch. However, other events during the day led to my moving my allegiances away from Blackpool just at the point when I should have been tied to them for life.

Just as for the Swindon match, the supporters' club two coaches were provided by - a luxury one, and a decrepit old boneshaker. Needless to say, the loyal supporters were made to travel on the old coach, whilst the 'dignitaries' had the use of the luxury one. This wasn't too bad, though, as we didn't really mind how we got to the game so long as we saw it. A couple of the regular girls, June Parkinson and her friend Joan were on the back seat, and we had a good laugh on the journey, with a few of us winding the Leeds-supporting girls up by chanting for Chelsea. The FA Cup Final a week earlier between Leeds and Chelsea had finished in a 2-2 draw, and we were pretending our allegiance was with the Stamford Bridge side for the forthcoming replay, which Chelsea did win, 2-1.

As we neared Oxford, we passed through Banbury and saw the team coming out of a pub. As they waved to us, it was obvious that some of them (such as Fred Pickering) were obviously the worse for drink, and it showed in their play once the match began. Nobody was too upset about the performance, though, as this was supposed to be the celebration after all of the hard work during the season. What upset all of the fans on our coach was what happened once we arrived at Oxford. Their supporters club had laid out a superb spread for after the game, including champagne, as a way of celebrating our promotion. We were soon told, however, that it was the patrons of the luxury coach who would be stopping after the game, and we would be leaving immediately the match had finished, although we were promised our usual stop-off point at another supporters' club somewhere on the way back. We protested, but to no avail, and grudgingly we had to go into the ground, standing on the Oxford end.

Some London lads came and stood with us - they were Arsenal and Chelsea supporters, and they'd come down to teach Blackpool fans about 'life in the First Division'. There was also an element of revenge in their plans, for our FA Cup defeat of Arsenal, and our League Cup defeat of Chelsea three seasons earlier. Chelsea fans still remembered this game as it had also resulted in Peter Osgood's leg being broken after a fair challenge by Emlyn Hughes. These lads were fine with our small group, but the Blackpool fans on the visitors' end were less fortunate as they were set upon throughout the game.

At the start, things looked promising for Blackpool, as Lucas cleared a Suddick flick off the line. After this, though, Blackpool seemed to lose interest in the game. Sloan headed on a Hatch cross and Clayton side-footed the first goal home, and the second came when Hatch's shot from a narrow angle went between Thomson's legs. Once the game had finished, we had a long walk back to the coaches, and it turned into a nightmare, with London or Oxford fans all over the place looking for trouble. I found out the next day that one of my friends, Mick Webb, had got a very bad kicking after he tried to hide behind a garden wall. Eventually, though, we got back to the coach and began the journey home, and to really compound the events of the day, the driver refused to let us have our promised stop at a supporters' club en route. He didn't want to make any stops at all, but eventually he was made to stop outside a Midlands pub for five minutes while we bought a pie and a drink for our tea. The rest of our journey home was conducted in a very miserable atmosphere, and the whole sequence of events left an indelible impression on me.

In my anger, I reasoned that there was nothing to be gained by following a team through thick and thin, spending every spare penny I had watching them, if the end-of-season 'band-waggoners' were going to get all the glory. Although I still watched a lot of games in the following season, my move away from my hometown club really began on this Saturday in April 1970.

Oxford v Blackpool ticket from 1996 (left);
Lincoln City (h) – first league home game
1962 (below left); Barrow (h) – record 7-0
league victory 1964 (below centre); 1-0
victory v Manchester United, 1974-5 –
(below right)

Preston North End (h) FA Cup
Sixth Round 1964 – record
attendance 22750

Queens Park Rangers, 1986
Football League Cup Final

Blackburn Rovers (h) FA Cup
Fifth Round 1964

Chelsea (h), Full Members Cup
Southern Final 1985-86

Headington United v Bolton
Wanderers, FA Cup Fourth
Round 1954

Aston Villa (h), Football League
Cup Semi-Final 1986

Pre-league Oxford (Headington)
at Peterborough, FA Cup 2 1958

Chelsea (a), Full Members Cup
Southern Final 1985-86

Darlington (a), September 1962
– first League season

First Footing Volume 02
Steve Wilson

First Footing
Volume Two
By: Steve Wilson

Barbara outside Ibrox, home of Glasgow Rangers, in October 1978

Contents – Volume II

No.	Date	Match Details	Comp	Crowd
49	250577	Liverpool (1)3 [McDermott, Smith, Neal penalty] *Final in Rome* Borussia Monchengladbach (0)1 [Simonsen]	EC	60237
		Season 1978-79		
50	111078	**St Mirren** 0 Glasgow Rangers 0	SLC2	20000

Athletic ₂v ₀ Blackpool

Saturday, 25th April 1970   Kick-off 3-15 p.m.

at Boundary Park

Attendance 2793

OLDHAM	BLACKPOOL
Tangerine Shirts, Blue Shorts Blue Stockings	All White

	OLDHAM		BLACKPOOL
1	John Roberts	1	Harry Thomson
2	Ian Wood ↳ Great shot 38 mins	2	Jimmy Armfield
3	Maurice Whittle	3	Henry Mowbray Peter Nicholson
4	Jim Bowie	4	John McNicholas + (above)
5	Alan Lawson	5	Glyn James
6	Arthur Thomson	6	David Hatton
7	Reg Blore	7	Mick Burns John Murray (withdrawn)
8	David Shaw	8	Ronnie Brown
9	Jim Fryatt ↳ Good header 89 mins	9	Fred Pickering
10	Alan McNeill	10	Alan Suddick
11	Keith Bebbington (Swannock)	11	Tommy Hutchison
12	G. Schofield Robbins	12	To be announced Mick Burns
		13	Harry Mowbray

Referee : Mr. A. Parker (Oldham)

Linesmen : Mr. J. Maxon, Mr. D. Brown

NEXT HOME MATCH

ATHLETIC v BURY

Tuesday, 28th April 1970   Kick-off 7-30 p.m.

L. V. Lawlor, Printers, Oldham.

---

26. Oldham Athletic v Blackpool

Played at **Boundary Park** on 25th April 1970

Friendly Match

Oldham Athletic (0)2 [Wood, Fryatt]
Blackpool 0

Attendance 2,797

Blackpool's 1969-70 season continued for one more week, as they had arranged a friendly away to Fourth Division Oldham, giving me a chance to see a tenth Blackpool away win of the season. I had already seen Oldham play during the season, for they had sent the first team squad for the Lancashire Senior Cup tie at Bloomfield Road a couple of months earlier. Having won that game against a Blackpool reserve side, Oldham were after the scalp of the Blackpool first team to complete a double over the Seasiders.

After all of the coach problems of a week earlier, on this occasion we were given a free trip to Oldham. Blackpool chairman Billy Cartmell had donated 100 free coach tickets as a thank-you to the supporters for following the club throughout the season – that didn't change anything for me, though, for my quarrel was with the supporters club, not the football club.

The game was played in torrential rain, causing us to buy a transfer so we could go into the covered stand. Blackpool didn't seem to be interested in the game, and we lost it 2-0. Thompson had denied Fryatt on several occasions before the deadlock was finally broken two minutes from time, with Wood hammering the ball home after receiving McNeill's pass thirty yards from goal. Fryatt headed the second goal almost from the restart to bring down a rather anti-climactic end to a successful season. It had been good, but not great - compared to 1967-68, there were too many poor performances at home by Les Shannon's team, and we achieved promotion despite gaining five fewer points.

Oldham were perennial lower-league strugglers, yet for a short-time in the 1990's they were one of the most talked-about sides in football. Apart from an FA Cup semi-final in 1913, and a league runners-up position in 1915, success eluded them until the 1989-90 season, even being on the receiving end of the league record aggregate score on Boxing Day 1935 when losing 13-4 to Tranmere Rovers, Bell netting nine for Rovers. Their own record victory also arrived on Boxing Day, in 1962, when Southport were trounced 11-0, with Lister scoring six of the goals. They began the 1989-90 campaign by setting a League Cup record when Frankie Bunn emulated Lister by scoring six goals in Athletic's 7-0 victory over Scarborough, and after knocking Arsenal out and trouncing West Ham 6-0 in the first leg of the semi-final, Oldham found themselves in the final against holders Nottingham Forest. It was almost a glorious weekend for the town, as the Oldham Rugby League club were up against Wigan in the Challenge Cup semi-final, with the prize being a first ever Wembley appearance for them as well. With the Rugby final on the Saturday, and the football on the Sunday, the townspeople of Oldham were preparing for a big weekend in London until Wigan ended their hopes. The football team also suffered disappointment, going down 1-0 to Forest. There seemed to be another chance of Wembley later in the season, when Oldham faced Manchester United in the FA Cup semi-final. Athletic were very unlucky to only draw 3-3 in the first game, being victims of a bad refereeing decision over a disallowed goal, and United took full advantage by winning the replay. Four years later, history repeated itself in a Wembley semi-final, with Oldham 1-0 ahead of United until the last minute of extra time when Hughes' equaliser brought another replay, and ultimately another final appearance for United.

Nottingham Forest at Wembley,
1990 League Cup Final

Manchester United, FA Cup
Semi-Final 1990

Manchester United, FA Cup
Semi-Final Replay 1990

Manchester United, FA Cup
Semi-Final 1994

Manchester United, FA Cup
Semi-Final Replay 1994

West Ham United (h) 1990
Football League Cup Semi-Final

West Ham United (a) 1990
Football League Cup Semi-Final

Scarborough (h), Football
League Cup Third Round 1989

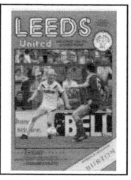

Leeds United (a), 1987 Play-Off
Semi-Final

| Oldham v Blackpool stand ticket 1970 and car park ticket 2002 | Match draw ticket | Southport (h), 1962-63 – Lister's game |

| St Mirren (h), 1978 Anglo-Scottish Cup Semi-Final | Oldham v Blackpool ticket from 2000 | Banik Ostrava (h), 1990 |

| Burnley (a), Anglo-Scottish Final 1978-79 | Southampton (a), Texaco Cup Semi-Final 1974 | Aston Villa (h), FA Cup quarterfinal 1990 |

27. Manchester City v Blackpool

Played at **Maine Road** on 26th August 1970

Football League Division One

Manchester City (2)2 [Lee, Bell]
Blackpool 0

Attendance 37,197

One of the early matches on Blackpool's return to the top flight was a difficult night game away at Manchester City. City had won the League Championship in 1967-68, the FA Cup in 1968-69 and the League Cup and European Cup Winners Cup in 1969-70, so they could truly claim to be the top team in England at the time. City almost retained the Cup Winners Cup, only losing to eventual winners Chelsea in the semi-final after being ravaged by injury. They had also had other periods of success, with an initial championship in 1937 (followed by relegation twelve months later!) and earlier FA Cup victories in 1904, 1934 (when Frank Swift fainted at the final whistle of their game against Portsmouth) and 1956 (when Bert Trautman played for the closing minutes with a broken neck). City also set a league record in the 1957-58 season, scoring 104 goals and conceding 100 to become the only side in league history to notch such a double century.

After the purple-patch period of success in the late 1960's, further success eluded them apart from a 1976 League Cup final victory over Newcastle, and they had to live in the shadow of Manchester United as their city rivals went from strength to strength both at home and in Europe.

Our game was played on a beautiful summer's day, hardly appropriate for a football match. Despite my fall-out with the club over the coach to Oxford at the end of the previous season, there was still really no alternative to using their transport to matches, so I caught the supporters' club coach to Manchester along with my best friend from school, Phil Whitehead.

We were really expecting City to give us an early roasting, and figured that if we could survive the first twenty minutes we would have a chance in the game. In fact Blackpool began the brighter and almost took a shock lead when Booth cleared a Suddick effort off the line. However, when City were awarded a penalty after fifteen minutes our worst fears seemed to be confirmed, but Harry Thomson saved magnificently from Francis Lee, and I began to think that we had survived the onslaught. However, City kept the pressure on and five minutes later Lee put them ahead, sweeping the ball in following a Summerbee shot. On thirty-three minutes, Bell crashed the second home following a run that took him from his own penalty area to the Blackpool goal. Pickering had a chance to reduce the arrears, but Corrigan saved his weak effort easily. City almost had a third in the second half, when Summerbee flicked Lee's right wing cross on to Young, but the striker just failed to reach the ball and turn it in. We managed avoid any further damage, but had learnt a brutal lesson about the quality of finishing of First Division sides.

Liverpool v Everton, FA Cup Semi-Final at Maine Road, 1977, and Newcastle United (a), title clincher in 1968

10

Portsmouth, 1934 FA Cup Final

FC Schalke 04 (h), 1970 European Cup Winners Cup Semi-Final

Leicester City, 1969 FA Cup Final

West Bromwich Albion, 1970 Football League Cup Final

Newcastle United, 1976 Football League Cup Final

Gornik Zabrze, 1970 European Cup Winners Cup Final

Chelsea (h) 1971 European Cup Winners Cup Semi-Final

Chelsea (a) 1971 European Cup Winners Cup Semi-Final

Bologna (h) 1970 Anglo-Italian League Cup Winners Cup

Coach ticket for Blackpool 1970,
Match ticket v Blackpool 1997

Manchester United (h), FA
Charity Shield 1956

Manchester City v Liverpool
ticket from 1982

Front Row—seated from left to right : Fred Pickering, Tommy Hutchinson, Alan Suddick, Jimmy Armfield (Captain), Tony Green, Henry Mowbray, Ronnie Brown. *Middle Row* : John Craven, Terry Alcock, Adam Blacklaw, Harry Thomson, Graham Rowe, Glyn James. *Back Row* : Dave Hatton, Tony Coleman, Bill Bentley, Peter Nicholson, John Hughes, Johnny Johnson, John Murray.

Signed Blackpool team from the programme from 1970

28. Manchester United v Blackpool

Played at **Old Trafford** on 26th September 1970

Football League Division One

Manchester United (1)1 [Best]
Blackpool (0)1 [Burns]

Attendance 46,647

Blackpool's next local away game was also in Manchester, against United. This time I didn't need to go on the club coach, as I went along with Phil Whitehead and his father in his dad's car. We called at Phil's grandmother's house in nearby Oldham before Phil and I caught the bus into Manchester. We stopped off at a park in Piccadilly, and were a little worried when we heard some nearby chanting. At the time, there was an advert for eggs at breakfast time which went "E for B 'cos eggs are best", but it was usually sung as "E for B and Georgie Best" by United supporters. We soon realised, though, that it was the Blackpool fans chanting 'E for B and John Murray' as they 'borrowed the slogan.

We joined with the group to get the bus to the ground, and outside Old Trafford I got the autographs of cricket's Basil d'Oliveira and the television presenter Gerald Sinstadt, who was commentating on the game for Granada Television. Inside the ground, the Blackpool fans gathered on the Scoreboard End, although just before kick-off the notorious hooligan element who followed United attacked and shifted most of the group.

In the first half, a George Best flick produced an opening goal following a bit of magic on the wing in a move involving Fitzpatrick and Morgan, while Charlton missed a couple of chances to score the goal that would have made him United's leading post-war goalscorer. Armfield went off injured for Blackpool at half time, but we more than deserved the second half equaliser from Mickey Burns that gave us a 1-1 draw. 'Pool played out the last quarter of an hour with ten men after Green was also forced to leave the pitch through injury.

United, formerly known as Newton Heath, were about to embark on a period of little success in an otherwise glorious career. League Champions on seven occasions up until 1967, they had to wait a quarter of a century before the championship again returned to Old Trafford – although once it did, in 1993, United went on to capture it eight times in eleven seasons. They also had major success in cup competitions, winning the FA Cup on ten occasions (with League and FA Cup doubles in 1994, 1996 and 1999), the League Cup once, the European Cup Winners Cup once and the European Cup twice. The European Cup victories meant the most to people at Old Trafford, for it was on the club's return from a European tie in Belgrade in February 1958 that their plane crashed at Munich airport, killing many of their star players. It was ten years later that they defeated Benfica at Wembley to lift the trophy for the first time (even though a programme was printed for the 'replay'), and in 1999 they added the cup to the League and FA Cup trophies in their cabinet when turning a 0-1 deficit against Bayern Munich into a 2-1 victory when Sheringham and Solsjkaer both scored injury time goals. They became the first British side to win the World Club's Championship in Tokyo late in 1999, before embarking on an ill-advised and fruitless tournament in Brazil in January 2000 at the expense of defending the FA Cup. They won the FA Cup again at Cardiff in 2004, defeating Millwall 3-0.

| Bus tickets for the trip to Old Trafford, and ticket for Red Star (a), February 1958 | Red Star Belgrade (a) February 1958 – the Munich disaster | Sheffield Wednesday (h), FA Cup Fifth Round 1958 – first game after Munich |

Liverpool (h) 1910 – first game at
Old Trafford (left) and
Newton Heath programme and
fixture card from 1890 (right)

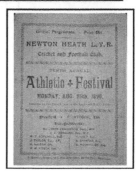

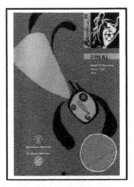

Benfica, 1968 European Cup Final at Wembley

Programme printed for a possible replay in 1968

Bayern Munich, 1999 European Cup Final in Barcelona

Estudiantes de la Plata (h) World Clubs' Championship 1968-69

Estudiantes de la Plata(h) ticket, World Club's Championship 1968-69

Estudiantes de la Plata (a) World Clubs' Championship 1968-69

Red Star Belgrade, 1991 Super Cup Final

Barcelona, 1991 Cup Winners Cup Final in Rotterdam

Lazio, 1999 Super Cup Final in Monaco

Palmeiras, World Clubs'
Championship, Tokyo 1999-00

World Clubs' Championship in
Brazil, 2000

Real Madrid (h), 1957 European
Cup semi-final

Borussia Dortmund (a) 1997,
European Cup Semi-Final

AC Milan (h), 1958 European
Cup Semi-Final

Partizan Belgrade (a), 1966
European Cup Semi-Final

Partizan Belgrade (h), 1966
European Cup Semi-Final

AC Milan (h), 1969 European
Cup Semi-Final

AC Milan (a), 1969 European
Cup Semi-Final

Blackpool, 1948 FA Cup Final

Liverpool, 1977 FA Cup Final

Everton, 1985 FA Cup Final

Chelsea, 1994 FA Cup Final

Liverpool, 1996 FA Cup Final

Newcastle United, 1999 FA Cup Final

Nottingham Forest, 1992 League Cup Final

Bayer Leverkusen (a), 2002 European Cup Semi-Final

Autographed back cover of the 1970 Blackpool programme

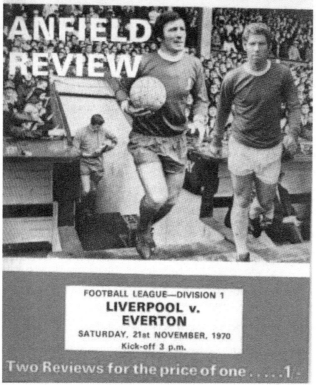

29. **Liverpool** v Everton

Played at **Anfield** on 21st November 1970

Football League Division One

Liverpool (0)3 [Heighway, Toshack, Lawler]
Everton (0)2 [Whittle, Royle]

Attendance 53,777

29 Liverpool - Anfield

Over the previous few weeks, Phil Whitehead and I had become more and more interested in Liverpool. At school, we stuck photographs of their players on the walls of the 'Book Room' as we tidied it up, and we decided to try and get tickets for the Everton game at Anfield on November 21st. We took the Friday of the week before the game off school, as we had found out that the tickets were on general sale then, and we caught the coach to Liverpool to join the queue. I felt lousy all day, with terrible stomach pains, and spent most of the journey stretched out flat on the back seat of the coach. I was hardly in the best condition for standing in a queue for five hours - we arrived at Anfield at 12:30 and the tickets weren't going on sale until 5:30. Even that early, the queue stretched right around the longest side of the ground. We joined the queue at the spot where the new main stand was being constructed. During the afternoon, new signing John Toshack walked past the ground with his wife Sue - and she was wearing a *blue* coat! The crowd let John know that blue was taboo as far as Liverpool were concerned, and I'm sure he got the message.

Once the time for selling the tickets arrived, the queue moved quite quickly, and we got our tickets after going into the ground via the Kop turnstiles before setting off back to catch our coach home. On the bus back to Lime Street we had our first experience of one-man buses - the driver must have thought we were mad as we just got on the bus and sat down, expecting the conductor to collect our fares.

Eight days later, we caught the coach into Liverpool, and Phil bought himself a bar-scarf in the city centre. I was trying to get one of the University-style scarves, and decided to leave it until I reached Anfield. Unfortunately, they were only selling the old-style ones there as well, so I ended up without one for the game.

Phil and I entered the ground and took our places on the famous Kop. Being first-timers at Anfield, we didn't realise that the one place *not* to stand was in the middle of the gangway. We soon found out our mistake though! I remember one tall coloured lad, who I was to see regularly in the middle of the Kop over the next few years, and he seemed fully at home with all of the surges up and down the terrace, while Phil and I were still struggling to keep our feet. Despite the swaying, it was a dream come true to be at Anfield at last. Once before, I had planned to come, when a coach from Blackpool was 'arranged' for a cup-tie with Leicester in 1969, but nothing actually came of it. I had walked past the ground on one of my visits to Goodison two years earlier, but this was the big day I had been waiting for. The ground was packed several hours before kick-off, with both sets of supporters in full voice.

It didn't seem as if it would be a happy 'debut' for me as the game unfolded. The first half was littered with some fifty free kicks for fouls, and champions Everton were taunted with chants of 'How Did You Win The League' from the Koppites. In the second half, football won and Everton made the most of some sloppy defending to take a 2-0 lead, Whittle and Royle scoring and prompting their fans to respond with "That's How We Won The League".

I was really impressed by the level of support, as the chanting had been continuous since the gates had opened at noon, and yet there was no physical violence offered either inside or outside the ground. I had resigned myself to a Liverpool defeat, being too used to Blackpool's habit of capitulating under pressure, and began to hope that we would score one just so I could have something to cheer. My wish was granted when Steve Heighway picked up the ball on the left wing, cut inside and unleashed a vicious shot to the near post that scorched into the net. The Kop erupted, and Phil and I were both half-crushed on the barriers because of the sway, although neither of us cared in the least. That goal changed the entire face of the game, as Liverpool bore down on the Everton goal to a background of a 28,000-strong Kop giving incredible vocal support. Heighway received the ball on the left wing again, and this time he swung over a perfect cross, allowing John Toshack to rise majestically above Brian Labone and head the equaliser - what a time to get his first goal for the club. If I had thought the noise was incredible after the first goal, it was absolutely unbelievable now. The Kop was a sea of red and white scarves, as honour appeared to have been saved. There was a slight scare when Ray Clemence dived to save brilliantly at the Anfield Road end as Everton fought back, but Liverpool were in the ascendancy now and another attack produced a corner. The Kop was in the middle of singing its anthem "You'll Never Walk Alone" as the ball came over, but the singing was replaced by a deafening roar as Chris Lawler stabbed the ball into the Everton net for goal number three.

That ended the scoring, and concluded an incredible debut game for Phil and myself. For all the major Liverpool games that I was to see over the years at Anfield, Wembley and in Europe, this initial derby game has to stand alone at the top of the tree. I bought myself a scarf after the game in central Liverpool, although it was still a bar-scarf like the one Phil had. I eventually gave that scarf to a lad called Dave Bamber as we went to see Liverpool play Nottingham Forest at Wembley in the 1978 Football League Cup Final. It wasn't until the following summer that I managed to get one of the University-style ones that I really wanted, and I kept it until I laid it on the Anfield pitch as my tribute to the victims of the Hillsborough disaster over seventeen years later.

Our coach trip back to Blackpool was one of almost permanent smiles on our faces, especially when we had just left Liverpool and we passed groups of Evertonians in the streets. The following day, Granada television broke with tradition when broadcasting highlights of the game by showing the 'second' game first and ending with the derby - after all, how could you possibly follow such a game?

For Liverpool, the years around 1970 were a solitary low point in a glorious history. League Champions seven times up until 1966, they had also finally achieved cup glory in 1965 with an FA Cup triumph over Leeds, 2-1 after extra-time. A year later, after clinching their seventh League Championship title, they lost in the European Cup Winners Cup Final to Borussia Dortmund at Hampden Park, again by a 2-1 scoreline after extra time. After this successful season, though, Liverpool were without a trophy for seven years. When they did finally break that barren spell in 1973, the floodgates opened, with eleven more League Championships in seventeen years, and by the end of the century another four FA Cup victories, alongside five League Cup triumphs, had filled the Anfield trophy cabinet. This, though, was relatively insignificant when compared with their exploits in Europe, where two EUFA Cup triumphs and four European Cups made Liverpool into the strongest team in the world during the 1970's and 1980's. Several years of double successes added to the tally of trophies won, and in 1984, Liverpool recorded the treble of League Championship, League Cup and European Cup. If it hadn't been for the aftermath of the Heysel tragedy, who knows what further overseas successes Liverpool could have claimed. They won the League and FA Cup double for the first time in 1986, pipping Everton to both trophies. The twenty-first century began with a second Liverpool treble, when the FA Cup, League Cup and EUFA Cup were won, the latter in a marvellous golden goal game against Alaves that finished 5-4. With the Charity Shield and the Super Cup also being won in 2001, Liverpool picked up an incredible *five* trophies in that one year. The League Cup was captured again two years later for a record seventh time, Manchester United being defeated 2-0 at Cardiff.

Amongst all of this success, Liverpool also set several records, including surpassing Millwall's run of home matches without defeat. Between 1978 and 1981, Liverpool went sixty-three league games undefeated at Anfield, eighty-five including cup matches, before Leicester City ended the run with a 2-1 victory. Unlike Millwall, though, the Liverpool fans gave Leicester a standing ovation following their win.

| Special 'Liverpool mints' pack from early 1970's | England v Wales, 1905 | Autographed reverse of Liverpool mints packet |

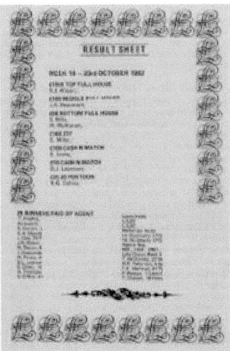

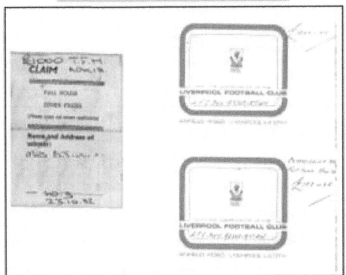

As a Liverpool FC agent, a ticket I sold Barbara won the top prize on one occasion, getting the top prize plus a ten per cent commission for selling the winning ticket.

**The Hillsborough memorial
alongside the Shankly Gates**

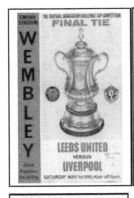

Leeds United, 1965 FA Cup Final

Everton, 1986 FA Cup Final

Newcastle United, 1974 FA Cup Final

Everton, 1989 FA Cup Final

Sunderland 1992 FA Cup Final

Hamburg (a) 1977 Super Cup Final

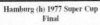

Hamburg (h) 1977 Super Cup Final

Anderlecht (a) 1978 Super Cup Final

Anderlecht (h) 1978 Super Cup Final

West Ham United, 1981 Football
League Cup Final

West Ham United, 1981 Football
League Cup Final replay

Tottenham Hotspur, 1982
Football League Cup Final

Manchester United, 1983
Football League Cup Final

Everton, 1984 Football League
Cup Final

Everton, 1984 Football League
Cup Final replay

Bolton Wanderers, 1995
Football League Cup Final

Manchester United, 2003
Football League Cup Final

Borussia Monchengladbach (h),
1973 EUFA Cup Final

Borussia Dortmund, 1966 Cup Winners Cup Final, Hampden	FC Bruges (h), 1976 EUFA Cup Final	FC Bruges (a), 1976 EUFA Cup Final

Bruges, 1978 European Cup Final	Inter Milan (h), 1965 European Cup Semi-Final	Inter Milan (a), 1965 European Cup Semi-Final

Flamenco, 1981 World Clubs' Championship in Tokyo	Independiente, 1984 World Clubs' Championship in Tokyo	Juventus (a), 1985 Super Cup Final

Alaves, 2001 EUFA Cup Final, Dortmund

Manchester United, 2001 FA Charity Shield

Bayern Munich, 2001 Super Cup Final, Monaco

Leeds United (h), 1971 European Fairs Cup Semi-Final

Paris St Germain (a), 1997 Cup Winners Cup Semi-Final

Paris St Germain (h), 1997 Cup Winners Cup Semi-Final

Liverpool v Everton ticket from 1970

Liverpool bingo ticket

Leicester City (h) 1985 – end of the unbeaten home record

Fleetwood Football Club Limited
Season 1970-71

Northern Premier League Cup
Semi-Final 2nd. Leg

FLEETWOOD
V.
WIGAN ATHLETIC

Tuesday, 2nd. March
Kick-Off 7-30 p.m.

Official Programme 2½p.
Highbury Avenue

30. Fleetwood v Wigan Athletic

Played at Highbury Avenue on 2nd March 1971

Northern Premier League Cup Semi-Final, Second leg

Fleetwood (3)4 [Cooke 2 penalties, Bowker 2]
Wigan Athletic (1)2 [Koo, Fleming]

Attendance 2,500

30 Fleetwood – Highbury Avenue

At the beginning of March 1971, I went to see my first non-league match, a Northern Premier League Cup semi-final between Fleetwood and highly fancied Wigan Athletic. Even though the first leg at Wigan had ended with the scores level, the 'Latics' had high expectations, having reached the third round of the FA Cup before narrowly losing 1-0 at Maine Road to Manchester City in front of a crowd of over 45,000.

It didn't turn out as Wigan anticipated. Cooke opened the scoring for Fleetwood with a penalty after twenty minutes, and Bowker added two more goals before Koo reduced the arrears before half time. Koo was a replacement for former Blackpool forward Graham Oates, which was a minor disappointment for me. Cooke restored the three-goal margin with his second penalty early in the second half, awarded after Wigan's goalkeeper Reeves had clashed with Fleetwood's Ollerton. Although Fleming added a second goal for Wigan it was too little and too late.

Much had been expected of Wigan's highly rated striker Geoff Davies, but he had an unimpressive game and Fleetwood caused a major upset with their 4-2 victory, taking the tie 5-3 on aggregate. This was the brightest moment in Fleetwood's recent history, the only one coming close to it being an FA Cup replay defeat to Rochdale in the mid-sixties.

Fleetwood continued their unexpected success with a victory in the final over Macclesfield, who as FA Trophy winners in 1970 were expected to win with some ease. For Fleetwood, this was a rare moment of triumph in a stormy history. In the years following, they found themselves slipping further down the league hierarchy, even going out of existence on a couple of occasions. There were, however, still occasional high-points, such as an FA Cup First Round tie against Blackpool, where Fleetwood surrendered home advantage to guarantee a bumper payday, and a Wembley appearance in the FA Vase in 1985, when they lost to Halesowen Town 3-1.

Poster for game v Stafford Rangers in 1974

FOOTBALL AT HIGHBURY, FLEETWOOD

WATNEY PREMIER CUP - 1st Round

SUNDAY, 10TH MARCH

STAFFORD R.

KICK OFF 3-0P.M. ALL PAY

ADMISSION ADULTS 25P O.A.P's & BOYS 15P STAND EXTRA

Rochdale (h), FA Cup First
Round 1965

Rochdale (a) FA Cup First
Round Replay 1965

Macclesfield Town (h) NPL Cup
Final 1971

Exmouth Town (h), FA Vase
Semi-Final 1985

Fleetwood draw ticket

Halesowen Town, FA Vase
Final 1985

Mossley, HFS Loans Cup Final
1985

Fleetwood Speedway Ticket,
1948

LES LATCHAM

the claret & blue

BURNLEY F.C. OFFICIAL MATCH MAGAZINE · VOL. 1. MATCH 20. 5p

Burnley

Claret with Blue collar and cuffs.
White shorts and stockings.

1. Tony WAITERS
2. John ANGUS
3. Les LATCHAM
4. Arthur BELLAMY
5. Martin DOBSON
6. Geoff NULTY
7. Dave THOMAS
8. Ralph COATES
9. Paul FLETCHER
10. Frank CASPER
11. Steve KINDON
Sub:

Blackpool

1. Neil RAMSBOTTOM
2. Terry ALCOCK
3. Dave HATTON
4. Henry MOWBRAY
5. Glyn JAMES
6. Peter SUDDABY
7. Micky BURNS
8. Tony GREEN
9. John CRAVEN
10. Alan SUDDICK
11. Tommy HUTCHISON
Sub:

Any late changes will be
announced over the Public
Address System.

Referee: Mr. J. K. Taylor
(Wolverhampton)

Linesmen:
Mr. H. P. Hackney (Red Flag)
Mr. G. N. Cochrane
(Yellow Flag)

---

31. Burnley v Blackpool

Played at **Turf Moor** on 10th April 1971

Football League Division One

Burnley (0)1 [Fletcher]
Blackpool 0

Attendance 14,498

31 Burnley – Turf Moor

On Easter Saturday Blackpool travelled to fellow strugglers Burnley, and lost 1-0 to an eightieth minute Paul Fletcher goal, the striker converting Docherty's pass. Ramsbottom played heroically for Blackpool and didn't deserve to be on the losing side. His performance was even more remarkable when it was revealed after the game that he had broken a bone in his left arm during the first half, yet he carried on until the end! The closest Blackpool came to a goal was when a Craven shot hit the underside of the bar but stayed out.

The victory failed to do the Turf Moor side much good though, as they were relegated along with Blackpool at the end of the season. There was little to enthuse about in the game, and the only other memory I have of the day is of seeing a group of about twenty *Liverpool* supporters outside the ground before the game. Whether they were true Liverpool fans or just a group of Burnley supporters who also followed Liverpool I don't know. On reflection, though, as Liverpool were in action at Stoke, where they won 1-0, and as this was a fairly 'local' game, I would have expected the true fans to be down at the Victoria Ground.

Burnley were yet another of the town clubs who had suffered as a result of the abolition of the maximum wage. They hadn't achieved an awful lot before the war, an FA Cup Final victory over Liverpool in 1914 and a League Championship seven years later being the sum of their achievements – although after losing the first three matches of their Championship season, they went on to set a league record of thirty unbeaten games. After the war, they reached Wembley in the FA Cup Final of 1947, losing to Charlton, but they reserved their best for the years between 1960 and 1962. Champions again in 1960, they reached the quarterfinal of the European Cup and the semi-final of both the FA Cup and the League Cup in 1961, going a stage further the following year when they faced Tottenham at Wembley in the Cup Final. Unfortunately for them, Spurs were too good on the day, and Burnley's slide out of the limelight commenced. Apart from a couple of League Cup semi-final appearances in 1969 and 1983 and an Anglo-Scottish Cup triumph in 1979, they generally found everything a struggle, and in 1987 they needed to win their last game, against Orient, to remain in the league at all. They did, narrowly, and gradually began the long climb out of the lower reaches of the Football League, making Wembley appearances in the Sherpa Van Trophy and the play-offs.

Ticket for England Under 21 v Latvia Under 21 at Turf Moor, 1995

Tottenham Hotspur, 1962 FA Cup Final

Tottenham Hotspur, 1961 FA Cup Semi-Final

Hamburg (h) 1960 European Cup quarterfinal

Hamburg (a) 1960 European Cup quarterfinal

Liverpool (a) 1983 Football League Cup Semi-Final

Liverpool (h) 1983 Football League Cup Semi-Final

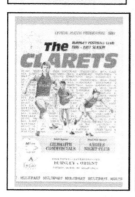

Orient (h) 1987 Division Four

Stockport County, Division Two Play-Off Final, 1994

Oldham Athletic (a) 1978-79 Anglo-Scottish Final

Aston Villa at Old Trafford, 1961 FL Cup Semi-Final Replay

Wolverhampton Wanderers (h), FA Charity Shield 1960

Liverpool, 1947 FA Cup Semi-Final Replay

Burnley v Blackpool ticket from 1998 and coach ticket from 1971

Aston Villa (a), FA Cup quarterfinal 1959

Rail ticket to Burnley in 1973

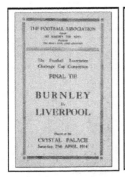

1914 FA Cup Final v Liverpool

32. Liverpool v Arsenal

Played at **Wembley** on 8th May 1971

FA Cup Final

Liverpool (0)(0)(1)1 [Heighway]
Arsenal (0)(0)(1)2 [Kelly, George]

Attendance 100,000

41

32 – Wembley Stadium

I became a regular at Anfield as the season wore on, and watched them reach the FA Cup Final by defeating Everton 2-1 at Old Trafford. The Wembley opponents were Arsenal, giving Liverpool the opportunity to avenge their 1950 defeat by Arsenal at Wembley, and I set myself the near-hopeless task of trying to get one of the 16,000 tickets that were allocated to Liverpool.

Wembley had been the home of the FA Cup Final and England International matches since it had been opened in 1923, and remained the premier ground in England until its closure for rebuilding in 2000.

With just a week remaining to the cup final, I still hadn't been able to get hold of a ticket. Ian Carden was studying Mathematics at Imperial College in London, and I arranged to contact him as he said he'd try and get a ticket in London, although with Arsenal in the final he didn't rate his chances very highly. I tried Blackpool FC, but their entire allocation went to people inside the club. One ticket was available through the supporters' club, but Sam the barman claimed it (even though he had no real interest in either side contesting the final). I contacted Ian towards the end of the week, hoping for some good news, but found that he'd had no luck whatsoever. Arsenal had just clinched the league championship by winning 1-0 through an eighty-seventh minute Ray Kennedy goal at local rivals Tottenham, with 50,000 in the ground and *another* 50,000 locked out! Apparently Arsenal fans were trying to swap cup final tickets for a ticket for White Hart Lane from anyone they found who had such a match ticket, but as Ian didn't have one of those either he was unable to take advantage of that situation. Now that the league had been clinched, the prospect of the double meant that Wembley tickets were in even greater demand, if that were at all possible.

There was a lad at school, Paul Deakin, who claimed to have had a ticket, although he often had fanciful stories that I didn't believe. He said on the Monday following the final that he had driven down my street on the Friday night, but as he didn't know which house I lived in, he hadn't been able to call to give it to me! I think he was disappointed when he failed to upset me by his 'news'.

I realised I wasn't going to be able to get a ticket before I went down, but I decided I was going anyway. I went to catch the overnight coach to London, which left Blackpool just before midnight on the Friday, and I arranged to meet Ian at Victoria station early on the Saturday morning.

On the Friday night, I went to Blackpool's Coliseum coach station to catch the coach, taking with me my entire post office savings of around £13. There were nearly a hundred people waiting for the 52-seater coach, and when it reached the stand the driver said that only people with tickets could get on, but I climbed on anyway. I was worried that if I didn't catch this one, I wouldn't be able to get to London at all, although as it turned out an additional coach was laid on for the rest of the queue of passengers. Fortunately for me, the driver didn't check the tickets right away, waiting instead until we stopped at Preston bus station. I claimed that I hadn't heard him when he said it was a ticket-only coach, and he allowed me to stay on for the trip, but he wasn't able to sell me a return ticket. Instead, he sold me a single ticket for the journey to London, and told me to see him in London the following night to catch the return coach. The only problem I had now was that the cost of the two single tickets (which was more than the standard return cost) had cut into my finances more than I had allowed for.

There were quite a lot of Liverpool fans on the coach, and at each of the service stations where we stopped for a break, but although I asked around, nobody had any spare tickets. We arrived at Victoria at around 6 a.m., and I had a short wait until Ian arrived to meet me, as the London Underground didn't begin operating until around 7, but by 8 o'clock we were at Wembley Park tube station. I had been hoping that he would meet me at Victoria and immediately produce the elusive ticket, but reality took over and we decided to try and get tickets outside the ground. Even though he was solely a Blackpool fan, as he was coming this far with me, he decided that he might as well try and go to the match as well.

Friday evening in Blackpool had been cold and wet, so I had travelled down wearing my heavy Parka jacket. In contrast, Saturday morning in London saw the hot sun blazing down on us, and we sweltered in the heat as we walked up and down Wembley Way searching in vain for anyone who had tickets to sell. I noted how you could see through the iron bars into the ground at certain places, and thought that at least I'd had a glimpse of the Stadium if I was unable to get in for the match, but it wasn't really any consolation to me. We had so little spare money that all we had to eat and drink were a bag of chips, a can of coke, and an ice cream, which was absolutely essential, for as the morning wore on so the temperature soared. One thing I did notice about London was the fashion-conscious girls, most especially as we sat at the entrance to the tube station for a rest and a couple of them walked past us wearing the most incredibly tight hot-pants, a sight to boost our flagging spirits!

There were hundreds of Liverpool fans along Wembley Way, and every single one of them seemed to be asking the same question - 'Any spares, lad?' As the morning wore on, some Arsenal fans came along, and at first everything was pleasant, with a game of football going on between the rival fans, but soon a much larger Arsenal mob arrived and the atmosphere changed. The Liverpool supporters at the top of Wembley Way charged towards the Cockneys, and somehow Ian and myself found ourselves near the front of this charging group. The Arsenal fans responded by charging towards us, and we suddenly realised that most of the Liverpool fans had done what they expected the Arsenal fans to do, and turned back. The small group of us who were still running at the Londoners had to make a hurried sideways dash to try and avoid the bricks that were being hurled at us. The morning continued with further charges between the groups, with each charge consisting of more and more fans from each side. Any touts who were crazy enough to try and sell their tickets ran the risk of being set upon by hundreds of Scousers and 'relieved' of them. This even applied to a vicar, who had to be rescued by the police when all he was trying to do was to give away a spare ticket that he had!

The sun was now so hot that I had to lie down for a rest around lunchtime before resuming our search for a ticket. We went right up to the ground, where the huge group of Scousers were chanting, "If you haven't got a ticket clap your hands", and every single one of us joined in the clapping. One group was trying to kick the gates down, and we hung around them in the hope that they might succeed, but the police moved them on before they had any success. Some other lads climbed a sheer wall to clamber through a very narrow unbarred window some twenty feet high, being pulled through by colleagues inside who'd been fortunate enough to get tickets, but the police soon cut off that route. Fans inside the ground offered to sell their halves of the match ticket, to at least give someone a start to be able to get in. At one stage somebody managed to grab a box of ticket stubs from one of the turnstiles, but there were so many people outside looking for tickets that we never got a chance of getting hold of one of these. Even those who got one wouldn't have been able to get past the second check inside, where the other half of the ticket was needed, but at least they would have been inside, and with a chance of getting to see the game.

Eventually, we resigned ourselves to missing the match, and we walked down Wembley Way again to try and find a colour television so we could see the game, as there were now only around thirty-five minutes to go to kick-off. As we walked past a few people, one of the group turned and walked away, shaking his head. We just asked him if he'd any spare tickets, and he said no, but the group he'd been talking to had some. We ran and caught them up, and they told us they did have some spare. We had to go with them between some coaches, a stupid thing for us to do really, as we could easily have been mugged, but at the time that thought was far from my mind. They asked us where we were from, made small talk about Blackpool, and then showed us two tickets that they were prepared to sell for £15 each. They were standing tickets, which had a face value of £1. I only had just over £10 left from my starting sum, but Ian lent me the rest to make up the asking price, and suddenly, after almost seven hours of constant asking, we had our tickets. The only problem now was that they were for the Arsenal end, but that didn't prove to be a problem as we managed to swap with a couple of Arsenal fans who had tickets for the Liverpool end. Those tickets were stamped on the back with the name of the Army Football Assocaition, and had possibly come from touts as well, but that didn't bother me in the least. At 2:45, Ian and I stood at the very top of the Wembley terracing at last, and all I could think was how tiny the people on the pitch looked!

Arsenal fans were singing their 'Good old Arsenal' song that they'd had written specially for them, as they had been unable to come up with a suitable song themselves, and Liverpool turned the song round into a 'Poor old Arsenal' version which extolled how they weren't going to win anything. It must have been a particularly worrying time for Arsenal captain Frank McLintock, as he had been a four-time loser at Wembley - twice with Leicester City in FA Cup finals, and twice with Arsenal in League Cup finals. I was desperately hoping that his run would be extended to five.

My lack of sleep, combined with the day's activities, was now catching up on me, and a lot of the game passed me by. I was alert enough to note that Peter Storey flattened Steve Heighway three times in the opening ten minutes, and after that a lot of the flare vanished from Liverpool's play and we rarely seemed to be in the game. In truth it was a very poor game, with the score still 0-0 at the end of ninety minutes, and Liverpool only began to look the part after Peter Thompson replaced Alun Evans near the end of the second half. Two minutes into extra-time, though, it all changed. Steve Heighway raced down the left wing after taking a ball from Thompson and scored past Bob Wilson with a low shot to the near post that clearly surprised the Arsenal goalkeeper. It was an almost exact replica of the goal he had scored against Everton at Anfield six months earlier on my first visit to the ground. I was perhaps the last person to realise that Heighway had scored, as I was almost too tired to notice, but in a few seconds the realisation hit me and I joined in the exultant celebrations. For the next few minutes, it was all Liverpool, with Hughes shaving the bar with one shot, but they failed to get the second goal that would have settled the game. Arsenal weren't champions for nothing, and they quickly equalised with a scrappy goal from Kelly that Graham went for and missed, but his presence was enough to wrong-foot Clemence in the Liverpool goal. The goal seemed to knock all of the fight out of Liverpool, and the travelling Kop was silenced. It came as no surprise when George hit a stunning goal to win the game for Arsenal in the second period of extra time, and consign me to my first ever Liverpool defeat.

The most abiding memory of the day, though, came immediately after the game had finished, when the Kop began singing "You'll never walk alone" - a very poignant moment, and I found that I was so choked up that I could only manage to sing about a third of it. We left the ground and waited for what seemed like ages outside the players' entrance until the Liverpool coach came out, so we could cheer the lads as they left the ground. We then went back across London to Ian's lodgings by the University, where he borrowed some money off a college friend to pay for my coach fare back to Blackpool. I met up with the same driver at Victoria, and eventually arrived home at 6 a.m. on the Sunday, to bring to an end my first, unforgettable, visit to Wembley.

Printer's proof of programme for a possible replay

Stafford Rangers' Jim Arnold saves a penalty from Scarborough's Jon Woodall during the 1976 FA Trophy Final

Travel tickets for subsequent visits to Wembley

Hotel voucher for 1992 visit

Ticket for 1974 FA Cup Final, Liverpool v Newcastle United

Tranmere v Bolton ticket, Third Division Play-Off Final 1991

Blackpool v Scunthorpe Ticket, Fourth Division Play-Off Final 1992

Stafford v Barnet ticket, FA Trophy Final 1972

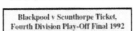

Ticket for Liverpool v Leeds, 1975 FA Charity Shield

Ticket for Liverpool v Nottingham Forest, 1978 League Cup Final

Ticket for Liverpool v Bruges, 1978 European Cup Final

Ticket for Liverpool v Everton, 1984 Milk Cup Final

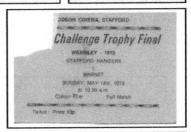

Cinema ticket for showing of Stafford Rangers v Barnet, 1972 FA Trophy Final

Song sheet from the Cup Final

Previous Arsenal v Liverpool
FA Cup Final of 1950

Tottenham v Arsenal, May 1971

1971 FA Cup Final Ticket

England v Germany, 2000 –
Last Game at Wembley under
the famous twin towers

1971 FA Cup Final Ticket – back
with 'Army' stamp

Nº 20834

Official
Programme 5p

LEEDS UNITED
A.F.C.
TOKEN

LIVERPOOL
6
1971-72

LEEDS UNITED
versus LIVERPOOL

Saturday, 18th September, 1971   Kick-off 3 p.m.
at ELLAND ROAD, Leeds

Leeds United   1
Colours :
WHITE SHIRTS, WHITE SHORTS

1. GARY SPRAKE
2. PAUL REANEY
3. TERRY COOPER
4. BILLY BREMNER
5. JACK CHARLTON
6. NORMAN HUNTER
7. PETER LORIMER (63)
8. ALLAN CLARKE Chris Galvin
9. MICK JONES Rod Belfitt
10. JOHNNY GILES
11. PAUL MADELEY

Sub. Jo. S-Aramen (for Madeley, 83)

Liverpool
Colours :
RED SHIRTS, WHITE SHORTS

1. RAY CLEMENCE
2. CHRIS LAWLER
3. EMLYN HUGHES
4. TOMMY SMITH Ian Ross
5. LARRY LLOYD
6. JOHN McLAUGHLIN
7. KEVIN KEEGAN
8. PETER THOMPSON
9. STEVE HEIGHWAY
10. JOHN TOSHACK
11. IAN CALLAGHAN

Sub.

REFEREE :
Mr. M. KERKHOFF, Bicester
LINESMEN :
Mr. M. LOWE, Sheffield
RED FLAG
Mr. R. M. HIMSWORTH, York
YELLOW FLAG

---

33. Leeds United v Liverpool

Played at **Elland Road** on 18th September 1971

Football League Division One

Leeds United (0)1 [Lorimer]
Liverpool 0

Attendance 41,381

33 Leeds United – Elland Road

I began watching Liverpool as my first choice side during 1971-72, and one of the early away games I went to was at Leeds. Although the game was played in mid-September, this was Leeds' first actual home match of the season. Following a pitch invasion and crowd trouble at the West Bromwich game towards the end of the 1970-71 season, the FA had ordered their ground to be closed for the first four home matches. Leeds had played these first four home games at other Yorkshire grounds, such as Hillsborough.

Leeds were one of the biggest sides in the country, yet for all of their quality, they never quite won the respect or the trophies that their talents warranted. They won the League Championship in 1969, 1974 and 1992 (the last time it was Division One before the advent of the Premiership), and the FA Cup in 1972. Their first success was in the League Cup final of 1968, when they defeated Arsenal 1-0 – the same score that they defeated the Gunners by in the 1972 FA Cup Final. In Europe, they were beaten Fairs Cup Finalists in 1967, but defeated Ferencvaros in 1968 and Juventus in 1971 to capture the trophy. The Juventus victory marked the final time the Fairs Cup was competed for, and Leeds played a special challenge game against Barcelona, first winners of the tournament back in 1958, to celebrate the success of the competition. They also reached the Cup Winners Cup Final in 1973 and the European Cup Final in 1975, losing to AC Milan and Bayern Munich respectively.

On the train to Leeds, I met up with a lot of Liverpool fans and I walked to the ground with some of them. There had apparently been a lot of trouble in the city centre, and the police stopped our group on the way to the stadium. One of our group had to explain why he was carrying an umbrella, as the current trend was to use umbrellas as weapons at games. These hooligans were known as 'brolly boys', with a 'uniform' that also consisted of a bowler hat, the idea being borrowed from the cult film "A Clockwork Orange", starring Malcolm MacDowell, and subsequently banned for its portrayal of violence. The police couldn't do anything about our situation, as the lad claimed he'd only brought the umbrella in case it rained, but considering that it was in a very battered state, I would say that keeping the rain off was the last thing it was intended to do!

The match went to Leeds 1-0, with Lorimer scoring the only goal with one of his 'trademark' strikes midway through the second half, but the game was notable for the emergence of the singing of the theme from 'The Dambusters'. It was later to be sung universally (except by the Leeds fans) with the words "We all hate Leeds and Leeds and Leeds, Leeds and Leeds and Leeds and Leeds, and Leeds and Leeds and Leeds, We all f***ing hate Leeds". This all came about during the pre-match record playing, where apparently there was a new disc jockey at Elland Road, and as he became a little nervous and unsure of what record to play next, he kept resorting to playing the Dambusters theme. After about the third time it was played, the travelling Koppites latched on to it and started singing along with the "Da, da da dada da da" theme, and carried on for the rest of the day.

As soon as the match finished, we set off back to the station. I was right at the back of a large group of Scousers, and after we had been walking for a few minutes I looked behind for some reason and saw that immediately following me were several hundred more supporters. I thought at first that another Liverpool group had joined us, but suddenly noticed that they were all wearing Leeds colours. Next minute, half-bricks and other missiles were hurtling around our ears as the Leeds mob commenced their attack. The police, who were supposed to be escorting us back to the station did absolutely nothing to stop the Leeds fans as we ran for cover. One Liverpool supporter with blood pouring from a cut on the back of his head was pushed away by one officer as he went to him for help. However, the second that some Liverpool fans stopped and regrouped under a bridge in order to fight back, the supposedly impartial police moved in with their horses to prevent their getting at the instigators of the violence.

Eventually, we arrived back at the station, but there was still no end to the trouble, and any Leeds fan unfortunate to be there was set upon by groups of angry Liverpool fans set on revenge. I saw one lad sent flying to the floor, and his head made a terrific bang on the concrete, probably rendering him unconscious before the boots began to fly into his unprotected face and body. Finally, the train arrived and we set off back home via Manchester, and I was pleased to return to a land of sanity.

Rail ticket for the trip to Leeds

Arsenal, 1968 Football League
Cup Final

Bayern Munich, 1975 European
Cup Final in Paris

Arsenal, 1972 FA Cup Final

Dinamo Zagreb (h) 1967 Inter
Cities Fairs Cup Final

Ferencvaros (h) 1968 Inter
Cities Fairs Cup Final

Ferencvaros (a) 1968 Inter
Cities Fairs Cup Final

Juventus (h), 1971 European
Fairs Cup Final

Leeds v Barcelona ticket, 1975
European Cup Semi-Final

AC Milan, 1973 European Cup
Winners Cup Final

Barcelona (a) 1971 Fairs Cup Play-Off

Brochure for the 1967 Fairs Cup Final in Zagreb

Barcelona (h), 1975 European
Cup Semi-Final

Juventus (a), 1971 European
Fairs Cup Final

34. Stafford Rangers v Boston United

Played at **Marston Road** on 30th October 1971

Northern Premier League

**Stafford Rangers (3)4 [Williams 2, Barlow, Cullerton]
Boston United 0**

Attendance 2,730

34 Stafford Rangers – Marston Road

I moved to Stafford in October 1971, when I started studying at the North Staffordshire Polytechnic. In the early weeks I was there I came home to Blackpool at the weekend and went on to watch Liverpool, but at the end of October I stayed in the town instead of going to see Liverpool's match at Sheffield United.

That Saturday afternoon I chose to go for a walk to get to know the town a little more, and picked a route that I hadn't used before. As I went further along the street I was on, I saw a sign and realised that I was on Marston Road, home ground of Stafford Rangers. It was also just coming up to 3 p.m., although I still didn't know if they were playing at home or not. A few hundred yards further and I came across a group of supporters wearing black and amber scarves and realised that yes, there was a game on. I was only thirty yards from the ground, and once inside it I bought a programme and found out that the 'black and ambers' were the visitors, Boston United. Their supporters had gone onto the 'home' end, but they soon vacated the 'Shed' as the main Stafford support arrived in the ground.

I knew nothing at all about the respective league positions of the two sides, but soon found that Rangers and Boston were both going well at the top of the Northern Premier League, with Boston top and Stafford second with games in hand, so this was clearly an important match.

Rangers played as if they were in a different league to the visitors, triumphing 4-0 with Williams (with two), Barlow and Cullerton scoring the goals in front of a very healthy crowd of 2,730. I didn't realise it at the time, but I soon became an avid follower of the Rangers. I actually saw them more times during the season than I did Blackpool, and was able to see them lift the Northern Premier League title (when Wigan were defeated 3-0), the Staffordshire Senior Cup, and the FA Trophy, when Barnet were defeated 3-0 at Wembley.

This was, in fact, the beginning of the golden age for Rangers, for they reached Wembley in the Trophy twice more in the seventies, losing 3-2 to Scarborough in 1976 and defeating Kettering 2-0 in 1979. In addition, they had their best ever FA Cup run in the 1974-75 season, reaching the Fourth Round. And it could have been even better, for they lost 1-2 to Peterborough in front of over 30,000 supporters at Stoke's Victoria Ground despite hitting the bar twice. Rangers joined the newly formed Football Conference at the end of the decade, but by now their star was on the wane and they didn't reach such dizzy heights again in the twentieth century.

34 Stafford Rangers – Marston Road

Wigan Athletic (h), Northern Premier League title clincher 1972

Ticket for Stafford v Maidstone, Alliance Premier League 1980

Chelmsford (h), Play-Off between Northern and Southern Champions in 1972

Stoke City (a) Birmingham and District League 1909

Barnet, 1972 FA Trophy Final

Kettering Town, 1979 FA Trophy Final

Runcorn (h), 1975 Northern Premier League Cup Final

Leek Town (h), FA Trophy Semi-Final, 1990

Swansea City (h), Welsh Cup 1981

Peterborough United at Stoke, FA Cup Fourth Round 1975

Rotherham United (h), FA Cup Third Round 1975

Leek Town (a), FA Trophy Semi-Final, 1990

Rotherham United (a), FA Cup Third Round Replay 1975

35, West Bromwich Albion v Coventry City

Played at The Hawthorns on 15th January 1972

FA Cup Third Round

West Bromwich Albion (0)1 [Brown]
Coventry City (1)2 [Rafferty, Chilton]

Attendance 26,472

58

35 West Bromwich Albion – The Hawthorns

At the beginning of 1972, I had my first experience of hitchhiking to a game when I went to see Liverpool's match at Leicester with my flatmate Pete Gathercole. The nightmare ten-hour homewards journey we experienced was almost enough to put us off hitchhiking for life. The following week, we had originally planned to hitch to Oxford to see Liverpool's FA Cup tie there, but after the events of Leicester we changed our minds and instead decided to go to West Bromwich to see their Third Round tie against Coventry City. The reason we chose this game was because it was motorway almost all the way from our door to the ground, which we thought would make it easier for us to get a lift, and we got there with no problems at all. In fact, West Bromwich must be one of the easiest grounds in the country to get to, being just off the first junction on the M5. There was also an excellent transport café close to the ground that we went to. Lorry drivers were usually the best people to get lifts with, and one of them told us to go in the lorry drivers' side, where you got a mug instead of a cup of tea, at no extra charge. It always seemed to make the drink taste better to me when it was out of a mug, sat with the gentlemen of the road.

We stood with the Coventry fans for the game, and witnessed a 2-1 victory, Rafferty giving City the lead and Chilton restoring it in the second half after Brown had levelled matters. I was pleased, still having a liking for City, and my day was complete when I heard Liverpool had won their game at Oxford 3-0, with Kevin Keegan scoring twice.

West Bromwich were one of the major teams when professional football first began, winning the FA Cup in 1888 and 1892. League Champions in 1920, they had further FA Cup successes in 1931, 1954 and as recently as 1968, when a Jeff Astle goal defeated Everton. Albion had also won the League Cup in 1966, winning the two-legged final against West Ham, and been defeated finalists in the first Wembley final of the competition a year later.

(Left) Tranmere Rovers (h) 1995, Fiftieth Anniversary of VE Day (Right) Wolverhampton Wanderers (h), 1888-89 (inaugural Football League season)

Ticket for West Bromwich Albion reserves v Blackpool reserves 1987 (right) and West Brom v Nottingham Forest 1900, last game at Stoney Lane (below)

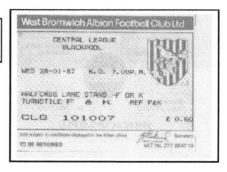

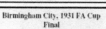

Birmingham City, 1931 FA Cup Final

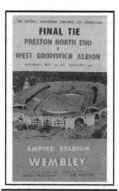

Preston North End, 1954 FA Cup Final

Everton, 1968 FA Cup Final

West Ham United (a) 1965-66 Football League Cup Final

West Ham United (h) 1965-66 Football League Cup Final

Birmingham City, 1968 FA Cup Semi-Final

FC Bruges (h) European Cup Winners Cup 1969

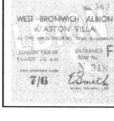

West Bromwich v Aston Villa ticket, 1958-59

Carl Zeiss Jena (a) EUFA Cup 1979

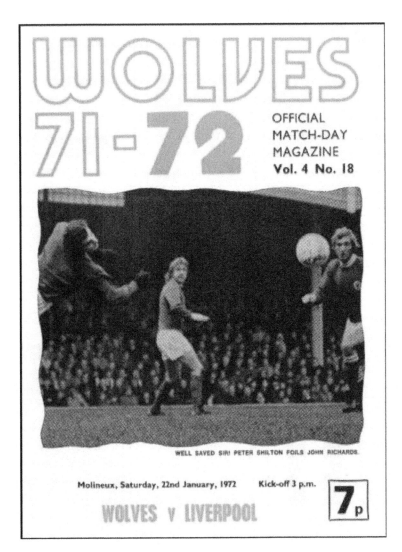

WELL SAVED SIR! PETER SHILTON FOILS JOHN RICHARDS.

Molineux, Saturday, 22nd January, 1972   Kick-off 3 p.m.

WOLVES v LIVERPOOL

7p

36. **Wolverhampton Wanderers** v Liverpool

Played at **Molyneux** on 22nd January 1972

Football League Division One

Wolverhampton Wanderers 0
Liverpool 0

Attendance 33,692

62

A week later, Pete and I were again thumbing our way down the M6, this time for the even shorter journey of Stafford to Wolverhampton. Again, we had little trouble either getting there or returning, but perhaps we would have been better if we hadn't made it this time, for the game was an awful goalless draw, although the reporter for the local evening newspaper, the "Sporting Star" considered it to be an exciting contest. Clemence dived to save an early Dougan header, while Keegan and Evans troubled the Wolves defence. Parkes had to be at his best to snatch the ball off Keegan's toes eleven minutes before the break, then the 'keeper dived to push a goalbound Evans effort away. Just before the interval, Wolves could count themselves unlucky when Shaw's first time effort came back off the angle of post and bar.

The second half saw a stalemate as Wolves were devoid of attacking ideas and Liverpool seemed content to sit and hold on to the single point. Wolves ought to have taken the lead on fifty-four minutes, when McCalliog slipped the ball through to Dougan, but with only Clemence to beat the Irish striker volleyed his shot over the bar. On the break, Lawler had a chance for Liverpool but Parkes was down quickly to save, and with just ten minutes to go the same combination saw Parkes tipping Lawler's back header over the bar.

Wolverhampton Wanderers were a famous name in football in the immediate post-war years, being league champions three times in the 1950's. They were also involved in famous European nights before the advent of the European Cup, one particular match against the mighty Honved, complete with Puskas, still being talked about. This was the 'final' of an unofficial European Cup competition, and Wolves won the game 3-2. Ironically, when the competition became official the next season, the shortsighted English footballing authorities refused to allow their league champions, Chelsea, to take part in it.

In cup football, Wolves were FA Cup winners in 1893, 1908, 1949 and 1960, the latter success almost completing a double, with Burnley just preventing Wanderers from completing three successive championships. Wolves reached the semi-final of the European Cup Winners Cup in 1961, losing on aggregate to Glasgow Rangers, and in 1972 they were EUFA Cup finalists, losing to Tottenham over the two legs. League Cup success was claimed in both 1974 and 1980, but after this Wanderers slipped down the leagues, eventually plummeting to the Fourth Division before beginning the long climb back. Whilst in the lower division, they defeated Burnley in a Sherpa Vans Trophy in front of a packed house at Wembley.

England v Ireland, 1903 and stub from the Liverpool game in 1972

63

Liverpool (h) 1976 – Championship-Relegation decider

Cardiff City (a) 1955 – record 9-1 away victory

Leicester City, FA Cup Final
1949

Blackburn Rovers, FA Cup
Final 1960

Honved (h) – 'unofficial'
European Cup Final 1955

Manchester City, 1974 Football
League Cup Final

Nottingham Forest, 1980
Football League Cup Final

Burnley, 1988 Sherpa Van
Trophy Final

Sheffield United, First Division
Play-Off Final 2003

Barcelona (a) European Cup
quarterfinal 1960

Tottenham (h) 1972 EUFA Cup
Final

Rangers (h) 1961 Cup Winners
Cup Semi-Final

Ticket for Ferencvaros EUFA
Cup Semi-Final in 1972

Rangers (a) 1961 Cup Winners
Cup Semi-Final

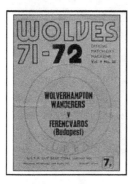

Ferencvaros (h), 1972 EUFA
Cup Semi-Final

Manchester United, 1949 FA
Cup Semi-Final

Bolton Wanderers, 1945 League
Cup Semi-Final

Leeds United, 1973 FA Cup
Semi-Final

Tottenham Hotspur, 1981 FA
Cup Semi-Final

Arsenal, 1998 FA Cup Semi-
Final

37. **Stoke City** v Tranmere Rovers

Played at **The Victoria Ground** on 9th February 1972

FA Cup Fourth Round Replay

Stoke City (1)2 [Bernard, Greenhough penalty]
Tranmere Rovers 0

Attendance 35,352

37 Stoke City – The Victoria Ground

The Fourth Round FA Cup replays in 1972 were played on a Wednesday afternoon as a result of the industrial dispute between power workers and the Heath government. In order to combat the strikes that were taking place, the government had banned floodlighting unless clubs had their own generators. On the Saturday, when the initial games were played, Merseyside had housed 120,000 supporters as all three sides were at home. Everton attracted 39,000 for their game against Walsall, Liverpool 56,000 for the tie against Leeds, and Tranmere a ground-record 24,000 against Stoke. Despite the awkwardness of the afternoon timing, Liverpool's replay at Leeds was still a complete sell-out. I knew I wouldn't be able to get to Leeds from college even if I could manage to get a ticket, so I decided to hitch with a classmate, Alan Fallows, to Stoke for their replay with Tranmere. We were fortunate to get a lift on a 'Corona' soft drinks lorry to its depot in Newcastle-under-Lyme, and walked from there to the ground up one of the steepest hills I've ever come across in my life.

We were part of an amazing crowd of more than 35,000, although relatively few of those were Tranmere supporters. They came through this replay without too much trouble, although the referee helped them immensely. Apparently, the first game at Tranmere had seen some ugly moments, with Rovers' Ron Yeats often involved. The same referee took charge of the replay, and when Yeats clashed with a Stoke forward after just five minutes, the referee immediately sent him off - surely a case of his being punished for his offences in the first game, not this one. Ten-man Rovers put up a superb fight, but eventually fell 2-0 to their First Division opponents, Bernard and Greenhough scoring. To complete a disappointing afternoon for me, Leeds won the replay with Liverpool by the same 2-0 scoreline. There would be no FA Cup final return to Wembley for me in 1972.

Stoke were on a cup 'high' at this time, having been FA Cup semi-finalists in 1971 – their first appearance at this stage since 1899 - and they followed up in 1972 by again reaching that stage, as well as winning the League Cup for good measure, to capture their first major trophy in over a century of existence. Arsenal had seen them off in both FA Cup semi-finals, needing a replay in each case – indeed, in 1971, only a controversial last minute penalty earned Arsenal a 2-2 draw in the first game and kept their hopes of a double alive. Further London opposition came up against City in the form of West Ham in the 1972 League Cup semi-final, and it took a wonder penalty save by Gordon Banks from Geoff Hurst before Stoke eventually came through, where they saw off Chelsea 2-1 in the final.

Stoke were perhaps just as well known, though, for being the club with which Stanley Matthews both began and ended his football career, a calling that spanned four decades. On his return to Stoke from Blackpool, he was instrumental in crowds rocketing from 8,000 to 35,000 and he helped them achieve promotion shortly afterwards. He played on until just after his fiftieth birthday before hanging up his boots, and he was knighted for his services to football. He only achieved four main successes as a player, and they came at ten-yearly intervals. He helped Stoke to win the Second Division title in 1932-33 and again in 1962-63, while he helped Blackpool win the War Cup in 1943 and the FA Cup in 1953.

The Victoria Ground site, awaiting redevelopment in 2002

Chelsea at Wembley, 1972
Football League Cup Final

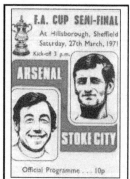

Arsenal, 1971 FA Cup Semi-
Final

Arsenal, 1971 FA Cup Semi-
Final replay

Arsenal, 1972 FA Cup Semi-
Final

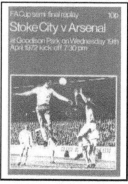

Arsenal, 1972 FA Cup Semi-
Final replay

West Ham (h) 1972 Football
League Cup Semi-Final

West Ham (a) 1972 Football
League Cup Semi-Final

West Ham 1972 Football League
Cup Semi-Final second replay

West Ham 1972 Football League
Cup Semi-Final replay

Ajax (h) EUFA Cup 1974

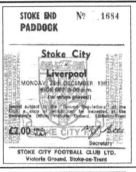

Stoke v Liverpool ticket from 1981

West Bromwich, Staffordshire County Cup Final, 1883

Manchester City (h), Football League Cup Semi-Final 1964

Ajax (a) EUFA Cup 1974

Port Vale (h), Autoglass Trophy North Semi-Final 1993

Real Madrid (h), Centenary Match in 1963

Stanley Matthews Farewell game in 1965

Sunderland in Canada, 1967

38. **Derby County** v Liverpool

Played at **The Baseball Ground** on 1st May 1972

Football League Division One

Derby County (1)1 [McGovern]
Liverpool 0

Attendance 39,420

38 Derby County – The Baseball Ground

With two league games remaining to the end of the season, Liverpool had an excellent chance of the championship. They had entered on a long unbeaten run following their cup defeat at Leeds, and the title was now between Liverpool, Leeds and Derby. Our next game, though, was at Derby, and a lot of controversy surrounded the build-up to the game. Not surprisingly, it was made all-ticket and Liverpool were only allocated 6,000 out of the 40,000 tickets - which was understandable if not exactly what we would have liked. The game should have been played on the Saturday, but England took on West Germany in a European Championship match that day, and league games were called off to accommodate the international. Liverpool released Emlyn Hughes to play for England, and he turned out to be our lone star in a sorry 3-1 defeat, with Gunther Netzer outstanding for the Germans. Derby, however, refused to release the 'injured' Roy McFarland for England duty, but he nevertheless managed to make a complete recovery two days later for the big league game!

I went to Derby via Uttoxeter with a mixture of hitching (from Stafford to Uttoxeter) and train (from Uttoxeter to Derby). I don't think the guard believed me when I told him I had only got on the train at Uttoxeter, but he sold me a ticket anyway. I hadn't got a match ticket, but I managed to buy one at Derby station for 50p - it was a 15p 'boys pen' ticket, and obviously something of a risk as I was a 6 foot tall nineteen year old! I had assumed that all tickets for the game had been sold, but at the ground, I was able to buy another of these 'boys pen' tickets at cost price from the ticket office. I decided to get it just in case I was ejected from the ground once for being over age, as it gave me a second chance to get in.

As I was walking around waiting for the gates to open, I bumped into John, a Cockney from college who lived in the same block of flats as I did. I hadn't realised he was a Liverpool supporter before, and meeting him solved one of my problems, as he'd driven down and he offered me a lift back to Stafford after the game.

When the gates opened I went into the boys section with some other over-age Liverpool fans, and we all sat down at the back in an attempt to try and remain inconspicuous - successfully, as it happened. Liverpool's long unbeaten run came to an end here, a John McGovern goal in the second half being the only goal of a game in which young Steve Powell, 16, was the Derby star. Derby had won the Central League Championship, and the Texaco Cup (defeating Airdrie in the final) so they were going for a unique hat-trick, but it all might have been so different as Chris Lawler was just inches away from getting the equaliser. At the end of the game, with Leeds defeating Chelsea at Elland Road in the other match played, the title now seemed to be just a pipe dream. As I left the ground and found John, there were some ugly clashes outside the ground, caused mainly by Derby fans looking for Liverpool supporters in the streets, and I had to hide my scarf as I walked back with John to his car.

Derby did go on to win the championship after this game, a triumph they repeated three years later. Apart from these successes, a European Cup semi-final appearance in 1973 and an FA Cup victory in 1946 when Bert Turner scored for both sides in the final against Charlton, success at the highest level eluded Derby, with perhaps their biggest triumph being to remain in the top flight of soccer for so many years. They were losing FA Cup Finalists in 1898, 1899 and 1903, conceding thirteen goals in the three finals, and in the League Cup they reached the semi-finals in 1968 before losing to Leeds.

The Baseball Ground after Derby moved to Pride Park, and my train ticket from Uttoxeter to Derby

Charlton Athletic, 1946 FA Cup
Final

Manchester United, 1970
Watney Cup Final

Cremonese, 1994 Anglo-Italian
Cup Final

Leeds United (h) 1968 Football
League Cup Semi-Final

Leeds United (a) 1968 Football
League Cup Semi-Final

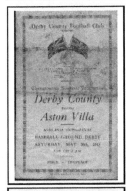

Aston Villa (h), 1945 Midland
Cup Final

Manchester United, 1948 FA
Cup Semi-Final at Hillsborough

Manchester United, 1976 FA Cup Semi-Final at Hillsborough

Juventus (a), 1973 European
Cup Semi-Final

Derby v Liverpool ticket, 1972

Juventus (h), 1973 European
Cup Semi-Final

West Ham United, Charity
Shield 1975

Juventus (h), 1973 European
Cup Semi-Final – VIP Edition

Blackburn Rovers (h) 1992 Play-
Off Semi-Final

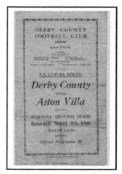

Sheffield Wednesday (a), FA
Cup quarterfinal replay, 1993

Juventus (a), 1973 European
Cup Semi-Final – Juve Edition

Aston Villa (h), FA Cup
quarterfinal, 1946

39. **Arsenal v** Liverpool

Played at **Highbury** on 8th May 1972

Football League Division One

Arsenal 0
Liverpool 0

Attendance **39,289**

Liverpool's final game of the season was away to Arsenal at Highbury. Arsenal were one of the most famous names in football, even having a London Underground station renamed after them once the club dropped its 'Woolwich' prefix. Although relatively slow starters (they didn't win their first League Championship title until 1931), Herbert Chapman's side soon made up for lost time, with further titles in 1933, 1934 and 1935 before the war started. Post-war, they continued their domination of English soccer with seven further titles, including league and cup doubles in 1971, 1998 and 2002. Nine FA Cup victories, the first in 1930, two League Cups, a EUFA Cup win and victory in the European Cup Winners Cup added to their trophy cabinet, although they also suffered defeat in European finals on occasion. In 1993, they achieved a strange cup double when they defeated Sheffield Wednesday in both the FA Cup and League Cup finals. Perhaps their greatest success, though, came in the league in 1989, when they went to Anfield for the final match needing a two-goal victory to take the title at Liverpool's expense, and at the same time prevent Liverpool from completing the double in the year of the Hillsborough disaster. As the game entered injury time, Arsenal led 1-0, and then Michael Thomas (ironically, later a cup final scorer *for* Liverpool) scored the goal that changed the destination of the title. In many respects it was fitting, for Arsenal had backed Liverpool following the tragedy, postponing their match against Wimbledon out of respect for the dead even though the Football League initially refused to allow clubs outside Merseyside to cancel games. They risked the loss of vital match points in their determination to offer whatever help to Liverpool that they could, and so in the end they received their due reward.

I was hoping to go down to London with John, but at the very last moment he had some car trouble and decided against risking it on such a journey, so I caught the train down instead. Relatively few Liverpool fans travelled down, probably due to the apparent hopelessness of the task awaiting us. For us to lift the title, we had to win (which shouldn't have been an insurmountable problem) but in addition Leeds had to lose at Wolverhampton. This latter requirement seemed much more unlikely, as Wolves were now concentrating totally on their forthcoming two-legged UEFA Cup final against Tottenham. Arsenal had just been defeated two days earlier by Leeds in the FA Cup final, a diving Alan Clarke goal taking the trophy to West Yorkshire for the first time in the club's history. With Arsenal facing us in the league it was almost a reverse of 1971, where Arsenal decided the fates of Leeds (in the league) and Liverpool (in the cup) in their final two games. Our game at Highbury was also scheduled for May 8th, exactly a year after our cup final meeting. As Leeds had reversed their 1971 setback two days earlier, I was confident that we would complete the 'retribution' on Arsenal.

On the train to London, I met up with Ann and Kath from Preston, who I had seen at several other games in the past, and we went to the game together. When we arrived at Highbury, we entered the ground on the North Bank (Arsenal's end), but quickly realised that Liverpool fans were at the other end of the ground. We decided to leave, go round to the correct end and pay again to get on to the Clock End with the rest of our supporters - so the official attendance of 39,289 was really three too many! The first half seemed to be pretty much end-of-season fare, as the players seemed as resigned as the fans were to the hopelessness of our task, and the only highlights came when we hit the bar and Ball hit the post for the Gunners. Arsenal ended the half in the ascendancy, but at half time the news came through that there was still no score at Wolverhampton, so we did still have a chance.

The second half saw a complete transformation in the game, and then the news filtered through that Wolves had taken the lead. Liverpool started to tear into Arsenal as the travelling Kop let the players know the situation with chants of "Leeds are losing". Minutes later, there was a second eruption as the news came through that Wolves had scored again. The whole ground celebrated this score, as Arsenal fans desperately hoped Leeds wouldn't win the title, in part for revenge for the cup final, and in part to prevent Leeds from joining Arsenal as one of the elite group of clubs that had won the double. Liverpool laid siege to the Arsenal goal in wave after wave of attacks, but nothing would go right for us. There were just three minutes remaining when one of the most controversial incidents I have seen at a game happened. A sloppy Arsenal defensive pass went straight to Kevin Keegan who was just outside the penalty area. As the goalkeeper advanced to meet him, Keegan slipped the ball sideways to John Toshack who slammed it into the empty net. We went crazy, the team went crazy, the coaching staff and manager went crazy and were dancing on the pitch - but referee Kirkpatrick just stood there, blew for offside and gave Arsenal a free kick. The Arsenal fans near us on the Clock End were laughing and jeering at us as they realised before we did that the goal had been disallowed. Despite all of the protests, the referee stuck to his decision. There was neither the time nor the spirit left for us to get another scoring chance, and Kirkpatrick blew the final whistle with the score at 0-0 and the Liverpool fans watching silently in their despondency. Leeds did manage to pull a goal back at Wolves, but it wasn't enough for them either, and Derby (who were on holiday in Majorca) were gifted the title. Once again, May 8th had left me feeling totally dejected.

After the game, Ann, Kath and myself waited outside the players' entrance for the teams to come out. One aged Arsenal official came out and proclaimed "Derby are the league champions, and that's all there is to it" - a remark which didn't endear him to us in the slightest. Liverpool supporter Tony Booth, an actor from television's "Till Death Us Do Part", and father of Cherie, future wife of Labour Party Prime Minister Tony Blair, was at the back of the waiting queue. When the police tried to push us all away from the players' entrance, he shouted at them to 'leave the fans alone'.

I had managed to get myself to the front of the queue, right by the door to the Liverpool coach, and as the crestfallen players emerged I ducked under the head of a police horse to get to them and give each of them a well-deserved pat on the back. Last out was the great man himself, Bill Shankly, and he came up to me and threw his arms round me in a big hug - a great gesture that typified the legend.

We eventually left Highbury to go back to Euston, and I caught the train to Wolverhampton, as there wasn't one that stopped at Stafford at that time of night. The police at Wolverhampton station thought I was a drunken Liverpool fan who had got off at the wrong stop as I left the station, but I had decided to hitch home as I wasn't prepared to wait until 3 a.m. for my Stafford connection. I came across a bunch of equally crestfallen Leeds supporters in Wolverhampton, and had a quick word with them - there wasn't any trouble, as for once we were both in the same situation. Despite the early hour, I had no problems getting a lift back to Stafford. In college the next day, I displayed my affiliations by wearing all *four* of my Liverpool scarves, giving further credence to all those who already thought I was a complete and utter lunatic.

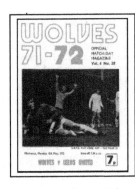

| Wolverhampton v Leeds on the same night | Arsenal v Blackpool ticket from 1999 | Real Madrid (h) 1962 |

Arsenal museum ticket, and rail ticket for my trip in 1972

Woolwich Arsenal v Manchester
United, 1908

Charlton Athletic, 1943 War
Cup Final South – pirate version

Liverpool, 1987 Football League
Cup Final

Manchester United, 1979 FA
Cup Final

Newcastle United, 1998 FA Cup
Final

Chelsea, 2002 FA Cup Final

Southampton, 2003 FA Cup
Final

Anderlecht (a), 1970 European
Fairs Cup Final

Anderlecht (h), 1970 European
Fairs Cup Final

Valencia, 1980 Cup Winners
Cup Final

Parma, 1994 Cup Winners Cup
Final

Real Zaragoza, 1995 Cup
Winners Cup Final

Galatasaray, 2000 EUFA Cup
Final in Copenhagen

AC Milan (h), 1994 Super Cup
Final

AC Milan (a), 1994 Super Cup
Final

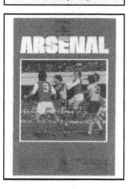

Juventus (h), 1980 Cup Winners
Cup Semi-Final

Paris St Germain (a), 1994 Cup
Winners Cup Semi-Final

Liverpool (a), 1989 League Title
'decider'

League
Division 1

Official
Programme 6p

IPSWICH

v

STOKE CITY

SATURDAY 16th SEPTEMBER 1972
Kick-off 3.00 p.m.

---

40. Ipswich Town v Stoke City

Played at **Portman Road** on 16th September 1972

Football League Division One

Ipswich Town (1)2 [Belfitt 2]
Stoke City 0

Attendance 17,810

Just before I returned to Stafford for my second year at college, I went to stay for a few days with Phil Whitehead, who was working at a hotel in Aldeburgh. After spending a few days there, I left to come home on the Saturday morning, hitching to London to catch my coach back to Blackpool. If I arrived early enough, I planned to go to Highbury to watch Liverpool play Arsenal. By lunchtime, though, I had only made it as far as Ipswich, and so I decided to stop off and go to the game at Portman Road between Ipswich and Stoke. I left my case in the club shop before going to see Rod Belfitt score twice as Ipswich won 2-0. It seems that I didn't miss much by not getting to Highbury, for Liverpool played out a 0-0 draw in a game that will only be remembered because one of the match officials picked up an injury during the game. Television summariser Jimmy Hill, a former player and qualified referee, took over the duties of running the line for the remainder of the match.

There were two unusual occurrences during the game I saw. First, and most bizarre, was the sending off of Stoke's England World Cup hero Geoff Hurst, one of the game's milder players. In fact there were some people in the crowd who must have doubted that he had actually been dismissed, for he all-but sprinted from the playing area, as opposed to the more usual slow, dejected walk to the dressing room. The other happening of note saw Concord pass over the ground soon after kick-of - a quite awesome sight.

I considered asking some of the Stoke supporters for a lift back to the Potteries to ease my journey a bit, but in the end I opted against this and resumed heading for London after the game. I managed to get a lift from a man who actually took me to his home and made me some tea before dropping me off at Victoria in time for my coach home. I did wonder a little as to whether there were any ulterior motives, but in truth he was just a genuinely nice person. I suppose the fact that I was dressed differently from usual, wearing a jacket and tie instead of my usual Wrangler jacket and Levi jeans, helped make me seem more presentable.

For Ipswich, an unfashionable club from East Anglia, these were good years. Promoted to the First Division for the first time in their history in 1961, Town had shocked everybody by winning the Championship at the first attempt, helped immensely by the scoring power of their twin strike force Ray Crawford and Ted Phillips. Although they were relegated again within two seasons, they maintained their link with the top flight, and in 1978 they defeated Arsenal at Wembley to win the FA Cup, Roger Osbourne scoring the only goal of the game. They also tasted European success in 1981, when they defeated Dutch side AZ Alkmaar in the EUFA Cup Final, with John Wark setting a scoring record for the competition, and retained an unbeaten home record in Europe for more than forty years. In the League Cup, they were beaten semi-finalists in 1982 and 1985.

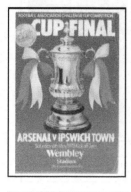

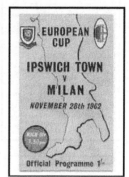

Arsenal at Wembley 1978 FA Cup Final

Southend (h) 1938, First League Game

AC Milan (h) European Cup 1962

Floriana (a) 1962 European Cup

AZ 67 Alkmaar (h) EUFA Cup Final 1981

AZ 67 Alkmaar (a) EUFA Cup Final 1981

Norwich City (h) 1985 Football League Cup Semi-Final

Ipswich v Nottingham Forest ticket from 1993

Norwich City (a) 1985 Football League Cup Semi-Final

Liverpool (h) Football League
Cup Semi-Final 1982

Liverpool (a) Football League
Cup Semi-Final 1982

FC Cologne (h) 1981 EUFA Cup
Semi-Final

West Ham United, 1975 FA Cup Semi-
Final

West Ham United, 1975 FA Cup
Semi-Final replay

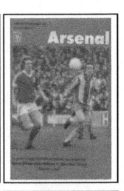

West Bromwich Albion, 1978
FA Cup Semi-Final

Manchester City, 1981 FA Cup
Semi-Final

Nottingham Forest, FA Charity
Shield 1978 at Wembley

Tottenham Hotspur (h), FA
Charity Shield 1962

SOUTHAMPTON FOOTBALL CLUB

Notts County goalkeeper Roy Brown dives, but the ball scraped the post
from this header by Ron Davies

LIVERPOOL

Saturday 14 October 1972

NEXT HOME MATCH
Saturday 28 October 1972   ko 3 pm
WEST BROMWICH ALBION

OFFICIAL PROGRAMME
and
THE FOOTBALL LEAGUE MAGAZINE

5p

---

41. Southampton v Liverpool

Played at **The Dell** on 14th October 1972

Football League Division One

Southampton (0)1 [Channon]
Liverpool (1)1 [Lawler]

Attendance 24,100

41 Southampton – The Dell

For Liverpool's away fixture at Southampton, I booked on the special train from Lime Street. I hitched to Liverpool on the Friday evening, sleeping on the floor at Ray Hart's University Halls of Residence. Ray was an ex-schoolmate of mine from Blackpool who was studying medicine at Liverpool.

Southampton were experiencing life in the top flight for the first time, joining the First Division as recently as 1966. It didn't take them too much longer to have trophy success, with Bobby Stokes scoring the goal that defeated Manchester United in the 1976 FA Cup Final. They were back at Wembley three years later, only to lose to holders Nottingham Forest in the Football League Cup Final, and they reached the Millennium Stadium in Cardiff for the 2003 FA Cup Final, going down 1-0 to Arsenal.

The trip to the south coast was reasonably uneventful, although over-reacting railway police threatened to turn the train back to Liverpool unless the high-spirited antics of some of the Scousers were curbed. I actually thought that this was happening as we left Birmingham, for we began travelling back along the same track we had used to enter the station, until I realised that we were just moving on to another line before continuing on the journey through Reading to Southampton.

Once we arrived, I went with the people from the special to the ground but then managed to lose contact with most of them after walking round it. I ended up on the Southampton end amongst a large group of Liverpool fans from the south, many of them coming from nearby Portsmouth. The main travelling support was on the opposite end of the ground, so Liverpool had effectively got both ends of the ground under their control. As I was telling some of the fans around me that I came from Blackpool, a lad who was stood just in front of me turned round and said that he was from the Fylde coast too, although we'd never met before. His name was Rocky, and I was to see him regularly at Liverpool matches over the next thirteen years, including outside the Heysel Stadium in Brussels following the end of the 1985 European Cup Final.

The Southampton police were clearly 'homers', as just like those at Leeds the previous season they kept threatening to eject Liverpool supporters from the ground. At Southampton the 'offence' was 'jumping up and down', whereas at Leeds it was for the much more serious crime of going for a half-time cup of tea two minutes before the interval! They could do nothing to prevent us from jumping up though when Chris Lawler shot us ahead from a corner in the first half, but we were much more subdued in the second half when the equalising goal went in from Mike Channon.

The game finished in a 1-1 draw, and we made our way back to the station, with the Southampton fans conspicuous by their absence on the streets. While we waited for the special, I talked with some of the 'Pompey' reds, including some very foul-mouthed skinhead girls. The trip back to Liverpool was also fairly uneventful, although I must admit that I never felt completely at ease until we arrived back in the city and I got off the train at 'Mossley Hill for Aigburth', such was the reputation of Liverpool people in general. I met up with Ray again at his room, and the plan was for him to give me a lift back to Lime Street to catch the last train back to Stafford. Unfortunately, I managed to miss the train back to Stafford due to our getting stuck in Liverpool's one-way traffic system. It was incredibly frustrating, as on more than one occasion, we could actually see the station but every road we turned down took us further away from it. We even found ourselves heading down the tunnel towards Birkenhead after one wrong turning! I ended up spending a second night on Ray's floor, and I finally got back to Stafford on the Sunday lunchtime.

Ticket for the football special

Manchester United, 1976 FA
Cup Final

Napoli (h) Anglo-Italian Cup
Winners Cup Final 1976

Nottingham Forest, 1979
Football League Cup Final

Nottingham Forest, 1992 Zenith
Data Systems Final

Manchester United, 1963 FA
Cup Semi-Final

Anderlecht (h), European Cup
Winners Cup quarterfinal 1977

Liverpool, FA Cup Semi-Final
1986

Southampton v Blackpool FA
Cup ticket, 1976

Anderlecht (a), European Cup
Winners Cup quarterfinal 1977

F.A. CHALLENGE TROPHY - 1972-73
SEMI-FINAL TIE

VALE PARK, BURSLEM
SATURDAY, 31st MARCH, 1973
Kick-off 3-0 p.m.

WIGAN ATHLETIC
versus
STAFFORD RANGERS
(HOLDERS)

WIGAN ATHLETIC (Blue & White)		STAFFORD RANGERS (Black & White)
DENNIS REEVES	1.	MILIJA ALEKSIC
KEN MORRIS	2.	BOB RITCHIE
BILL SUTHERLAND	3.	JOE CLAYTON
MIKE TAYLOR	4.	JIMMY SARGEANT
ALBERT JACKSON	5.	STAN ASTON
IAN GILLIBRAND	6.	MICK MORRIS
PAUL CLEMENTS	7.	MICK CULLERTON
GRAHAM OATES	8.	STUART CHAPMAN
JOHN ROGERS	9.	BRIAN FIDLER
JOHN KING	10.	TERRY BAILEY
MICK WORSWICK	11.	GERRY JONES
COLIN CHADWICK	12.	MIKE COLLINS
Manager : LES RIGBY		Manager : ROY CHAPMAN

OFFICIAL PROGRAMME — 5p

---

42. Stafford Rangers v Wigan Athletic

Played at Vale Park on 31st March 1973

FA Trophy Semi-Final

Stafford Rangers 0
Wigan Athletic 0

Attendance 10,600

42 – Vale Park

I had been to Wembley to watch Stafford Rangers defeat Barnet 3-0 to lift the FA Trophy in 1972, although I hadn't originally intended going to see the match. My plan had been to cross London and watch Liverpool at West Ham, but by the time our coach arrived at the ground it was far too late to move to the East End, so I went to see the Rangers' match instead.

When Rangers reached the semi-final again in 1973, I intended to go and watch them *as well as* watching Liverpool. I was able to do this as the game was played on Grand National Day, and Liverpool's league match with Tottenham had been given a morning kick-off to enable people to go and watch the race afterwards if they wished. One of the lads I shared the house with, Gan from Manchester, had recently passed his driving test, and so the two of us, Spurs-fan Chris Crome and Diane Lancaster (who wanted to go shopping in Liverpool) set off on our journey in Gan's car.

The Tottenham game was a marvellous match, with Pat Jennings providing one of the greatest goalkeeping displays of all time, guaranteeing him a special welcome at Anfield in years to come as he took over from Gordon Banks as the Kop's favourite visiting goalkeeper. The bare facts of the game were that Tottenham scored early on through Alan Gilzean, before Jennings came into his own, making numerous 'impossible' saves. We were given a penalty, and Jennings saved Keegan's kick, and it seemed that we were never going to score past him until we equalised from a mis-hit Keegan shot. I suppose it was fitting that it was an 'accidental' goal, as it was just about the only way we were ever likely to beat Jennings. All of this occurred in the first half, as we attacked the Kop, but in the second forty-five minutes Liverpool were even more dominant, with Jennings performing more miracles until we were awarded a second penalty two minutes from time. Once again, Jennings saved the kick, which was this time taken by Tommy Smith, and the game finished at 1-1. Of all Jennings' saves, the best was a one-handed stop following a corner, and the two penalty saves were ordinary in comparison to some of the other stops he pulled out. But, despite the disappointment of dropped points, it was superb entertainment for the enthralled crowd of 48,477 spectators.

As soon as the final whistle blew, Gan, Chris and I raced back to the car, where we met up with Diane and her purchases, and set off back towards Vale Park, getting there just in time for the start of the game. All four of us went to this match, entering on the Vale end, which was full of the black-and-white colours of both Stafford and Port Vale. Apparently, the two sets of Staffordshire fans had joined forces to see off the Wigan supporters, but just before kick-off the Vale fans turned against the Stafford fans and cleared them off their end totally. We were nearly hit by one flying brick as we quickly headed for the safety of the paddock terracing.

On the pitch, it was almost as nasty as old vendettas appeared to be settled, with Stafford the chief offenders, and the goalless draw certainly wasn't a credit to football. The tone of the match was set after just three minutes when Stafford's Sargeant was booked for a scything tackle. Wigan had the better chances, with Aleksic keeping Stafford in the game with a magnificent one handed save before half time. He also had to be at his best to deal with a second half cross, and though Rangers had most of the play, especially in the first half, those saves undoubtedly gave them a second chance at Oldham.

There was one odd fact about this match, concerning the 'official' attendance. Vale Park could comfortably hold between 40,000 and 50,000, and the ground looked at least half-full, but the published attendance was a meagre 10,600 - I'm convinced that there was a gate 'fiddle' going on there somewhere.

A week later, Stafford and Wigan met again at Oldham in the replay, and by all accounts this was a classic match which restored all of the faith in the game for those unfortunate enough to see the first encounter, Wigan getting to Wembley with a 2-1 victory. It was as far as they were to go, though, with Scarborough winning the final 2-1.

| Liverpool v Tottenham in the morning | The replay at Oldham | Wigan v Scarborough, 1973 FA Trophy Final |

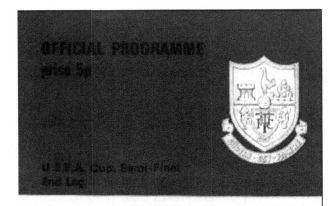

43. Tottenham Hotspur v Liverpool

Played at White Hart Lane on 25th April 1973

UEFA Cup Semi-Final Second Leg

Tottenham Hotspur (0)2 [Peters 2]
Liverpool (0)1 [Heighway]

Attendance 46,150

43 Tottenham Hotspur – White Hart Lane

Liverpool all-but clinched the league championship by defeating Leeds 2-0 at Anfield on Easter Monday. Before we could tie up the league title, though, we had to travel to London for the second leg of the UEFA cup semi-final against Tottenham. We had narrowly won the first leg at Anfield 1-0 in a game that I went to with Chris Crome. As the second leg was played during the Easter vacation I was still at home in Blackpool, so I hitched down to Stafford on the Tuesday afternoon and spent the night in Chris Crome's digs, before the two of us hitched to London on the Wednesday morning. We were lucky with lifts, arriving in the capital in the early afternoon thanks mainly to one lift we got in the back of a van driven by some gypsy women.

We spent a few hours in the vicinity of Trafalgar Square before moving over to North London. Not surprisingly, there was another big crowd at Tottenham, which eventually exceeded 46,000, but it was certainly one of the nastiest experiences I've ever had at a football match. On all four sides of the ground there were large groups of Tottenham fans looking for trouble and it took a long time before Chris and I could find somewhere reasonably safe to watch the game from, as we eventually stood close to a 'normal' family group. Even Chris felt uneasy, and he was a Tottenham fan. It was such a contrast to the atmosphere at Anfield where he had stood on the Kop in perfect safety.

The first half of the game was goalless, but overall Liverpool were in control. At the start of the second half, Peters put Tottenham ahead, but Liverpool responded almost immediately when Heighway equalised against the cup holders, sending me jumping up and down in delight. Chris wasn't too happy about this, but he neglected the fact that he had done just the same when Peters had scored! Spurs refused to give up, even though Heighway's away goal meant that they now had to score twice more, and Peters scored his second of the night to initiate a tremendous spell of pressure from the Londoners which all-but got them through to the final. Somehow, Liverpool survived this onslaught, and at the final whistle they accepted the generous applause that came from the majority of the White Hart Lane crowd.

As we left the ground, our journey back to the underground station reminded us once more of the dangers that we faced, with groups of Spurs fans lining the long route back to Seven Sisters station. We saw more than one Liverpool fan running from them for all he was worth, but once again we were fortunate enough to avoid the problems and we caught the tube to Edgware without any difficulties. From here, we weren't far from the M1 junction and we started to hitch back to Stafford, with our best lift coming when we saw a 'Blue Dart' lorry with a Stoke address at a service station and asked the driver if he could take us back. Not only did he agree to do so, but he also came off and detoured through Stafford, dropping us off in the centre at about 6 a.m. While we were still on the M6, still short of Stafford, the sun rose and lit up a layer of mist that seemed to cover the road like a filmy blanket for a height of about two feet - a strange and somehow quite beautiful sight.

I stayed at Chris' for a few hours to get some rest before completing my journey to Blackpool, and went immediately to get myself a one-year passport so that I could go to the final against West Germany's Borussia Monchengladbach.

This defeat was a rare cup defeat for cup-kings Tottenham. They were FA Cup winners in 1901, 1921, 1961, 1962, 1967, 1981, 1982 and 1991, League Cup winners in 1971, 1973 and 1999, EUFA Cup winners in 1972 and 1984, European Cup Winners Cup winners in 1963, as well as being League Champions in 1951 and 1961. Their record attendance came in an FA Cup tie as well, 75,038 watching their single goal defeat against Sunderland in 1938. In their only entry into the European Cup, they reached the semi-finals before losing by the odd goal on aggregate to Benfica, despite hitting the post or bar on several occasions in the second leg at White Hart Lane on a "Glory, Glory" night of European football. This era under Bill Nicholson's management was a golden age for Tottenham, and his first match – a 10-4 demolition of Everton in 1958 - gave full notice of their new manager's attacking intent.

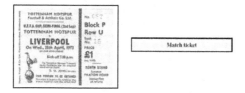

97

Sheffield United, 1901 FA Cup Final

Wolverhampton Wanderers,
1921 FA Cup Final

Chelsea, 1967 FA Cup Final

Manchester City, 1981 FA Cup
Final

Manchester City, 1981 FA Cup
Final replay

Nottingham Forest, 1991 FA
Cup Final

Aston Villa, 1971 Football
League Cup Final

Norwich City, 1973 Football
League Cup Final

| Sunderland (h) 1938 FA Cup quarterfinal – record crowd | Leicester City, 1999 Football League Cup Final | Everton (h) 1958, Nicholson's first game in charge |

| Gornik Zabrze (h), European Cup First Round 1961 | Feyenoord (h), European Cup Second Round 1961 | Dukla Prague (h), European Cup quarterfinal 1962 |

| Benfica (h), European Cup Semi-Final 1962 | Atletico Madrid in Rotterdam, 1963 Cup Winners Cup Final | Wolverhampton Wanderers (h) 1972 EUFA Cup Final |

Anderlecht (a) 1984 EUFA Cup Final

Anderlecht (h) 1984 EUFA Cup Final

Torino (h) 1971-72 Anglo-Italian League Cup Winners Cup

Barcelona (h) 1982 Cup Winners Cup Semi-Final

Ticket for Benfica European Cup Semi-Final, 1962

Pirate programme for the 1973 Liverpool EUFA Cup game

44. Borussia Monchengladbach v Liverpool

Played at **Borussenstadion** on 23rd May 1973

UEFA Cup Final, Second Leg

Borussia Monchengladbach (2)2 [Heynckes 2]
Liverpool 0

Attendance 35,000

Liverpool took a 3-0 lead in the first leg of the UEFA Cup final against Borussia. This game was played over two nights, as the initial match was abandoned after less than half an hour following a torrential storm. The short time that was played was enough for Bill Shankly to spot a tactical weakness in the German side, and he played John Toshack from the start the next night. Toshack's presence in the air unsettled Borussia to the extent that his strike partner Kevin Keegan scored two early goals. Keegan also missed a penalty, but as Ray Clemence saved a penalty at the other end after Larry Lloyd had added a third Liverpool goal, Keegan's miss didn't seem to matter very much. The fact that no away goal had been conceded would make the second leg that much easier.

I booked on a flight from Liverpool to Germany with Towns Travel, the travel agents who handled Liverpool football excursions. My only problem was how I was going to get to Speke airport for the early morning flight, as the only train that could get me there went on the Tuesday night from Stafford. That would have left me stranded in Liverpool for several hours until the early morning local transport system started up. In the end, housemate John Briscoe agreed to drive me to the airport and to return and collect me the following morning.

As John drove me to Liverpool in the early hours of Wednesday morning, traffic police on the M6 stopped us – they wanted to know what we were doing on the road at 3 a.m. It took a few moments before they believed what we were saying. I was beginning to get visions of being stuck in a cell while my plane took off, especially when John couldn't remember his car registration number for a moment! John was also stopped on the journey back to Stafford, yet he was an extremely careful driver, and drove a Morris Minor 1000 car, which was hardly a souped-up sports model, so there was really no reason for such action by the police. I, though, was happily unaware of his latest run-in with the law as I bought the book "2001: A Space Odyssey" by Arthur C. Clarke to read on the plane, and chatted to a lad from Leicester. I also met up with one of the lads I had met on the train going to an FA Cup tie at Burnley four months earlier.

We landed in Cologne at around 10 a.m. and boarded the coach that was going to take us on the hour-long journey into Monchengladbach. Borussia had resisted the temptation to move the game out of town to a venue where they would be able to attract a much larger crowd. Instead they banked on the atmosphere that would be generated in their own compact ground being sufficient to overturn our big lead, and they were so nearly proved correct. Five years later, when we met them in the semi-final of the European Cup, they did decide to move the game away from Monchengladbach, and I'm sure that made it easier for Liverpool ultimately.

We arrived about nine hours before kick-off, so I walked round the town with the lad from Leicester, going into such well known German stores as Woolworth! As it was my mother's birthday, I bought her a souvenir birthday present that I took back to Blackpool when I went home at the weekend. We lunched in a German pub on German sausage and sauerkraut and I spotted a poster on the wall advertising the game - I asked the landlord in halting German if I could buy it, and he let me have it for nothing. Near to the ground I bought myself a Liverpool flag and a Borussia flag, which was made of much better material and made a nice souvenir.

During our wanderings, we had managed to get ourselves a little lost, and had to ask a passing woman if she could direct us to the ground. Again trying out my schoolboy German, I asked her "Wo ist der fussball-grunde?" and I must have made some of the right sounds because she did eventually manage to understand what I was asking. I had no understanding, though, of her answer, as she tried to explain the way to me in fluent German. Finally she found a way I could understand her, as she pointed and said "Zo, und zo, und zo" indicating each change of direction that we needed to make with a wave of her arm at each "zo". Her directions proved faultless and we soon arrived back outside the ground. At tea-time we lay down and rested in a park by the ground, almost dozing in the hot sun while a soccer game between Liverpool fans and local lads took place in front of us, with the locals seemingly coming out on top. That was hardly a surprise, as most of the Liverpool fans had been drinking for several hours by now and were looking slightly the worse for wear.

We entered the ground well before the kick-off time. Anybody could have walked in, as all you had to do was show your ticket to a lone official at the top of a very wide set of steps. Once inside, we tried to find a programme seller, but there seemed to be none around. One of the lads near me spotted a steward with some, for they were apparently being given away free to fans, and he managed to get hold of a bundle of them. The lad I knew from the Burnley game managed to get some of the bundle, and he let me have three, one for myself, one for the lad from Leicester, and one I took back as a souvenir for Ian Carden. It turned out that very few Liverpool fans actually managed to find a programme, and on the flight home people were asking if anybody had any spare ones. On reflection, I ought to have let one of them have my spare copy, as at least they had been to the game.

As kick-off time approached, the weather suddenly changed and we were caught in the middle of a downpour. We were on the open end of the ground and were absolutely soaked to the skin. People behind were waving their Liverpool flags and it was very uncomfortable as these sodden pieces of cloth continually slapped me across the face. I was beginning to get really angry about this until the rain stopped and things began to get a little better. Out of the capacity 35,000 crowd, some 7,000 were Liverpool supporters, around half being British soldiers stationed in the area.

Once the game started, it was immediately evident that the Borussia side had a totally different attitude from the one that they had adopted at Anfield a fortnight earlier. They raced into a 2-0 lead in just over half an hour and it seemed that my big day out was going to end in disappointment. It also seemed likely that there might be some trouble on our end, as some of the less sober Liverpool fans were getting increasingly angry about the way things were going on the pitch, but fortunately that threat soon subsided. A fan behind me was trying to get the Liverpool crowd to rally behind the team, but we all seemed to be shell-shocked by the way things had turned in the Germans' favour. Gunther Netzer was in inspirational form for the home side, and we were happy to keep the score down to 2-0 by half time, Jupp Heynckes scoring both goals.

The odds must now have been heavily on Borussia to lift the cup, but Liverpool were defending the travelling 'Kop' end in the second half and Shanks must have uttered one of his inspirational half-time talks. The lads really buckled down to their job of defending the slender 3-2 aggregate lead, and for all their pressure Borussia hardly had a chance in the entire half. Phil Boersma came on as a substitute and could have put the result beyond doubt when he had a clear run at the German goal, but unfortunately he missed the chance. There was one moment a few minutes from the end when I thought Borussia had been awarded a penalty after one of their forwards went crashing to the ground in the area. It looked at first as if the referee was pointing to the spot, but thankfully he was just pointing for a goal kick.

And then the final whistle blew, and we went crazy. The team came back on to the pitch to receive the trophy and we all left the ground singing and chanting as we went back to our coaches. I even started some of the chants, the one and only time that I remember being a leader instead of a follower. The scarves that had been on sale before the match proclaiming "Liverpool, UEFA Cup Winners 1973" had not been prematurely produced after all.

When we returned to Liverpool airport, we were delayed in going through customs as the team plane was due to arrive back in a few minutes, and they were being given express clearance through the building. Hundreds of fans were waiting, even though it was after 2 a.m., amongst them John, Gan and Liverpool-fan Allan Orient, who had all come to pick me up for the return journey to Stafford. They had climbed through a gap in the fencing to get onto the tarmac inside the airport where they found me. As the team's plane landed and the door opened a few minutes later, we watched as Peter Cormack was the first player to come to the door - until he saw the waiting crowd and turned and went back onto the aircraft, obviously unprepared for such a reception. Years later, I heard Bill Shankly say that the reception at the airport was one of the most moving moments of his entire time at Liverpool. We didn't get to see the cup, just the tall brown wooden box that it was being transported in, but we cheered each of the players as they left the plane.

Eventually, we got fed up of all the waiting and left the airport by way of the same hole in the fence that John and the others had used. It doesn't say a lot for the security procedures at Liverpool airport in 1973! It had cost me just £30 to go to Germany, and I counted it as one of the best expenditures that I had ever made. Coming so soon after the disappointing ends to the 1970-71 and 1971-72 seasons, the double success in 1972-73 had more than made up for what had happened in the past.

For Borussia, this defeat was the first of three by Liverpool in big European games, with the European Cup final of 1977 and semi-final of 1978 being the others. They did, though, go on to have European success, defeating FC Twente Enschede on aggregate in 1975 after a 5-1 victory in Holland, and Red Star Belgrade on aggregate in 1979, before losing another final to fellow countrymen Eintracht Frankfurt in 1980.

| Twente Enschede (h), 1975 EUFA Cup Final | Twente Enschede (a), 1975 EUFA Cup Final | Red Star Belgrade (h), 1979 EUFA Cup Final |

| Red Star Belgrade (a), 1979 EUFA Cup Final | Eintracht Frankfurt (h), 1980 EUFA Cup Final | Eintracht Frankfurt (a), 1980 EUFA Cup Final |

| Dinamo Kiev (a) 1977 European Cup Semi-Final | Liverpool (h) 1978 European Cup Semi-Final | Liverpool (a) 1978 European Cup Semi-Final |

Borussia v Liverpool ticket (above), my passport, complete with stamp of entry to Germany and trip details (below)

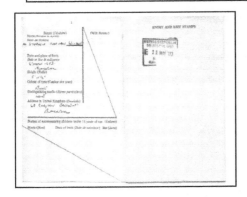

Borussenstadion Mönchengladbach

DFB-POKAL HALBFINALSPIEL gegen

Werder Bremen

15. Mai 20 Uhr

UEFA-POKAL FINALSPIEL gegen

FC LIVERPOOL

23. Mai 20 Uhr

Deutscher Pokalsieger 1960/61
Regionalmeister 1964/65
Deutscher Fußballmeister 1970
Deutscher Fußballmeister 1971

Mitglieder und Dauerkarteninhaber haben laut DFB Bestimmungen zu diesen Spielen keinen freien Eintritt.

45. Glasgow **Rangers** v Dundee

Played at **Ibrox Park** on 17th February 1974

Scottish Cup Fourth Round

Glasgow Rangers 0
Dundee (0)3 [Duncan 2, J Scott]

Attendance 64,762

45 Glasgow Rangers – Ibrox Park

My four hundredth game was also my very first Glasgow Rangers game, and it was played on a Sunday as the power strikes continued. The government had decided to allow games to be played on a Sunday, although I don't really see what difference that would make to power consumption. I had followed Rangers almost as long as I had watched football, ever since seeing a photograph of Rangers' Davie Wilson scoring for Scotland in their 3-9 defeat at Wembley in 1961. The fact that I had the same surname as him gave me an affinity with both him and his club. I had never had the opportunity to go and watch the side before, but a Blackpool branch of the Rangers supporters club had just been formed, and they had advertised a coach trip to the cup-tie against Dundee.

Rangers are Britain's most successful side, with more than a hundred trophies in their history. League Champions a world record fifty times, including nine in a row towards the end of the century, they also had a record-equalling thirty-one Scottish Cup victories and a record twenty-three Scottish League Cup victories. Domestically, they completed their seventh treble in 2003. They even recorded a Scottish Cup Final appearance against a fictitious side, Kilnockie, in the 2000 film "A Shot at Glory"! European success was also achieved after several near misses, when the Cup Winners Cup was won in Barcelona as Moscow Dynamo were defeated 3-2 in 1972. The game, though, was remembered more for the after-match riots that led to a ban on Rangers as they hoped to defend the trophy.

It did seem, though, as if Rangers were pre-destined to lift this trophy, as they won the competition despite not qualifying for it, and then being eliminated in an earlier round! They didn't actually qualify as Celtic defeated them in the 1971 Scottish Cup Final, but as they were also champions, Celtic entered the European Cup while Rangers took their place in the Cup Winners Cup competition. Then, Rangers played Sporting Lisbon and defeated them 3-2 in Glasgow before being behind after ninety minutes of the second leg by the same score in Portugal. Extra time was played, with both sides scoring again, and the referee then ruled that the game should go to penalties. It did, and Lisbon won, but after the game EUFA admitted that the referee had been wrong, as the goal that Rangers scored in extra time should have counted 'double' with the scores being tied, and Rangers were reinstated into the competition. Barcelona was also the venue when Manchester United won the European Cup in 1999, despite not qualifying for the tournament as champions of England, and to complete a trio of strange links, United's goalkeeper that evening was Denmark's Peter Schmeichel. He had been the goalkeeper in the 1992 European Championships, when Denmark defeated Germany in the final. Yet Denmark, too, hadn't qualified for that tournament, getting their chance when war prevented Yugoslavia from taking their rightful place amongst the finalists, and Denmark, as 'first reserves' were called up!

Tragedy has never been far from Ibrox, with disasters occurring on no less than three occasions. In 1902, at a Scotland versus England game, twenty-five people were killed and more than five hundred injured, and in 1961, at a Rangers versus Celtic match, two people died when crush barriers collapsed. By far the worst, though, came at the 'Old Firm' derby on January 2nd 1971. Celtic took the lead with a minute to go, and many of the Rangers fans began to leave the ground. From the restart, Rangers equalised, and the final whistle blew. Hearing the goal, those who were leaving turned back, just as the rest began to leave now that the game was over. The barriers collapsed and sixty-six Rangers supporters were crushed to death.

I turned up at the rear of the bus station for the coach, wearing my Liverpool scarf with the Rangers badge prominent on it, and met Charlie Mackay, the organiser, before going to sit with a couple of young lads for the trip. As well as all of the industrial problems caused by the miners' strike, there was also an oil crisis, and to conserve fuel a maximum speed limit on motorways of 50 mph had been imposed. On our way up to Glasgow, the coach broke down on the motorway somewhere near Carlisle, with half of the journey still to go, and we were delayed for well over an hour before it was repaired and we could set off again. Consequently, I was asked to act as a look-out for "Po-lice" from my seat at the back as the coach sped northwards at well over this speed limit in an attempt to regain some of the time that had been lost. I was visiting Scotland for the first time, and in my naivety I was totally unsure of whether or not I needed a passport as it was a 'foreign' country, so I had a nervous few moments until I realised that no such document was required.

We eventually reached Glasgow quarter of an hour before kick-off time, and received a torrent of abuse as we drove past Parkhead, where Celtic were at home to Stirling Albion in another cup match. By the time we finally reached Ibrox it was a few minutes past kick-off time. I had hoped to stay with the others from the coach, as after the match we were supposed to be going into the Rangers supporters club for the evening, but we all rushed for the queues and were separated. It was twenty minutes into the game before I got into the ground, with the score still 0-0.

45 Glasgow Rangers – Ibrox Park

The game was a big disappointment to me, with Rangers very poor. Dundee scored three times without reply in the second half, and the only things that Rangers goalkeeper Peter McCloy did better than I could have done were his massive goal kicks. Although the official attendance was given as 64,762, it didn't include season ticket holders, and there were actually close to 80,000 in the ground. The end I was on, the Copland Road, held 40,000, and made Liverpool's Kop seem tiny in comparison. The enormous Rangers support was quick to slate the team when things were going wrong, and they had plenty of opportunity during this dismal performance.

As I left the ground after the game, I bumped into a couple of the lads off the coach, and as one of them had an uncle living not too far away, we set off to walk to his tenement flat. On reflection it was a potentially hazardous walk through Glasgow to Govan. At one point there was a sudden rush to remove our scarves as he realised that we were now in Celtic 'territory'! We went by taxi for the final stage of the journey, and were made very welcome by his uncle when we reached his flat. He made us a very acceptable egg-and-chip tea, before we set off back to Ibrox, with his uncle's warnings of "Don't hang about and don't speak to anybody" ringing in our ears. He couldn't believe how foolish we had been to casually walk through such a dangerous city at night.

Once we arrived back at Ibrox, we tried to get into the supporters club to meet up with the rest of our party, but we weren't allowed in at that time. It was now around 10 p.m. so for the remaining hour and a half until the coach left we walked around the ground and coach park. Even at that late hour, on a cold February evening, small children were still hanging around the streets. Some were as young as five or six, and many of them were puffing away on cigarettes.

My first visit to Scotland had certainly proved eventful, and was a real eye-opener as I compared it to the relative peace of Blackpool and Liverpool. It was a very weary party that eventually arrived back at the bus station to find deserted streets at 3 a.m. There was just time for me to get home and get a couple of hours sleep before it was time for work - that highlighted a potential problem with Sunday football, in that there wasn't a day's grace to recover from a long journey.

Travel tickets for journeys to see Rangers

110

Ibrox as viewed from the Car Park

Official opening of the Blackpool branch of the Rangers Supporters Club, with Tom Forsyth as the guest, and the club handbook

Brochure for the official opening of the stand in 1929, tickets for journeys to see Rangers and programme for the game v Dundee United in January 1971, the first match since the Ibrox disaster

Celtic (h) 1947 – programme number 1

Rangers v Liverpool ticket, 1981, and car park ticket

Alternative version of Bayern Munich, 1967 European Cup Winners Cup Final

Eintracht Frankfurt (a) 1960
European Cup Semi-Final

Eintracht Frankfurt (h) 1960
European Cup Semi-Final

Fiorentina (h) 1961 European
Cup Winners Cup Final

Bayern Munich, 1967 European
Cup Winners Cup Final

Newcastle United (h) 1969 Inter
Cities Fairs Cup Semi-Final

Newcastle United (a) 1969 Inter
Cities Fairs Cup Semi-Final

Bayern Munich (h) 1972 Cup
Winners Cup Semi-Final

Dundee United, 1940 War Cup
Final

Hibernian, 1946 Victory Cup
Final

Third Lanark, Glasgow Cup
Final 1947

Celtic (h), 1971 'Ibrox Disaster'
match

Aberdeen 1946 Scottish League
Cup Final

Aberdeen, 1953 Scottish Cup
Final

Kilmarnock, 1960 Scottish Cup
Final

St Mirren, 1962 Scottish Cup
Final

Celtic, 1963 Scottish Cup Final

Celtic, 1963 Scottish Cup Final
replay

Dundee, 1964 Scottish Cup Final

Celtic, 1966 Scottish Cup Final

Celtic, 1973 Scottish Cup Final

Hearts, 1976 Scottish Cup Final

Aberdeen, 1978 Scottish Cup Final

Hibernian, 1979 Scottish Cup Final

Dundee United, 1981 Scottish Cup Final

Airdrieonians, 1992 Scottish Cup Final

Aberdeen, 1993 Scottish Cup Final

Hearts, 1996 Scottish Cup Final

Celtic, 1999 Scottish Cup Final

Aberdeen, 2000 Scottish Cup Final

Kilnockie, 2000 Scottish Cup Final for the film

Celtic, 2002 Scottish Cup Final

Dundee, 2003 Scottish Cup Final

Kilmarnock, 1960-61 Scottish League Cup Final

Hearts, 1961-62 Scottish League Cup Final replay

Celtic, 1964-65 Scottish League Cup Final

Celtic, 1970-71 Scottish League Cup Final

Celtic, 1975-76 Scottish League Cup Final

Celtic, 1977-78 Scottish League Cup Final

Aberdeen, 1978-79 Scottish League Cup Final

Dundee United, 1981-82 Scottish League Cup Final

Celtic, 1983-84 Scottish League Cup Final

Dundee United, 1984-85 Scottish League Cup Final

Celtic, 1986-87 Scottish League Cup Final

Aberdeen, 1987-88 Scottish League Cup Final

Aberdeen, 1988-89 Scottish League Cup Final

117

| Celtic, 1990-91 Scottish League Cup Final | Aberdeen, 1992-93 Scottish League Cup Final | Hibernian, 1993-94 Scottish League Cup Final |

| Hearts, 1996-97 Scottish League Cup Final | Celtic, 2002-03 Scottish League Cup Final | Hearts, 1961-62 Scottish League Cup Final |

| Everton (a), British Championship 'decider' 1963 | Aberdeen, 1946-47 Scottish League Cup Final | Everton (h), British Championship 'decider' 1963 |

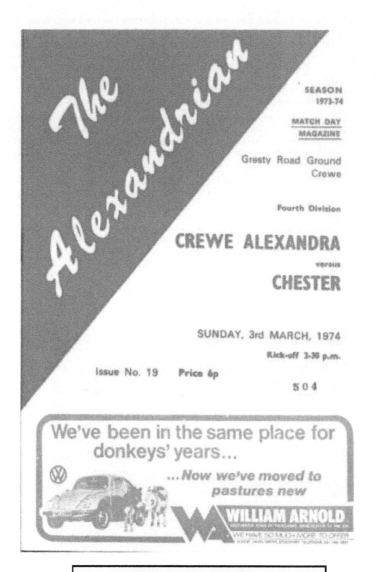

SEASON
1973-74

MATCH DAY
MAGAZINE

Gresty Road Ground
Crewe

Fourth Division

CREWE ALEXANDRA

versus

CHESTER

SUNDAY, 3rd MARCH, 1974

Kick-off 2-30 p.m.

Issue No. 19   Price 6p

5 0 4

---

46. Crewe Alexandra v Chester

Played at **Gresty Road** on 3rd March 1974

Football League Division Four

Crewe Alexandra (1)1 [Purdie]
Chester 0

Attendance 3,261

46 Crewe Alexandra – Gresty Road

As the Sunday matches continued, Rob Frowen took me to see Crewe take on Chester in the Cheshire derby. It took longer to reach Gresty Road than we anticipated, and we had only just got into the ground when Purdie scored after forty-one seconds. This strike was enough to win the game, with James having Chester's best chance to equalise when he had a penalty saved by Parker. In the Chester side was a winger called Terry Owen, who became famous a quarter of a century later through the footballing exploits of his son, for he was the father of Michael Owen of Liverpool and England fame. Terry, though formerly on the books of Everton, never attained the heights his son would aspire to, but probably laid the foundations for Michael's common-sense approach to the game.

One of the strange aspects of Sunday football was that it was illegal in England to charge admission to games. I found this surprising, as for years Rugby League had been played on a Sunday without any such problem. Clubs acted in different ways to overcome this problem, varying from Crewe's selling of a team sheet at 45p, the normal admission price, to other teams' special one-day club memberships! Preston's 'Sontag' club membership was perhaps the most memorable for its ingenuity.

Crewe were one of the 'Cinderella' clubs of league football, always hovering around the foot of the league until a resurgence in fortunes in the 1990's saw them achieve Wembley glory twice via the play-offs, as well as having a spell in the First Division. They also achieved national cup success twice, winning the Welsh Cup in 1936 and 1937, and were even FA Cup semi-finalists once, way back in 1888. In 1960, they held mighty Tottenham Hotspur to a 2-2 draw in the FA Cup Fourth Round – only to lose the replay *13-2*! The sides met again at White Hart Lane in the same round a season later, Tottenham's 'double' year, and this time Spurs only won 5-1!

York City, Third Division Play-Off Final 1993

Brentford, Second Division Play-Off Final 1997

Teamsheet for the Chester game

Liverpool team sheet for a Sunday fixture

Crewe v Liverpool FA Cup ticket from 1992

Preston North End Sunday 'Sontag' club and Blackpool temporary Sunday membership

Tottenham Hotspur (a) FA Cup 1960

Tottenham Hotspur (h) FA Cup 1960

Tottenham Hotspur (a) FA Cup 1961

47. Newcastle United v Liverpool

Scheduled for **St James' Park** on 28th December 1974

Football League Division One

Match postponed – high winds – but didn't find out
until I arrived at the ground

Just after Christmas, the lads I was now going to Liverpool matches with decided they were going to go up to Newcastle to watch Liverpool, and I agreed to go with them. Newcastle were one of the giants of old, but they had been a long time without any significant success. League Champions on four occasions, the last being in 1927, they ought to have made it five in 1996, when they threw away a twelve-point lead over Manchester United in February. United were involved in a high-scoring match shortly after the war, when Newport County were defeated **13-0**. Len Shackleton, the 'Clown Prince' of football made his Newcastle debut that day and helped himself to *six* of the goals. They were also a renowned Cup side, winning the FA Cup in 1910, 1924, 1932, 1951, 1952 and 1955. Since that last victory, though, their only success had been in winning the Fairs Cup final of 1969, defeating Hungary's Ujpest Dozsa 6-2 on aggregate, a tie in which non-scoring centre-half Bobby Moncur helped himself to three goals! Earlier in 1974 they had faced Liverpool at Wembley in the FA Cup Final, and had been totally outplayed in a humiliating 3-0 defeat. The 2003-4 season promised success for a while, only for Newcastle to fall to Marseille in the EUFA Cup Semi-Final.

Reasonably early on the Saturday morning, 'Roger' Hunt, Dave, Gary Ellis and myself set off in a car we had hired to go on the journey. We stopped off for lunch in a pub at Carlisle, then continued on our journey, leaving the pub just before 'Football Focus' began on the television. Had we stayed a few more minutes, we would have saved ourselves a long journey.

As we were going across country, we stopped to offer a hitchhiking Liverpool fan a lift. He was hitching with his mate, but he decided that they wanted a lift together, and as we only had room for one of them we carried on and left them to continue hitching. We arrived in Newcastle at just after 2 p.m., and I was amazed to see so little traffic around, as a very large crowd was expected at the game. When we parked near to the ground, we soon found out the reason why - strong winds had caused the game to be postponed for safety reasons. We went to a pub for the next hour or so, and managed to win enough tokens from a faulty one-arm bandit machine to buy us a crate of Newcastle Brown Ale for our return journey. As we'd gone for the game, we decided that we'd go up to the ground and try and get a match programme. There were a lot of Newcastle fans around the ground, and we had to pretend when asked that we were Geordies, but in the shop we explained that we'd travelled from Blackpool for the match and they allowed us to buy some of the programmes.

We set off back home and had another stay in a pub at Hexham, which was slightly friendlier territory than the vicinity of St James' Park. We also had a final pub stop in Garstang before we got home. By this time I was ready to get out of the car, as one of the bad effects of Brown Ale is that it is very gassy and tends to produce a noxious smell after it has been consumed in quantity -as it had been by Dave in particular!

The fuel gauge was showing empty as we reached Blackpool, but we were determined that we weren't going to put any more petrol in the car, and we actually ran out of fuel on the corner before we returned to the hire car offices. Our eventful day ended up with us pushing the car for the final hundred yards or so.

Ticket v Ujpest Dozsa, 1969 Fairs Cup Final (left) and England v Scotland programme, 1967 (right)

47 Newcastle United – St James' Park

After my visit to Hartlepool in October 1999, Newcastle United's St James' Park was the only Football League ground in the area between the Scottish border and Mansfield that I had still to visit, if I discounted that trip for the postponed match! I still hadn't been to some of the new grounds, such as Sunderland's Stadium of Light and Middlesbrough's Riverside Stadium, but I had visited those clubs at their former grounds.

I had managed to get tickets for the Monday night 'Sky' game between Newcastle and Derby, albeit on the Derby end, after ringing Derby when they went on general sale. I would have tried Newcastle first, but their tickets didn't go on general sale until a couple of days later, and I didn't want to risk missing out. I had the afternoon off work and set off with Craig at around half two. It was an ideal game to choose as Craig was on half term, and so it didn't matter what time we got back home. As Newcastle were Craig's 'other' team after Blackpool, for once he was keen to go with me on a long journey. I had previously thought of trying to get tickets for Newcastle's Sunday 'Sky' fixture against Sheffield Wednesday a few weeks earlier – if I had done, I would have see Alan Shearer score *five* times in an eight-nil victory!

The reason for our early departure from Freckleton was to give us plenty of time to find our way there, and we needed it after I misread the directions and took a wrong turn, resulting in a drive around Newcastle for almost an hour! We eventually found the ground, though, and parked near the Newcastle Brewery in Corporation Street. The football ground guidebook I was using said it was okay to park in the road, but as it was very quiet there, I checked with another fan who'd parked just in front of us. He told us it was fine, and we could get straight on to the A1M South afterwards, as he assumed we were Derby fans. I told him we were from Blackpool, but we still needed to go along the same road, so it was useful information.

We had seen the cranes used in the ground redevelopment round the ground from a long way off, yet the ground itself didn't initially appear to be a football ground as we approached it. We found the ticket office with help from a steward, and were able to swap our tickets for two on the Newcastle end after I explained to the girl in the office that Craig was a Newcastle fan and wanted to be able to cheer his team. There were a lot of people around the player's entrance, and we waited with them for a few minutes until the Newcastle team coach arrived. We had an excellent view as Shearer, Ferguson, Speed, Barton, Bobby Robson and the rest got off the bus. Shearer had been rated an injury doubt before the game, but from the looks of things he was going to be in the side.

We then went into the souvenir shop and bought a few mementoes of the day. After having a walk round the ground, we finally went in with still an hour to kick-off. I took time to look round the stadium, and once again it showed how football grounds could look. To our right, work was taking place to increase the capacity by another 14,000, but until that work was complete there was no roof either there or further round in the Derby section. As it began to rain, I was more than glad that we had exchanged our seats, for our corner was completely covered. I noticed also that our tickets were priced at £25.50, whereas I had only paid £24 for those from Derby, yet the girl didn't ask me for any more money when she gave them to me. The teams were announced, with Shearer in the starting line-up and Ferguson as substitute in a game that was of immense importance at the foot of the FA Premier League, with only Sheffield Wednesday below these two clubs. Just before kick-off, there were hundreds of empty seats, including the entire row in front of us, and all but our seats on the row we were on, but at the last moment, the ground filled, leaving just the row in front of us showing empty seats. There also seemed to be a fairly large empty group of seats in the Derby section.

The new building had caused much controversy over the past couple of weeks, with the Newcastle board in general, and despised director Freddie Fletcher in particular, trying to move the fans who had been in that section. Many of them had bought ten-year bonds during the time when Kevin Keegan was manager. Fletcher wanted to sell those seats at a much higher price to local businesses, and there was an angry response from the Geordies. The game began with all of the fans standing up, and it was a full fifteen minutes before the protest ended and people sat down, but throughout the game the fans sang anti-Fletcher songs.

Newcastle dominated play in the first half, with home goalkeeper Shay Given barely having a touch. A Shearer cross was headed over by Speed, Shearer headed another chance at Hoult, the goalkeeper then made a superb save to prevent a goal, before Solano found space out wide and his cross forced Eranio (under pressure from Shearer) to turn the ball into his own net. Warren Barton was very dangerous in his role as an attacking fullback, and at half-time Newcastle were well worth their one goal lead.

Derby began the second half more adventurously, but Newcastle were lightning fast on the break and Solano again found himself clear on the right. His cross fell invitingly, and saw Shearer almost pushing his team-mate out of the way to slam home the second goal – the one both Craig and I really wanted to see. Another quick break and Solano cross almost brought a goal for Speed, Schnoor miraculously clearing his full-blooded shot off the line, and Shearer glanced a header wide when he would normally have scored from that position. Shearer was winning everything in the air, and Gallagher was also having an excellent game, typified when he chased one seemingly lost cause, kept the ball in and set up another goal-scoring chance.

Derby, with Mikkel Beck prominent, were beginning to have more of the play without creating any clear cut chances, and they were always susceptible to Newcastle's breaks. Ferguson came on as substitute with ten minutes to go, and had the crowd in raptures with one delightful back-heel to change the direction of play. With five minutes to go, Solano was baulked in the box, but the referee ignored the fall and waved play on. I almost missed this, as hundreds of people were leaving the ground at this time. The 2-0 final score was no more than Newcastle deserved.

I soon found out the reason for the early leavers, as it took an age to get away from the ground due to the heavy traffic and the city-centre location of St James' Park. As we waited, we listened to the radio, and the tragic news that American golfer and current US Open champion Payne Stewart had been killed in a plane crash in America. During the recent Ryder Cup, which America won in contentious fashion, Stewart had remained the ultimate gentleman, picking the ball up to concede to Colin Montgomery when he was still a distance from the hole, in order to save him from further crowd abuse. He would be sadly missed.

We eventually got on our way, and managed to get home in good time, arriving back at just before one a.m. after a very enjoyable visit to Tyneside. As far as Craig was concerned, this more than made up for Newcastle's 3-0 defeat to Ajax at Goodison on the only previous occasion he had seen them play.

25th October 1999 – FA Premier League, Newcastle United (1)2 [Eranio own goal, Shearer] Derby County 0. Attendance 35,614

| Marseille (a), EUFA Cup Semi-Final 2004 | Marseille (h), EUFA Cup Semi-Final 2004 | Marseille (a), EUFA Cup Semi-Final 2004 alternate version |

Newcastle v Derby ticket from 1999 (left) and v Newton Heath, 1897 (right)

Aston Villa, 1924 FA Cup Final

Arsenal, 1932 FA Cup Final

Newport County (h),
Shackleton's debut 1946

Blackpool, 1951 FA Cup Final

Arsenal, 1952 FA Cup Final

Manchester City, 1955 FA Cup
Final

Ujpest Dozsa (h) 1969 Inter
Cities Fairs Cup Final

Ujpest Dozsa (a) 1969 Inter
Cities Fairs Cup Final

Derby County (h) October 1999

48. Glasgow Rangers v Glasgow Celtic

Played at **Hampden Park** on 10th May 1975

Glasgow Cup Final

Glasgow Rangers (2)2 [Stein, McLean]
Glasgow Celtic (2)2 [Wilson 2]

Attendance 70,494

I ended the 1974-75 season by going to the Glasgow Cup final between Rangers and Celtic at Hampden Park. I had telephoned a ticket agency in Glasgow to order my ticket, and after getting off the train I hailed a taxi to take me from Glasgow Central to the shop where my ticket was being held. Unfortunately, I chose the wrong time to get a taxi as there was a procession through the city centre and we were held up for a long time, with the meter accumulating its 'standing' charge for most of the wait before the driver finally switched it off.

I had better luck with the shop-owner, as he gave me a lift directly to Hampden, and he also gave me a programme from the Rangers v Aberdeen game that had just been played. The rain was torrential, yet despite this there was still a crowd of more than 70,000 at the game, two thirds of them being Rangers supporters. We were on the covered end, and the Celtic support was on the uncovered end, so most of their fans will have been drenched by the time they got home after the match. It seemed that Rangers and Celtic fans always kept to their own end when playing at Hampden, which meant that in some matches the Celtic fans would get wet while the covered end was barely populated by opposition supporters.

Although the game was in reality fairly meaningless, no 'Old Firm' derby is ever played with less than 100% commitment, and this one was no exception. The first half was exceptionally good, with Paul Wilson scoring for Celtic after only three minutes, Colin Stein equalising five minutes later, Wilson restoring the lead mid-way through the half and Tommy McLean equalising for a second time shortly afterwards. There was no further scoring, but the game still had plenty of action as both sides threatened to get on top at different periods, with Rangers shading the first half and Celtic the second. At the final whistle, honours were even and the trophy was shared between the sides. I only saw one minor bout of trouble, when a Celtic fan was being punched in the face as he got off the train from Mount Florida at Central station.

The train back to Preston was packed with Rangers fans, and there was almost a confrontation back at Preston station when a trainload of Manchester United fans arrived, returning from a 3-2 defeat in their final Second Division game at Notts County. I also met up with a couple of Liverpool supporters from Kirkham, Alban and Brian, on the train from Preston to Kirkham, although they were clearly the worse for drink that evening. Brian 'borrowed' my Rangers v Aberdeen programme to read, and I had to remind him that it was mine as he put it in his inside pocket!

| Rangers v Celtic, Glasgow Cup Final of 1970 | Rangers v Hibernian Scottish Cup Final ticket from 1979 | Scotland v France, 2000, opening of all-seater Hampden |

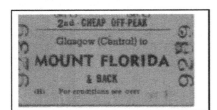

Rail ticket for the journey between Glasgow Central and Hampden

49. Liverpool v Borussia Monchengladbach

Played at **The Olympic Stadium, Rome** on 25th May 1977

European Cup Final

Liverpool (1)3 [McDermott, Smith, Neal penalty]
Borussia Monchengladbach (0)1 [Simonsen]

Attendance 60,237

49 – The Olympic Stadium, Rome

As season 1976-77 drew to a close, Liverpool were in line for an unprecedented treble. They clinched the league title on the second Saturday in May, leaving just Manchester United in the FA Cup at Wembley and old foes Borussia Monchengladbach in the European Cup in Rome to overcome to collect all three trophies. I went to Liverpool now regularly with 'Alex' Lindsey Henderson and Kevin Diggle from Preston. Despite being regulars at Anfield, not one of us were able to get a ticket for Wembley. Kevin was the hardest done to, as he saw 41 out of the 42 league games played by Liverpool, only missing the final game at Bristol City five days before the final. One chap I worked with, Mike Thompson (an ex-pro with Preston, Barrow and Blackpool) had tickets for the final that he was going to sell, but he refused to let me buy any as he said I wouldn't be able to afford his price! He went down to Wembley and as far as I know he sold them on Wembley Way. He suffered a lot of back trouble, presumably as a result of his earlier football career, and after this incident I always felt a little happier when I knew that he was in pain.

Immediately before the final home league game, I went into the Development Shop to enquire about my application to join the 'Anfield Travel Club', which was supposedly a pre-requisite before I could travel on the official trip to Rome. The official who I spoke to thought I was enquiring about becoming an agent for the club, and gave me a batch of tickets to sell, warning me though that it was too late to qualify me for a Cup Final ticket against Manchester United. If only I had known about this in advance, I could have been an agent all season and would have had my ticket without any problems at all. I took the tickets home, sold them, returned the cash and asked them to send me another lot of fifty, but didn't hear any more from the club - neither did I hear about the travel club membership, but fortunately it didn't seem to be a requirement after all.

After a fairly lengthy period of correspondence with 'Towns Travel' of Liverpool, I eventually booked Alex and myself on a £85 one-day flight to Rome. We could have gone on a rail trip, costing under £50, but it left on the Monday and didn't get back until the Friday, with most of that time spent on the train as it had to take several diversions due to industrial action taking place in France. It had seemed at one point that we would be unable to get the flight we wanted, but at the last minute an extra plane was put on, and we were allocated seats on it. It was hardly much of a trip, as it was almost literally straight there and back again. I had also entered a competition in the 'Daily Mirror' to try and win a trip, in which I had to submit a caption to a cartoon. The cartoon showed two Liverpool fans talking as they walked past some seated German fans, and my caption read "Joey and Tosh will be the only 'glad bachs' in Rome tonight". I was surprised when it didn't win the prize!

We lost 2-1 to United at Wembley, although we were the better side throughout and were clearly unlucky to lose. The dejected looks of the players and fans alike didn't bode too well for the trip to Rome four days later, but by the Monday, I think most had recovered quite well. I realised that unlike most other defeated cup finalists we had a bigger prize to chase after. I still hadn't received the tickets for Alex and myself, but got a letter from Towns Travel telling me that I needed to collect them at the airport on the day of the flight. Early on the Wednesday morning I set off to Lytham to meet my fiancée, Barbara, and she walked with me to the coach stop to wait for the 8 a.m. express to Liverpool. Alex was already on the coach, wearing his new red trousers that he'd bought for the day (and never wore again as far as I know).

On the coach, the new song that the Koppites had penned was going through my mind. Adapted from 'Arrivederci Roma', it went - "We're on our way to Roma, On the twenty-fifth of May, All the Koppites will be singing, Vatican Bells they will be ringing, Liverpool FC will be singing, When we win the European Cup". We were on our way at last. We got off the bus at Walton Hospital, and waited for a local bus to Speke and the airport some ten miles away. We met a chap there who was a few years older than us, and had a bad leg, and he stayed with us throughout the day. I didn't see him again until eight years later, when he was on our trip to Brussels and Kevin and I had to help him climb a fence while we tried to get back to our coach as we attempted to avoid any trouble outside the stadium following the game. There were no thoughts of this, though, in 1977 and we were in a happy mood as we made our way to the airport. On arrival I went to the desk to collect our tickets, and the clerk looked all of the way through her pile without finding ours, then she started again and found them straight away - just as the panic alarms were starting to go off inside me!

Our flight was scheduled to take off at lunchtime, but there were delays and it was almost two o'clock before we took off on our two-and-a-half hour flight to Italy, arriving in Rome at 5:30 Italian time - less than three hours before kick-off. My first impression on leaving the plane was of the incredible heat. We took a couple of photographs outside the coaches, before we boarded them and sat in even more sweltering heat as we waited for them to set off. Our flight had landed at Fiumicino, the airport designated for the German supporters – the main Liverpool support used Rome's other airport, but with almost 30,000 Liverpool supporters at the game, I suppose there had to be some overlapping. The Germans were great supporters of their national side, but at club level they didn't seem anything like as committed.

The coaches went directly to the ground, so I didn't have much chance to get a look at Rome, and it took about an hour to reach the coach park next to the Olympic Stadium. As we drew up at the stadium, all I could see was a mass of red-and-white, and it was a truly marvellous sight. I was hoping to be able to buy a souvenir for Barbara but though there were plenty of souvenir stalls around, there was nothing I felt was suitable on sale. After looking around for a while we decided to go into the ground, even though there was still quite a long time before kick-off. There was a tight security check for tickets and a search of all bags at the perimeter fences surrounding the ground. Once inside, we sat centrally behind the goal fairly near to the back and watched a schoolboy match that was being played as part of the pre-match entertainment. We sat next to a couple of Italians who didn't speak any English, but we managed to converse with them somehow. They were Roma supporters who were supporting Liverpool, and at the other end were Lazio supporters who were backing Monchengladbach - both Lazio and AS Roma shared the Olympic Stadium as their home ground. Borussia certainly needed this support as their green and white colours were swamped by the red-and-white of Liverpool. All of the gloom of Wembley seemed to be light-years away now.

As the game began, the mood on the field matched that on the terraces with Liverpool dominant. There had been a lot of kidology before the game about the fitness of John Toshack and Jupp Heynckes. Toshack was much feared by the Germans, ever since the 1973 UEFA Cup final between the sides, and I'm sure Liverpool kept the Germans worrying about whether or not he would play even though he never really had a chance of being fit. The Germans, on the other hand, risked playing Heynckes and it was obvious that he wasn't fully fit. After ten minutes of the game, Ray Kennedy hit the German bar, and twelve minutes later (in their first serious attack) Bonhof beat Clemence but fortunately for us his shot came back into play off the post. Twenty-seven minutes had been played when Steve Heighway slid a lovely ball through the German defence that Terry McDermott took in his stride and shot low into the corner of the Borussia net - and thirty thousand Liverpool fans went absolutely crazy. At half-time, the score was still 1-0, but a few minutes into the second half disaster struck as a short Jimmy Case back-pass was intercepted by Borussia's Danish star Allan Simonsen who lashed the ball into the roof of the net for the equalising goal. Almost immediately, Simonsen put a close-range header wide, and for the next few minutes, Liverpool were struggling. One through ball to Stielike brought a brilliant blocking save by Ray Clemence to keep us level. Gradually, we got over this shaky spell and began to get back on top, and from a Steve Heighway corner Tommy Smith rose to head the ball powerfully past Knieb into the net - what a way to celebrate what was expected to be his last game for Liverpool. It seemed to me that the action was in slow motion before the ball hit the middle of the net. Smith was literally 'over the moon' about this goal, and the experience prompted him to change his mind about retiring, spending another year at Anfield and then going on to play for John Toshack when he was manager of Swansea City.

The goal also stopped the threat of some trouble behind our goal, as a group of Italian fans had started barracking Liverpool after the Borussia equaliser, and the Liverpool supporters didn't take too kindly to this. The rest of the game seemed to me to last forever. I kept on looking at the huge clock at the back, and each minute seemed to last for hours. Then Kevin Keegan, who had put on probably his best display of the season in his final game for the club, took the ball in the centre of the field and advanced towards goal. He kept Bertie Vogts away from him, and just as he was about to shoot Vogts brought him down for a penalty. For Keegan this performance did a lot to answer the critics who had torn into him about his attitude, especially after his inept performance in the FA Cup final four days earlier. In fact he played against Borussia sporting a black eye, reputedly given to him by Jimmy Case after that final as he accused Keegan of being only interested in his own future. Phil Neal stepped up to take the penalty and coolly stroked the ball into the right hand corner of the net to seal the game at 3-1. The tension was lifted now, but had Ray Clemence not performed heroics to keep the score at 1-1 (as well as making another important save to keep us 2-1 in front) it might have been a very different story.

At the final whistle, the Roma Kop erupted again. I gave one of my scarves to one of the Italians who we had been sat with, as he had been asking for it before the game. Emlyn Hughes collected the cup, and then set off on a memorable lap of honour, with Joey Jones having his finest moment, wearing an enormous hat and almost climbing over the terracing fences to join with 'his people'. He lived up to the message on the banner that proclaimed, "Joey ate the frogs legs, made the Swiss roll, and now he's munching Gladbach". After the first lap of honour had ended, he brought the team back again to our end to set off on another one, and it was a long time before he left the field.

We eventually left the ground, rather reluctantly, and went to the coaches for the journey back to the airport. We were made to wait a long time, as the German flights all seemed to leave before ours did, and while there we walked around and shook hands with some of the German supporters. I also bumped into an ex-school colleague in Ian Henderson, who I had seen on the Kop on occasions. The flight home, although it was tiring, was full of celebrations, with bottles of champagne on sale. They had sold out by the time they reached Alex and myself, although I did get covered in the spray from the bottle bought by the chap in the seat in front of me! I bought a bottle of 'Ma Griffe' perfume to give to Barbara, but unfortunately when I opened it the next evening it had all leaked out and I had to write to the airline before I eventually got a replacement.

We arrived back in Liverpool at shortly after 3 a.m., to be met by hundreds of supporters who were cheering us for the part we had played in helping Liverpool lift the prestigious trophy – I saw Martin Catterall there, and I thought that he hadn't been to the game, but apparently his plane home had landed just before ours. As soon as we left the airport, we got a taxi to Alex's aunt's. Alex was staying there for the rest of the night, having taken the Thursday off work. We got there at about 3:30 a.m., and after having some rest and a breakfast his uncle drove me to the station so that I could catch the first train out of Liverpool at 6 a.m.

It was a great journey back, as I was talking to the railway guards at both Liverpool Exchange and Ormskirk stations about the game, and they seemed really impressed that I had actually been there myself. I did, however, feel a little out of place on the train from Preston to St Annes as I was still dressed in my red-and-white colours amongst a bunch of 'works' people in their smart suits. I eventually arrived back at my flat at 8:50, just as my lift arrived to take me to work! I just took time for a quick wash and change before going in, though I didn't actually do much work that day as nearly everybody wanted to talk to me about the game.

Bob Paisley was interviewed at length about Liverpool's successes after the match, and I remember his saying that the last time he had entered Rome, it was to liberate it during the war and he was in a tank on that occasion! This time, he just had the awesome red machine with him.

 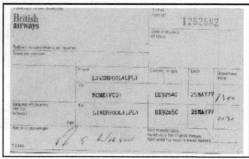

Boarding passes for the flight

Alex and his red trousers, and by the coach doors is 'the man with the limp', who I saw again at the Heysel Stadium in 1985

Liverpool v Borussia match ticket and Stadium edition of the match programme

50. **St Mirren** v Glasgow Rangers

Played at **Love Street** on 11th October 1978

Scottish League Cup, Second Round, Second Leg

St Mirren 0
Glasgow Rangers 0

Attendance 20,000

Barbara and I were away in Scotland for a week's touring holiday during October 1978. We reached Paisley in mid-week, and had a look inside the St Mirren ground during the afternoon before going to see Rangers defend their 3-2 first leg lead in a Scottish League Cup tie. Rangers had won the treble in 1977-78, and were seeking a second consecutive hat trick as well as aiming for success in the European Cup. The hat-trick had seemed unlikely at one stage in the first leg, as St Mirren took a 2-0 lead, but Rangers fought back to take a narrow advantage into this second leg fixture.

The 'Buddies', in the shadow of their neighbour Glasgow giants, had nevertheless achieved some measure of success themselves. They won the Scottish Cup three times, in 1926, 1959 and in 1987, and they also won the Anglo-Scottish Cup in 1980. They were also runners-up in the Scottish Cup in 1908, 1934 and 1962, and in the Scottish League Cup in 1956.

St Mirren had a first minute penalty claim turned down, but Rangers had the chance to take the lead on twenty-six minutes when a Parlane header fell to Johnstone only for the striker to shoot wildly over the bar. St Mirren pressed for the goal that would level the aggregate scores, and Bone headed over from a Stark cross. At the beginning of the second half, McCloy had to make a brilliant save – from a Jardine back-pass! The 'keeper also held a Bone header at the far post as Rangers held out for a 0-0 draw, thus progressing in the competition on their way to retaining it.

Barbara had been a little apprehensive about the match, having heard all about the bad reputation that Scottish football followers seemed to have, but there was no trouble at all, and both sets of supporters mingled together both inside and outside the ground. Most of the 20,000 crowd were Rangers supporters, and her main memory of the game was of the police who walked round and round the perimeter of the pitch during the game - she was certainly more interested in watching them than in watching the rather tedious football.

The following day, we moved on to Glasgow, and paid a visit to Ibrox, where we were invited by a doorman to come inside and look around the trophy room. We spent a good few minutes inside, looking at the numerous trophies that Rangers had amassed, including the three domestic trophies that they currently held, before walking onto the pitch itself. Barbara even sat in the trainers' dugout while I continued on my walk all around the famous ground.

The redeveloped Love Street in 2000, and the Ibrox trophy room

Aberdeen, Scottish Cup Final 1959

Dundee United, Scottish Cup Final 1987

Bristol City (h), Anglo-Scottish Cup Final 1977

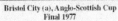

Bristol City (a), Anglo-Scottish Cup Final 1977

Bristol City (h), Anglo-Scottish Cup Final 1980

Bristol City (a), Anglo-Scottish Cup Final 1980

St Mirren v Celtic ticket from 2000

Slavia Praha (h), EUFA Cup 1985

Slavia Praha (a) EUFA Cup 1985

Motherwell, 1955 Scottish League Cup Semi-Final

Rangers (h) 1980-81 Scottish League Cup Semi-Final

Rangers (a) 1980-81 Scottish League Cup Semi-Final

Celtic, 1971-72 Scottish League Cup Semi-Final

Aberdeen, 1982 Scottish Cup Semi-Final

Rangers, 1983 Scottish Cup Semi-Final

Rangers, 1983 Scottish Cup Semi-Final replay

First Footing Volume 03
Steve Wilson

First Footing
Volume Three
By: Steve Wilson

1981, Barbara with Iain in the trophy room at Anfield – and the European Cup

Contents – Volume III

No.	Date	Match Details	Comp	Crowd
70	020592	**Lincoln City** (1)2 [Carmichael 2 penalties] Blackpool 0	Div 4	7884
		Season 1993-94		
		(Divisions 'upgraded' with the emergence of the FA Premier League, so Division 3 now becomes Division 2 etc.)		
71	050294	**Wigan Athletic** 0 Colchester United (0)1 [Dickens]	Div 3	1695
		Season 1994-95		
72	230794	**Southport** (0)1 [Quinlon] Blackpool (1)4 [Sheedy, Rodwell, Goulding own goal, Brown p]	Mrsdn Cup	1287
		Season 1995-96		
73	290795	**Rochdale** 0 Blackpool (0)1 [Ellis]	Mrsdn	1265
		Season 1996-97		
74	270796	**Morecambe** (2)2 [Ceraelo 2] Blackpool (1)3 [Bradshaw, Quinn, Thorpe]	Mrsdn	1692
75	290796	**Squires Gate** (1)3 [Barnes 2, Arnold] Tranmere Rovers XI (3)3 [Walker 3]	Frndly	80

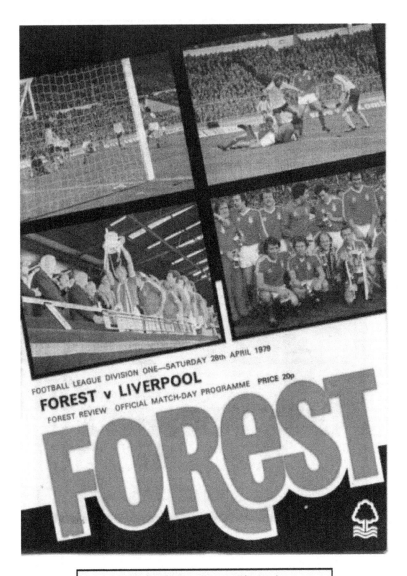

51. Nottingham Forest v Liverpool

Played at **The City Ground** on 28th April 1979

Football League Division One

Nottingham Forest 0
Liverpool 0

Attendance 41,898

51 Nottingham Forest – The City Ground

As Liverpool moved closer towards the league title in 1978-79, they had to go to the home of the reigning champions, Nottingham Forest, towards the end of April. I went to the game with Kevin by train, and endured one of the worst journeys that I have ever had the misfortune to take. Nottingham was a difficult place to get to, and we had to change at Crewe and catch the local service train through Stoke, Uttoxeter, Derby and on to Nottingham. This train was absolutely packed to the rafters with Liverpool fans, with no room even to stand without stepping on somebody else.

At some stations along the way, Forest fans were waiting, but for some reason they chose not to get on when our train stopped at the platform! On arrival in Nottingham, the local police herded us like cattle towards the ground, taking us past the Notts County ground and crossing the Trent along the way. We were all treated as if we were hooligans, and it doesn't surprise me when people treated like this often behave in that stereotyped fashion. Indeed, we did hear of quite a lot of trouble in the city as Liverpool fans took their 'revenge' on Forest for recent cup defeats, and as we were waiting to go into the ground we saw blood-spattered Forest fans on the way to their own end.

There were 42,000 in the ground, with a good 10,000 from Liverpool, and many more were locked out. One of those who didn't get in was Paul Molyneux, a Liverpool fan we knew from Maghull, who had gone with us on the train but decided to go for a drink instead of going straight into the ground. At first, there were no programmes available, but shortly before kick-off a seller came round and I just managed to get one before they had all sold out again.

In a bright beginning, Dalglish missed a first minute chance after Heighway had beaten two men and set up a chance for Souness. Souness' shot was blocked and spun to Dalglish, who inexplicably shot over the bar. Heighway then headed a Case cross towards goal, but it didn't trouble Shilton. When Forest attacked, Clemence made a hash of one Anderson cross, and it needed Thompson to head Robertson's far post effort away. Apart from this isolated Forest chance, Liverpool totally dominated the match, with Terry McDermott twice hitting the bar (one of them a superb long range shot that hit the underside and bounced down and out again) but once again we failed to score against our bogey-side. Even so, we could claim a moral victory from the 0-0 draw, and Forest needed a win more than we did if they were hopeful of closing the gap that existed between us. Forest were chanting more about the European Cup than anything else, with "To Munich, To Munich" (using the tune from "Top of the Form") and "Were you crying Liverpool?" being the height of their originality. We responded with the same chants they had aimed at us at Anfield the previous May - "You're not champions any more" and "Hand it over, Hand it over, Hand it over Nottingham". At the final whistle we left the ground while the Forest fans were kept in the ground on their Trent End as we walked along the banks of the river on our way back to the station. When we got there, the few Forest fans waiting for trains were chased all over the place by rampaging Scousers, with one terrified lad screaming "They're after me, they're after me" as he dived on to a goods train.

Eventually our train for Crewe left, and once more it was packed out. Although most of the passengers were Liverpool supporters, there were a few local people travelling as well, yet the railway police decided to lock all of the carriage doors - one more example of their total disregard for people as individuals. Perhaps they thought we were all going to run riot at every station we stopped off at on the journey back, but there was no basis for this, as there had been nothing like that on the journey to Nottingham. In our carriage, there were an elderly gentleman and two teenage girls, all of them Forest fans, and they had a good-natured chat with all of us. When the train stopped at Uttoxeter, their local station, they tried to get off but found that all of the doors were locked and there was nobody around who could open them. After trying for a few minutes, the train started off and the old man pulled the communication cord as he was obviously very concerned about being able to leave the train. This, of course, caused the train to pull up suddenly, and when the police came to investigate the three locals were eventually allowed off, although not before the police 'booked' the old man for pulling the cord without there being an emergency - what utter garbage!

The old chap was met at the station by his lift, and they sat in the car and waved to us, little realising that their pulling of the cord had jammed the wheels of the train, condemning us to be stuck at the station for the next couple of hours. Not surprisingly, this didn't please us and a lot of the Liverpool fans (including Brian and Alban) climbed out of the train windows (for the doors to the carriages were still locked) and went into Uttoxeter. A little later, we heard police sirens and not long after that some of these fans came running back on to the train, loaded down with rings and watches from a jeweller's shop that they had broken into. Although the police came back onto the train, I don't think that they managed to recover any of the stolen items and eventually we were allowed to resume our journey. I finally got back home at around midnight, a good three hours later than I had expected, and too late to watch the highlights of the afternoon's match that I had been so looking forward to. I later found out from Alban that he had got back to the station with Brian just as the train was leaving, and they had waited for the next one along with a lot of other Liverpool supporters. Unfortunately for them, the riot police had arrived while they were waiting and their investigations into the robbery had been brutal to say the least as they questioned the waiting Scousers. Without doubt, though, none of this would have happened if the police hadn't locked those carriage doors.

Forest were experiencing the most successful period in the history of the club. Promoted from the Second Division by a very narrow margin in 1977, they surprised everybody by winning the First Division title *and* the League Cup in 1978. They followed this success by retaining the League Cup in 1979, and reaching the final again in 1980, but their biggest successes came in Europe. They lifted the European Cup in Munich in 1979, a Trevor Francis goal defeating Malmo, and retained it in Madrid a year later when a John Robertson goal defeated Kevin Keegan's Hamburg. Prior to this, Forest's only real successes had come with FA Cup wins in 1898 and 1959. They had further League Cup successes in 1989 and 1990 before once again slipping out of the limelight and top-flight football.

Derby County, 1898 FA Cup Final

Match ticket

Luton Town, 1959 FA Cup Final

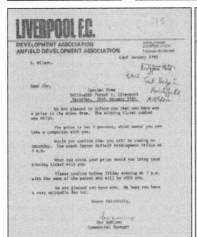

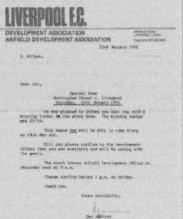

Letters re. the draw for a trip for two to Nottingham Forest v Liverpool in 1980 for the FA Cup Fourth Round fixture – I won one of the prizes, and as the agent selling the winning ticket, I won a third ticket

Draw ticket for the free trip for two to Nottingham Forest v Liverpool in 1980 for the FA Cup Fourth Round fixture

Malmo, 1979 European Cup
Final in Munich

Hamburg, 1980 European Cup
Final in Madrid

Nacional, 1980 World Clubs'
Championship, Tokyo

Another v Nacional, 1980 World
Clubs' Championship, Tokyo

Liverpool, 1978 League Cup
Final replay at Old Trafford

Liverpool, 1978 League Cup
Final at Wembley

Valencia (h) 1980 Super Cup

Valencia (a) 1980 Super Cup

Barcelona (h) 1979 Super Cup

52. Tranmere Rovers v Liverpool

Played at **Prenton Park** on 29th August 1979

Football League Cup Second Round First Leg

Tranmere Rovers 0
Liverpool 0

Attendance 16,759

52 Tranmere Rovers – Prenton Park

The draw for the Second Round of the League Cup competition in season 1979-80 featured Liverpool against Tranmere Rovers, a pairing that I had been waiting a long time to see. I got a ticket for the first leg, in Birkenhead, and went with Kevin. We had arranged to meet up with Alex when we got there, although we failed to see him at the meeting point, so we caught the ferry across to Birkenhead from the Pier Head and took a bus from there to Prenton Park. The match programme was one of those awful newspaper-style affairs that I hated so much, but that were becoming popular amongst clubs at the time.

It wasn't quite a full house, but most of the 16,759 crowd were Liverpool supporters. Johnson in the home goal was the hero of the night, with a string of fine saves keeping Liverpool out. After half an hour, he stopped a thirty-yard Alan Kennedy drive that was heading for the top corner, diving and tipping the ball over the bar. Four minutes later he gave a repeat performance, this time foiling a Jimmy Case effort. Johnson then made a fine save from Terry McDermott's goal attempt, and Ray Kennedy poked the rebound wide from ten yards. The 'keeper then saved at Souness' feet as he almost took Liverpool on single-handed. Bramhall appeared to have conceded a penalty when he brought Dalglish down four minutes into the second half, but the referee waved play on. Tranmere's two best chances of scoring came late in the game. First, on seventy-two minutes, Flood put in a cross-shot that eluded everybody in the area, and in the last minute O'Neill raced on to a Lumby through ball, forcing Clemence to emulate Johnson and block the shot, preventing a shock Tranmere victory. Tranmere played well above their station and took a lot of credit for holding on to the 0-0 draw.

We set off after the game to walk back to catch the ferry across to Liverpool again, and found ourselves right in the middle of one of the most frightening episodes of my soccer 'career'. Although there weren't that many Tranmere supporters at the game itself, it seemed that every youth in Birkenhead had come on to the streets with the sole intention of getting at the hated Scousers from across the water. As we walked along there were scuffles, fights and mobs running and hurling missiles all over the place, and one Liverpool lad who ran across the road to get away from a chasing Birkenhead pack was hit by a car and knocked over. He was left sitting in the road while the woman driver (who had no chance of being able to avoid him) was crying her eyes out. His friends stayed with him while the Birkenhead youths who had caused the accident stood watching and waiting a few yards away.

It was becoming obvious to us that the ferries would be the site of a major battleground, and we considered altering our plans and trying to catch a train back on the Wirral and Mersey line. We heard later that we wouldn't have been able to get one anyway, as they were only letting passengers on if they had already bought return tickets for the underground. Just as we were considering our options, a mini pulled alongside us. Fortunately for us the driver was Bruce, a lad we regularly saw at matches, and who had recognised Kevin. He shouted to us to get in and then drove us through the tunnel away from all of the trouble and back to Preston.

A week later, the return leg was played at Anfield, and revenge was uppermost in the minds of a lot of the Liverpool supporters. On the pitch, Liverpool strolled home by four goals to nil, and towards the end of the match an announcement was made that the last ferry would be leaving the Pier Head in five minutes time. Clearly the ferry operators had decided that they had seen enough trouble last time, and they weren't prepared for the same to happen again. We heard afterwards that there had been an awful lot of trouble at the Pier Head, and the previously untarnished reputation of Merseyside football supporters lay in tatters after this two-legged 'war'.

Tranmere had been the poor relations on Merseyside throughout their career, almost all of which had been spent in the bottom two divisions. In 1987, they found themselves one game away from dropping out of the league, and yet this proved to be the springboard for an unprecedented period of success for Rovers. Within a year, they were the star performers in the Football League Centenary Tournament at Wembley, defeating First Division sides Wimbledon and Newcastle, and losing to Nottingham Forest on penalties in the semi-final. Four more Wembley visits followed, two in the Leyland Daf Final (a 2-1 victory over Bristol Rovers followed by a 3-2 defeat against Birmingham) and two in the Third / Second Division play-off final (a 2-0 defeat to Notts County followed by a 1-0 victory over Bolton). Promoted to the newly-renamed Division One, Rovers confounded the critics by prospering and reaching the play-offs for three consecutive seasons, as well as losing a League Cup semi-final on penalties to Aston Villa and reaching three FA Cup quarterfinals, narrowly losing to Newcastle, Liverpool and Millwall. Newcastle were also the opponents in an incredible match in the Zenith Data Systems trophy in 1991 – the game finished 3-3 after ninety minutes, and an unbelievable 6-6 after xtra time before Rovers triumphed on penalties! The culmination of all of their achievements was to make a major cup final appearance, when they fought gallantly against Premiership Leicester in the Worthington Cup Final of 2000 before succumbing 2-1, David Kelly going down in Prenton Park history for scoring the Rovers' Cup Final goal. Rovers *had* reached a National Cup final prior to this, in fact, but that was the *Welsh* Cup Final. In 1934, they lost 3-0 to Bristol City, and the following year they defeated Chester 1-0 – and not a Welsh club in sight in either final!

Bristol Rovers, Leyland Daf Final, 1990

Leicester City, Football League Cup Final 2000

Football League Centenary Tournament, 1988

Aston Villa (h), League Cup Semi-Final 1994

Aston Villa (a), League Cup Semi-Final 1994

Wrexham, Isle of Man Tournament Final 1994

Liverpool (h) FA Cup quarterfinal 2001

Newcastle United (h), Zenith Data Systems Trophy 1991

Cremonese (h), Anglo-Italian Cup 1992

Ticket for Tranmere v Liverpool, 1979

Tranmere draw ticket

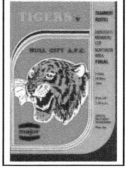

Hull City (a), 1984 Associate Members Cup Final (North)

53. Brighton and Hove Albion v Liverpool

Played at **The Goldstone Ground** on 10th November 1979

Football League Division One

Brighton and Hove Albion (0)1 [Clarke]
Liverpool (1)4 [R. Kennedy, Dalglish 2, Johnson]

Attendance 29,682

53 Brighton and Hove Albion – The Goldstone Ground

Brighton had won promotion to the First Division at the end of the 1978-79 season, fulfilling their aim of being the top seaside club in the Football League. Kevin's sister lived in the town and we arranged to go and stay there for the weekend prior to going to the game. Kevin was going to stay both Friday and Saturday nights, while Barbara and I were just going to stay over on the Friday. I set off with Barbara on the Friday morning and we spent a very pleasant day walking around London in the warm November sunshine. We visited several of the tourist attractions, including Westminster Abbey, with its poppies there in readiness for the following day's Remembrance Day service. On one of the multi-laned roads we had one tricky moment when trying to cross, where the traffic lights were slightly offset and I didn't realise that the red stoplight was for traffic coming from a different direction. It was almost like my close escape at Blackburn in 1968, as we stepped into the road and found four lanes of traffic heading for us, with us being unable to go either forwards or backwards for a few heart-stopping moments.

We eventually managed to negotiate our way round London towards Victoria Station, and had tea in a Wimpy bar near the station before meeting up with Kevin. He had travelled straight down to London in the afternoon, and we caught the train from Victoria to Brighton. Kevin's sister Mary worked in a pub close to the station on the sea-front, and we spent the evening there before going to her flat.

The following morning we went back with her to the pub before Kevin, Barbara and I left her to go to the station to meet Alex off the train - he had only set off on the Saturday morning from Blackpool. I noticed at the station that there was a poster proclaiming the virtues of our adversaries from Nottingham Forest, Clough and Taylor, who had 'enjoyed' a brief and unsuccessful spell at the helm at the Goldstone Ground. Results while they were in charge included a 0-4 home defeat by Walton and Hersham in the FA Cup, and a 2-8 home defeat in the league by Bristol Rovers. One of the people from the pub who we had been talking to gave us a lift to the ground, and as Kevin had a ground ticket while Alex had obtained stand tickets for the other three of us, Kevin left us while we went into a nearby pub.

The pub was packed out with Liverpool supporters, and during one of the many sing-songs one Liverpool supporter climbed onto a table and dropped his trousers, but fortunately (for her!) Barbara had gone to the toilet and so missed this 'action'. There was a sell-out crowd of approaching 30,000 at the game, and many more watched from outside the ground on a hill overlooking much of the pitch. Liverpool were far too good for the division's new boys and won in a canter 4-1 with Ray Kennedy, Dalglish with two, and Johnson all finding the net. Brighton's goal, from Clarke, made the score 2-1, and there did appear at the time to be a slight threat to our hopes of victory, but that was soon snuffed out. Indeed, we all thought that Terry McDermott had made it 5-1 but for some unknown reason the referee ruled the goal out. McDermott was later booked for a clash and then substituted to avoid his getting into any further trouble.

After the game had finished we walked back to the station, passing a scuffle in the park near to the ground that appeared to be started by Liverpool supporters. One chap near to the station asked us the result, and when I said 4-1 to Liverpool Barbara looked surprised as she thought we had won *3-1*. I could have understood it better if she thought we had won 5-1 considering the confusion over the disallowed goal! The Liverpool team were travelling on the same train as us from Brighton to London, but their compartment was locked to keep supporters away from them. I couldn't help but contrast the open access that there was when I travelled back from London with the Blackpool team a decade earlier. Back at Victoria station, we noticed a lot of West Ham skinheads hanging about, but we didn't stay around to find out whether or not they were waiting for Liverpool fans. The weekend had been too good to be spoiled at this late stage.

This particular period was the most successful in the history of Brighton, sandwiched between long periods of lower league activity. League Cup quarterfinalists in 1979, they came within inches of lifting silverware in 1983, when they played Manchester United in the FA Cup Final at Wembley. With the scores level at 2-2 and the game entering its final moments, Gordon Smith found himself one-on-one with United goalkeeper Bailey. Smith had scored the opening goal for Brighton, but faced with a match-winning scenario luck deserted him and Bailey saved with his legs. Reprieved, United went on to ease through the replay 4-0. To add salt to the wound, Brighton were without their influential captain Foster for the first game, due to a suspension that the club had unsuccessfully attempted to overturn. Back for the replay, he was run ragged, and the United supporters taunted him with chants of "What a difference you have made".

Brighton's tenure at the top level ended shortly after this momentary success, and in little more than a decade they found themselves waging a desperate fight to retain their league status, a cause not aided

16

by their having to play home matches at Gillingham, sixty miles from Brighton, due to the selling off of their Goldstone Ground home at the end of the 1996-97 season.

Manchester United, 1983 FA Cup Final

Sheffield Wednesday, 1983 FA Cup Semi-Final at Highbury

Manchester United, 1983 FA Cup Final replay

Millwall (h), 1991 Play-Off Semi-Final

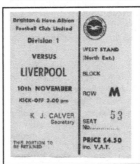

Brighton v Liverpool ticket from 1979

Notts County (h), Sherpa Van Southern Semi-Final 1987-88

54. Norwich City v Liverpool

Played at Carrow Road on 9th February 1980

Football League Division One

Norwich City (2)3 [Peters, Reeves, Fashanu]
Liverpool (2)5 [Fairclough 3, Dalglish, Case]

Attendance 25,624

54 Norwich City – Carrow Road

For the second time I decided I'd travel on the football special to watch Liverpool in action. The game was at Norwich City in February 1980, and we met up with Paul Molyneux at Lime Street. It was an uneventful journey across country to East Anglia, but it was far from an uneventful game.

We managed to get separated from Paul in the ground, as he had to finish all his cans of beer before the police would let him in. The away terracing was in an awful location, and we were barely able to see because of the wire meshing which separated us from the pitch, although we were still able to view clearly as Norwich scored in the first minute through Martin Peters. David Fairclough equalised, then put us 2-1 ahead before Reeves added to Peters' goal to level the scores at half time. Fairclough completed his hat trick in the second half, only for Justin Fashanu to level the scores again with a stunning volley that deservedly won the BBC's 'Goal of the Season' award for 1979-80. With two minutes remaining a 3-3 draw seemed to be the likeliest result, but then Kenny Dalglish and Jimmy Case scored to turn it into a 5-3 victory.

Leaving the ground we heard even more good news as Wolves has won 1-0 at Manchester United, and Everton had been trounced 4-0 at home by Ipswich. There was one charge by Liverpool fans at Norwich supporters on the way to the station, but basically it was a very organised and well-behaved outing. We got back home at around midnight, and despite it being a long day it was more than worth it.

Fashanu's goal was my fourth 'Goal of the Season' in five years, the others being Mickey Walsh's in 1975 for Blackpool against Sunderland, Terry McDermott's in the 1977 FA Cup semi-final against Everton, and Graeme Souness' volley against Manchester United in 1978.

The Norwich team of 1980 were in the midst of the most successful period in the club's history. Apart from reaching the FA Cup semi-final as a Third Division side in 1959 – eliminating previous season's finalists Manchester United 3-0 along the way - and winning the League Cup in its second season in 1962, they had achieved little until the early seventies. Following promotion to the First Division for the first time in 1972, they reached the Football League Cup finals of 1973 and 1975, losing to Tottenham and Aston Villa, before they lifted the trophy ay Wembley by defeating Sunderland 1-0 in 1985. They were also defeated FA Cup semi-finalists in 1989, but their defeat by Everton was totally overshadowed by the tragic events of the other semi-final between Liverpool and Nottingham Forest at Hillsborough. Three years later, they lost another FA Cup semi-final – Sunderland gaining revenge for the 1985 defeat – and Norwich won the Anglo-Scottish Cup in 1977.

Norwich v Nottingham Forest
FA Cup quarterfinal ticket 1991,
and visitor pass

Sunderland, 1985 Football
League Cup Final

Manchester United, FA Cup
1959

Luton Town, FA Cup Semi-
Final 1959

Luton Town, FA Cup Semi-
Final replay 1959

Everton, FA Cup Semi-Final
1989

Sunderland, FA Cup Semi-Final
1992

Inter Milan (h), EUFA Cup 1993

Football Special details

Ipswich Town (a), Texaco Cup
Final 1973

55. Arsenal v Liverpool

Played at **Hillsborough** on 12th April 1980

FA Cup Semi-Final

Arsenal 0
Liverpool 0

Attendance 50,174

55 – Hillsborough, Sheffield

The FA Cup Semi-Final at Hillsborough against Arsenal on Barbara's twenty-second birthday certainly brought some relief from the tensions of Liverpool's pursuit of the league title, only to generate an entirely new set of nervous problems! Kevin, Alex, Martin and myself made the journey to South Yorkshire for my first visit to the ground. We were all quite confident of success despite the hiccup of a league defeat at Old Trafford, as our recent form was impressive enough otherwise. Arsenal were going for their third consecutive FA Cup final appearance, and the atmosphere around Hillsborough was good as we went to a 'Kentucky Fried Chicken' outlet for dinner before going into our seats, which Alex had obtained for us from his friend at the Football league, Lee Walker.

Frankly, the game was a great disappointment, mainly due to very windy conditions and a hard pitch, and not surprisingly it ended up 0-0. Even below their best, Liverpool were by far the better side, and Case headed wide of a gaping goal before Lee swept a simple chance wide after just seven minutes following a Souness–Johnson combination. Johnson also missed a good chance in a first half of Liverpool dominance. In the second half, Lee robbed Brady and presented Ray Kennedy with a glorious chance, but the ex-Arsenal man's right foot shot went wide of both Jennings and the post. Right at the finish, Arsenal nearly stole the game when Talbot sent in a chip shot and everything seemed to be taking place in slow motion as the ball dropped and landed on top of the bar.

As we left the ground and joined the crush of other Liverpool fans on the steps leading from the terracing we heard that Everton had drawn their tie with West Ham as well, 1-1 in their case. I do remember thinking how dangerous it was leaving the ground due to the steepness of the steps and the fact that we were merging with the fans from the Leppings Lane terraces. Even so, little did I think that such a disaster as that which would happen in the Semi-Final between Liverpool and Nottingham Forest in 1989 would ever occur at a game. The tie was replayed at Villa Park, and again finished level at 1-1. A second replay at Villa also finished 1-1, before Arsenal finally triumphed 1-0 in the third replay at Coventry to set up a Wembley date against fellow Londoners West Ham.

First replay at Villa Park

Second replay at Villa Park

Third replay at Highfield Road

Liverpool v Nottingham Forest
1988 Semi-Final at Hillsborough

Ticket for the 1980 Semi-Final

Liverpool v Nottingham Forest,
1989 – Hillsborough Disaster

56. Crystal Palace v Liverpool

Played at Selhurst Park on 26th April 1980

Football League Division One

Crystal Palace 0
Liverpool 0

Attendance 45,583

56 Crystal Palace – Selhurst Park

After the first replay with Arsenal we had to resume our campaign for the league title. The final league game before the resumption of semi-final action was at Crystal Palace. Kevin didn't go to this one, and that left me 'one up' on him over the season as I went with Alex, Martin and his policeman-friend Paul. It was a long journey to London as Paul's car had a top-speed of only 50mph. At one motorway services we met some Blackpool fans going to Reading and I saw Ian Carden there - Blackpool achieved a vital 1-0 victory down at Elm Park in their bid to stave of relegation to Division Four.

At Selhurst Park a massive crowd approaching 46,000 gathered to watch the champions-elect. Liverpool, without Case and McDermott, were fortunate to survive as Palace dominated the game. Clemence saved when Murphy put Walsh in on goal, and another Murphy through pass saw Flanagan sweep the ball wide of the post. In the second half, Liverpool showed a bit more urgency, and when Johnson managed to get in behind the Palace defence, ex-Blackpool goalkeeper Burridge had to scramble around desperately before the ball was cleared. Palace claimed a late penalty when Kennedy seemed to be all over Flanagan, but the referee ignored their claims and the last chance of a goal had disappeared.

So Liverpool came away with a vital championship point in a goalless draw, and although it was not a very impressive performance it was still one that left us level on points with Manchester United. We had a better goal difference than United, and in addition had two games left to their one.

For Crystal Palace, their time was yet to come. They were relegated to Division Two, but after defeating Blackburn in a two-legged play-off final in 1989, Palace returned to the top flight. Their return wasn't the happiest, including a 9-0 thrashing at Anfield against Liverpool, yet they managed to reach the FA Cup Semi-Final where their opponents were Liverpool again. In a marvellous match, Palace won 4-3 after extra time to set up a Wembley final against Manchester United. Two Ian Wright goals almost won the cup for Palace, but United equalised to force a replay after a 3-3 draw, and they went on to win at the second attempt by the only goal of the game. Palace did triumph at Wembley in 1997 in the First Division play-off final, and they encountered Liverpool in the semi-finals of the League Cup in 1995 and 2001, losing on aggregate on both occasions. They had also lost at that stage in 1993, and won silverware at Wembley by lifting the Zenith Data Systems Cup against Everton in 1991.

Reading v Blackpool April 26th 1980, and Palace v Blackpool ticket from 1968

Manchester United, 1990 FA
Cup Final

Manchester United, 1990 FA
Cup Final replay

Everton, Zenith Data Systems
Cup Final 1991

Liverpool, 1990 FA Cup Semi-
Final

Manchester United, 1995 FA
Cup Semi-Final

Manchester United, 1995 FA
Cup Semi-Final replay

Southampton, 1976 FA Cup
Semi-Final

Real Madrid (h), 1962

Sheffield United, First Division
Play-Off Final 1997

Liverpool (a) 1989 – the 9-0
trouncing

Blackburn Rovers (a), 1989
Play-Off Final

Liverpool (a), 1995 Football
League Cup Semi-Final

Liverpool (h), 1995 Football
League Cup Semi-Final

Liverpool (a), 2001 Football
League Cup Semi-Final

Liverpool (h), 2001 Football
League Cup Semi-Final

Arsenal (h), 1993 Football
League Cup Semi-Final

Verona (h), Anglo-Italian Cup
1973

West Ham United, First Division
Play-Off Final 2004

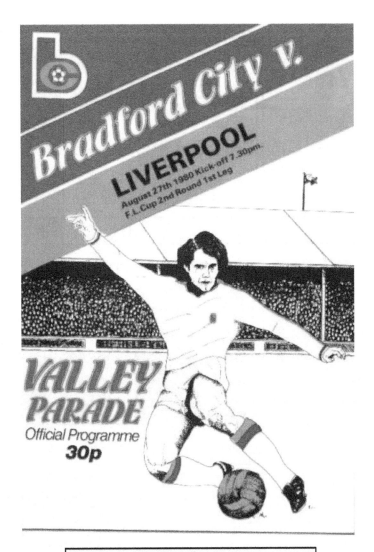

57. Bradford City v Liverpool

Played at **Valley Parade** on 27th August 1980

Football League Cup Second Round, First Leg

Bradford City (0)1 [Campbell]
Liverpool 0

Attendance 16,232

57 Bradford City – Valley Parade

The 1980-81 league season didn't get off to the best of starts for defending champions Liverpool, with an early 2-0 defeat at Leicester. Worse was to follow four days later as I left work at 4 p.m. to go with Kevin to Bradford City for the League Cup tie. It was to share similarities with the experience we had at Tranmere twelve months earlier, with the supporters of the smaller division club out to make a name for themselves against the biggest club in the land.

Things started to go wrong as soon as we came off the motorway in Bradford, when we took the wrong turning and had to come back after passing Bradford Northern Rugby League ground at Odsal. We eventually found Valley Parade and were able to park almost outside the ground, just fifty yards from the turnstiles. Our terracing was a disgrace for a Football League club, just a few yards in depth, and fortunately only a few Liverpool fans made the trip – otherwise, it could have been a disaster waiting to happen in there. Considering the awful state of the ground it was not really a surprise when they had the terrible fire in the main stand during the game against Lincoln in May 1985, when over fifty people died. The only thing in favour of Bradford came when Martin reckoned they served the best pies in the league!

Liverpool's performance on the pitch tended to match the state of the ground, even though they did dominate events. Clemence was brought into action for the first time with just twelve minutes to go when he failed to hold a Dolan free kick. The ball ran loose for Campbell, who hooked the only goal of the game in from a tight angle. That was enough for City, still without a victory in the Fourth Division, to defeat the League Champions. Prior to this goal, Smith had dived to hold a Johnson shot, and after Wood played a too-short back pass on seven minutes, Souness slipped the ball past the goalkeeper but hit the post with his shot from the by-line. Johnson drew Smith out of his goal but shot wide midway through the second half, and that was the closest Liverpool came to a goal in the final forty-five minutes. In truth, though, I wasn't too disappointed with the result, as with a second leg at Anfield still to come I didn't doubt that we'd get through - we did, winning 4-0. As soon as the final whistle blew we dashed for the car, getting there just as a mob of Bradford fans came charging around the corner across the waste ground, laden with bricks and other missiles. If we'd been just a minute later we'd have had no chance of getting away unscathed.

Better times were to come for Bradford, with promotions and a two-year spell in the Premiership at the turn of the century. They also had a Wembley success in the 1996 Division Two play-off final, after seeing off Blackpool in a momentous semi-final. Trailing 2-0 after the first leg in Bradford, the Yorkshire side surprised everybody by defeating Blackpool 3-0 at the seaside to set up the London trip. Their biggest success, though, came way back in 1911, when they defeated Newcastle United 1-0 after a replay to win the FA Cup, and to complete a successful season they attained their highest ever league placing of fifth in Division One. In the League Cup, they were quarterfinalists in 1965 and 1989. As mentioned above, though, tragedy struck in 1985 when a main stand fire at their final game against Lincoln changed a championship celebration into a lament for the dead as fifty-six people lost their lives.

Lincoln City (h) 1984-5 –
Bradford Fire Disaster

Match ticket

Bristol City (h), Football League
Cup quarterfinal 1989

Newcastle United, 1911 FA Cup Final

Newcastle United, 1911 FA Cup Final

Notts County, 1996 Division Two Play-Off Final

Blackpool (a), 1996 Division Two Play-Off Semi-Final

Blackpool (h), 1996 Division Two Play-Off Semi-Final

Middlesbrough (h), 1988 Play-Off Semi-Final

Middlesbrough (a), 1988 Play-Off Semi-Final

Southampton (h), 1976 FA Cup quarterfinal

The Bradford fire memorial

58. Sunderland v Liverpool

Played at **Roker Park** on 29th November 1980

Football League Division One

Sunderland (0)2 [Brown, Cummins]
Liverpool (2)4 [Johnson, McDermott, Lee 2]

Attendance 32,340

Liverpool's season was still a mixture of ups and downs. This was never better illustrated than in the final week of November. After a 2-1 victory at Anfield against champions-elect Aston Villa, they travelled to Wolverhampton on the Tuesday evening and were trounced 4-1, with old-boy Emlyn Hughes netting the final goal in the last minute. After such a crushing defeat, we were unsure about what to expect at Sunderland on the Saturday, for it could be either retribution or a continuance of the poor away form. Sunderland were very much a side with a glorious past but an almost non-existent present. League Champions on six occasions up to 1936, they were also FA Cup winners in 1937, but apart from another Wembley success in 1973, no other silverware reached the Roker Park trophy cabinets. The 1973 final, though, was one of those still talked about decades later, as Second Division Sunderland defeated hot favourites Leeds 1-0. Porterfield scored the game's only goal, but a double Montgomery save from Lorimer and Cherry, and a delighted dance on the pitch at the final whistle from manager Bob Stokoe are the images that spring most readily to mind. Further Wembley visits ended in defeats against Norwich in the 1985 League Cup Final, Liverpool in the 1992 FA Cup Final, and Charlton in the 1998 First Division Play-Off Final.

At first there was some doubt as to whether our game there would be played, as there was a lot of snow and ice about. By the morning of the game it seemed set to go ahead, so Kevin and I set off, picking up Paul Molyneux at Preston station. Paul had wanted Kevin to drive to Maghull to pick him up, a near thirty-mile detour, but Kevin told him he either met us at Preston or he would have to make his own way there. As we travelled up the A1 we saw one overturned car on the central reservation, evidence of the treacherous conditions, but in Sunderland it was cold but playable. We managed to lose Paul in the queue for the paddock as he went off to buy and sell programmes, only for him to come up to us in the ground just before kick-off. We didn't really want him to stand with us because he had a broad Scouse accent, and didn't have the sense to keep his mouth shut, but fortunately the people around us were a decent, knowledgeable football crowd who appreciated and applauded good football by either side.

There was certainly plenty to applaud from Liverpool that afternoon. David Johnson and Terry McDermott scored from two of the many chances that came along, and with under ten minutes remaining that seemed to be how the game would finish, when Sammy Lee clip-volleyed a brilliant goal to make it 3-0. Kevin then had to go to the gents, missing Lee repeat the shot to make it 4-0. Straight from the kick-off, Sunderland came back and made it 4-1 when Brown scored. Kevin was keen to make a quick getaway, so we left just as Sunderland scored again through Cummins to bring the score to 4-2, and a roar outside the ground indicated how close they'd come to pulling a third goal back. So an easy victory suddenly turned into a nerve-wracking final few minutes for the team and the few supporters who had travelled up to the Northeast.

On our journey home we were a little concerned about running out of fuel, but by sticking to 40 mph we reached Scotch Corner for a fill-up and some chips. The only slight 'mishap' we had was going about twenty miles out of our way by following the motorway signs outside Leeds and heading for the M1, instead of going on the more direct route through Leeds. Given the tricky road conditions, though, we were probably better off on the motorway.

Preston North End, 1937 FA
Cup Final

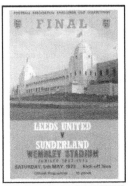

Leeds United, 1973 FA Cup
Final

Vasas (h), 1973 European Cup
Winners Cup

Fiorentina (h), Anglo-Italian
Cup 1970

Arsenal, 1973 FA Cup Semi-
Final

Vasas (a), 1973 European Cup
Winners Cup

Chelsea (h), 1985 League Cup
Semi-Final

Chelsea (a), 1985 League Cup
Semi-Final

Sunderland v Blackpool ticket
from 1974

59. Real Madrid v Liverpool

Played at **Parc des Princes, Paris** on 27th May 1981

European Cup Final

Real Madrid 0
Liverpool (0)1 [A Kennedy]

Attendance 48,360

59 – Parc des Princes, Paris

Liverpool again reached the final of the European Cup in season 1980-81. They had already won the Football League Cup for the first time in their history, and now they had the chance to crown a season that had so often seemed destined for disappointment. The final opposition was the mighty Real Madrid, with the game being played in Paris, but 'Pool made hard work of getting there. Liverpool seemed out of the competition after a goalless draw at Anfield against old adversaries Bayern Munich in the semi-final. However, a superb fighting performance brought a 1-1 draw in the second leg and Liverpool reached the final on the away goals rule – I flung my month-old son Iain into the air in delight as Ray Kennedy scored the late goal that sent us to Paris.

Real Madrid were the undoubted past masters of European football. They had won the European Cup in each of the first five years of the tournament, with Di Stefano, Puskas and Gento among the household names, but their sixth and last success had come fifteen years earlier and they were in desperate need of further European glory.

For the trip to Paris, Kevin, Dave and Martin went by train. Kevin had been beset with problems as he tried to get a passport from the office in Liverpool, and he eventually bought a one-year passport from a local post office to make sure that he could get to the game. For £112 I booked a flight to travel there on the day. I drove up to Speke Airport very early on the Wednesday morning, taking the motorway route down and arriving in good time. I had booked through Towns Travel, but hadn't yet received all of my tickets, and I was given the name of somebody on my trip who had my plane tickets. At the airport I made contact with the given person, which eased one slight worry.

At breakfast I bought a paper, which highlighted the trouble occurring overnight in Paris. We had only been allocated 12,000 tickets in the 48,000 capacity stadium, and with at least twice that many wanting to go (and going!) trouble seemed inevitable. I kept my ticket in my sock inside a plastic bag for much of the day, as I'd heard of all sorts of ways of 'removing' the ticket from pockets of unsuspecting fans. After a smooth flight to Paris, we boarded our coaches for the journey to the ground. The weather wasn't too good, with heavy clouds threatening a downpour and keeping the temperature cool. The coach went up to the 'Parc des Princes' stadium, then drove back towards the Eiffel tower, dropping us off at the Trocadero Metro station. We had been given return tickets from Trocadero to the stadium as part of our package. The coaches then left us, and I had some eight hours to spend, so I took the opportunity to look around and travel to the top of the Eiffel Tower.

I bought myself a pennant commemorating the game before finally deciding to head for the ground. There were a lot of Liverpool fans on the metro, and on arrival at the stadium the sight was of masses of red-and-white clad Liverpool supporters, most of whom it seemed were without tickets. Amongst the supporters, I saw John, a fan from Bolton who saw most of Liverpool's games and stood near me on the Kop. He was without a ticket, and not too optimistic about his chances of getting hold of one. There were hundreds of Liverpool fans around, but very few supporters of Real.

The atmosphere started to turn a little sour, as bottles of beer were being bought and consumed by the dozen and gradually the ticketless Scousers began to get belligerent. There were still no Real Madrid fans around but there were some French ticket touts trying to make some 'easy' money. Some Liverpool lads went towards one, and in a well-planned 'military' operation came out from behind the cover of a passing van and proceeded to kick him to the ground in unsuccessful attempts to get his tickets.

It was inevitable that the French gendarmes would become involved, but when they arrived they totally over-reacted, lining up with riot shields and huge truncheons. The Liverpool fans greeted their arrival with a hail of beer bottles, but the greater might and organisation of the gendarmes forced them away from the ground, and though they tried to come back in full circle they were met and repulsed there too. To make matters worse, the heavens opened and a torrential downpour soaked me to the skin. At one stage I was stood in the middle of a line of ordinary French police, with one indicating to me that I should cover up my Liverpool colours, whilst drunken Liverpool fans hurled bottles at the riot police lines in a scene that could have been taken from the television news from Ulster or some other war-torn province.

Eventually a semblance of order and sanity was restored, with two and half hours still to go until kick-off time. The barriers erected around the ground to keep fans without tickets away from the stadium had two entrances, both heavily policed, and fans were let through to the ground one by one after strict checks. The organisation from here, though, became a disgrace and there was now a real danger of people being crushed in the melee. Lawrie McMenemy, one of the BBC's panel of 'experts' came through, and one fan shouted at him "why don't you report this disgraceful treatment on the tele" – although he nodded, I'm sure he didn't.

After at least half-an-hour, I was still nowhere nearer the front of the queue, then I noticed another entrance a couple of hundred yards away which was comparatively quiet. I went and joined that, and when I went to get my ticket from my sock I found I'd stuffed a piece of paper there instead, leaving my ticket in my front coat pocket all the time where anyone could have stolen it! I listened to a couple of lads talking in front of me, and they claimed that we were to be banned from Europe because of the trouble at the ground. Ironically, the newspapers back in England reported on the 'excellent behaviour' of the Liverpool fans and no action was ever taken by UEFA over the near-riot at the stadium.

Eventually I got inside the ground and found my seat, on the front row of the top tier of the stand. It was an excellent view, but unfortunately the seat and floor were under several inches of water from the heavy rain, so I took a seat on the row behind for a while. I spotted Kevin in another section and went to talk to him. He'd not had a good time because of his being with Martin and Dave. They wouldn't go with the Liverpool crowd from the railway station, going instead in a different direction while Dave tried to find a bank to get some French Francs, and consequently Kevin saw nothing of the Eiffel Tower or other parts of Paris. After chatting for a short while, I went back to my seat and waited for the game to start. The planned pre-match game between two boys' sides had been cancelled due to the state of the pitch so I just watched the crowd building up. Eventually the lad with my seat ticket came, and although I moved he kept shouting at me that I could have caused trouble for sitting in his seat. He was totally drunk, and at different times during the game he argued with other people, cried on his mate's shoulder, apologised to me and finally shook my hand!

There were more Liverpool fans than Spaniards, although they had a large and noisy drum and made an awesome noise with their chants of "Ma-drid, Ma-drid". We had a scare during the pre-match kick-about when a shot reared up and hit Ray Clemence in the face, but fortunately after treatment he was all right. In a dour first-half, Liverpool overcame early raids by Real's English import Lawrie Cunningham to dominate the game. Liverpool had three scoring opportunities in the first quarter of an hour, McDermott shooting over, Alan Kennedy bringing a diving save out of Agustin and from a Ray Kennedy free kick, Hansen heading the ball across for Dalglish to hit a shot on the turn that went straight at the 'keeper. The only scare at our end came when Juanito played a through ball for Camacho, but his poked effort went wide with Clemence scrambling across his goal line to cover. Agustin was by far the busier 'keeper, and he couldn't hold on to one Souness effort but managed to react quickly and dived on the loose ball.

Liverpool's domination was even more pronounced in the second-half, when, apart from one attack which led to Camacho hitting a lob over Clemence and the bar, Real were never in with a shout. Even so, extra time was beginning to look a certainty when we got a throw-in on the Real right and Ray Kennedy threw it quickly to Alan Kennedy. "Barney" chested the ball past two defenders, Cortes taking a fresh-air shot in an attempt to clear the ball, and unleashed an unstoppable shot past the Real goalkeeper into the corner of the net, instantly transforming us from a feeling of boredom to one of ecstatic delight.

I thought there were still ten minutes left, and sat there nervously looking at my watch, but just seven minutes later the final whistle went and we'd won our third European Cup in five seasons. The closest to a goal in those dying minutes came when Agustin made a fine save from a Souness shot – Real never once threatened to equalise. The Liverpool fans taunted deposed champions Forest with chants of "Are You Watching Nottingham", and you couldn't help but feel a little sympathy for Real's Stielike, on the losing side again against Liverpool after previously playing for Borussia Monchengladbach.

It was a joyous procession now on the way back to the metro station, with not a Real fan to be seen. A gendarme asked me for a scarf, and I gave him my silk one. Nobody wanted to throw beer bottles or wave truncheons now. On the train I saw John from Bolton, and to my delight I found he had got in, getting a ticket fairly cheaply outside. A rumour did circulate that the French authorities let all Liverpool fans without a ticket into the ground at kick-off time, as some blocks were still empty. Presumably they had been snapped up by the French people in the forlorn hope of making a profit on the black market! I rang Barbara when I got back to the airport, then had a long wait there until 3 a.m. before my plane took off. I eventually got home at about five thirty, although I almost fell asleep at the wheel at one stage as I drove home through the deserted streets of Liverpool. In total contrast to my first European Cup final trip in 1977 to Rome, I went into work later that afternoon and hardly anybody even knew I'd been to the game! A few months later, I took Barbara and Iain to Anfield and we were allowed into the trophy room to see the silverware that had been won by the club's various sides in the 1980-81 season.

My boarding passes, airport ticket. Metro ticket, coach transfer ticket, travel details and draw ticket

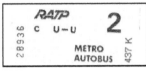

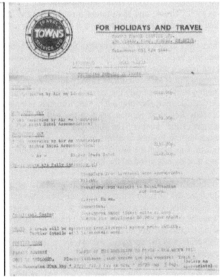

Real Madrid version of the final programme	Liverpool v Real Madrid match ticket	French version of the final programme

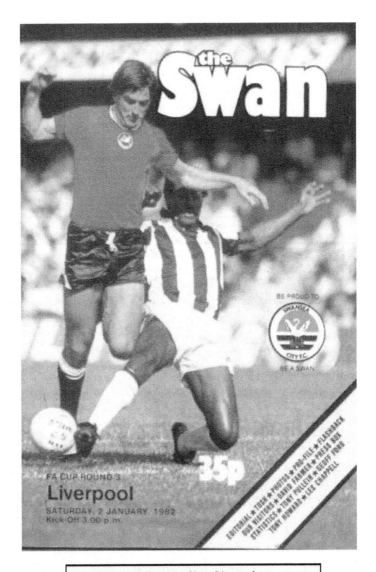

60. Swansea City v Liverpool

Played at **The Vetch Field** on 2nd January 1982

FA Cup Third Round

Swansea City 0
Liverpool (2)4 [Hansen, Rush 2, Lawrenson]

Attendance 24,179

1982 began with an FA Cup tie at high-flying Swansea, who were almost unbeatable at the Vetch Field. Since their promotion, they had taken the First Division by storm, and under the management of John Toshack they looked like they could take the leap from Fourth Division obscurity to Europe in their stride. They trounced Leeds United 5-1 in their first ever game in the top flight, Bob Latchford netting a hat trick, and topped the table for a considerable part of the season.

Their only previous claim to fame had come with victories in the Welsh Cup, and FA Cup Semi-Final appearances in 1926, when Bolton defeated them, and 1964, when they narrowly lost to Preston. They produced a major shock in the 1964 quarterfinal when they defeated Champions-elect Liverpool 2-1 at Anfield but couldn't quite do the same against Second Division North End. In the League Cup, their best displays saw them reach the Fourth Round in 1965 and 1977. Welsh Cup success in 1982 led to them defeating Malta's Sliema Wanderers 17-0 on aggregate in the European Cup Winners Cup, winning 12-0 at home and 5-0 away. After two seasons in the top flight under Toshack, with a championship appearing possible for most of 1981-82, they dropped back down through the leagues, although they did achieve Wembley success in 1994 when Huddersfield Town were defeated on penalties in the Autoglass Final. For such a major Welsh side, their total of ten victories in the Welsh Cup between 1913 and 1991 was surprisingly few.

The game looked a bit unlikely to take place as the Christmas freeze-up was followed by fog. By the Saturday morning, though, it had cleared a little and I set off for Preston. I was taking Kevin and Martin, and supposedly picking up Paul Molyneux at Preston station, but when I arrived at Kevin's, he said Paul's dad had rang to say he wasn't coming, so there were just the three of us. Martin usually only went as far as Newton-le-Willows, where he went with John, Ron and a few others. We decided to see if we could get a lift with them as well, but as they were full I drove the three of us down.

It was the longest journey I'd ever driven in one day, a round trip of 500 miles. In South Wales, as we approached Newport, the fog came down again quite thickly and it now seemed almost certain that the game would be off. We carried on to the coast anyway and conditions there were much better, so we parked up just away from the ground. John's car had passed us on the outskirts of Swansea, where one of the back seat occupants had 'mooned' to the locals. There was a huge crowd of 24,000 in the ground, with the masses from Liverpool packing our terracing ridiculing Wales, who had just failed to qualify for the 1982 World Cup finals in Spain.

John Toshack came on to the pitch to be presented with a local award before kick-off, but that was the last thing Swansea received that afternoon. Liverpool were so much on top that in the end the fact that they only scored four times was a bit of a disappointment. It took thirty-six minutes to get the breakthrough, Hansen heading home a right wing McDermott cross. Rush made it 2-0 on the stroke of half-time, tapping in after Whelan's header had hit the bar and bounced back into play. In the second half, Dalglish, Lawrenson and Whelan all went close before Souness put Lawrenson through for the third goal with less than twenty minutes remaining. Whelan and McDermott were denied goals by the woodwork before Souness and Rush exchanged passes to set up Rush for his second and Liverpool's fourth goal. Swansea's only real chance came when Grobbelaar failed to hold a Leighton James drive, and ex-Evertonian Bob Latchford delighted the Liverpool supporters by blasting the loose ball way over the bar.

Such was the dominance of Liverpool that the travelling Kop started singing "Oh, I had a wheelbarrow and the wheel fell off" - what relevance that had to football I don't know! After the game it took us a while to get out of Swansea, but once we managed to find our way we had a fairly uneventful journey home, as the driving conditions eased.

Hereford (h), Welsh Cup Final 1981

Liverpool (a), FA Cup
quarterfinal 1964

Preston North End, FA Cup
Semi-Final 1964

Huddersfield Town, 1994
Autoglass Final

Leeds United (h), First Division
debut, 1981

Chester (h) 1966 Welsh Cup
Final

Paris St Germain (h), Cup
Winners Cup 1982

Sliema Wanderers (h), 1982-83
European Cup Winners Cup

Hereford United (a), Welsh Cup
Final 1981

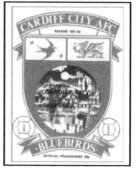

Cardiff City (a), Welsh Cup
Final 1982

Cardiff City (h), Welsh Cup
Final 1982

Cardiff City (a), Welsh Cup
Final 1956

Wrexham (h), Welsh Cup Final
1983

Wrexham, 1991 Welsh Cup
Final

Newport County, Welsh Cup
Semi-Final 1963

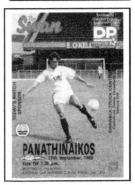

Panathinaikos (h), European
Cup Winners Cup 1989

FC Magdeburg (a), 1983
European Cup Winners Cup

West Ham United (a), FA Cup
Fifth Round 1980

Chelsea (a), Football League
Cup Fourth Round 1965

Merthyr Tydfil, Welsh Cup
Final 1949

Merthyr Tydfil, Welsh Cup
Semi-Final 1950

Stoke City (a), FA Cup Fifth
Round 1964

Wycombe Wanderers (h),
Autoglass Area Final 1994

Swansea v Liverpool ticket from
1982

Wycombe Wanderers (a),
Autoglass Area Final 1994

61. Notts County v Liverpool

Played at **Meadow Lane** on 20th November 1982

Football League Division One

Notts County (1)1 [Christie]
Liverpool (0)2 [Johnston, Dalglish]

Attendance 16,914

61 Notts County – Meadow Lane

Ian Rush had scored consecutive hat-tricks for Liverpool, and it set people wondering if he could emulate Jack Balmer's feat of three consecutive First Division hat-tricks, a record set way back in 1947. The game in which he attempted to equal this record was at Notts County, scene of Rush's first treble for the club ten months earlier.

Notts County were the oldest club in the Football league, having been founded in 1862, but for all of their age, they had achieved very little in terms of success. Apart from an FA Cup victory way back in 1894, their only other silverware of note came with a 1995 Wembley success in the Anglo-Italian Cup Final – a year after defeat in the same competition at the same stage. For most of the time, they had to play second fiddle to Nottingham Forest on the other side of the River Trent, but for a short period towards the end of the twentieth century, they did manage to claim the title of 'top dogs' in Nottingham. During their two-year spell in the First Division, they reached the FA Cup quarterfinals in 1984, only to go out by the only goal to eventual winners Everton. Their best League Cup performances came with quarterfinal appearances in 1964, 1973 and 1976.

I travelled to Nottingham with Dave, Kevin and Martin. County are the oldest club in the league, and their ground showed it as we walked round in the time before kick-off. Liverpool were allocated about a third of the open end, but we had a real struggle to find somewhere where we could see. Rush had a couple of early chances to open the scoring but fluffed them, and County gradually got to grips with our attacks and started to pile on the pressure, exploiting our lack of pace down the flanks. It was no real surprise that at half-time County led 1-0 through a Christie goal.

In the second-half, we gradually got back into the game, and Craig Johnston and Kenny Dalglish both scored from close range in a five-minute spell early in the period. After that, we held County at bay for the final half-hour without too much trouble. One unusual occurrence happened at the end of the game - like Forest in 1978-79, the County fans were locked in until we had been cleared away from the ground, allowing us to make a good getaway from Nottingham, a city that it is usually difficult to get out of. At most other venues, it was the away supporters who were kept in at the end.

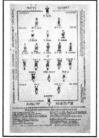

Notts County v Blackburn
Olympic, 1885 (left) and v
Burslem Port Vale, 1895 (right)

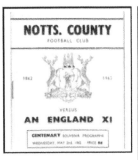

Ascoli, Anglo-Italian Final, 1995	An England XI (h), 1962 Centenary Match	Brescia, Anglo-Italian Final, 1994

Everton (h), FA Cup quarterfinal 1984	Chelsea (a), Football League Cup quarterfinal 1973	York City (h), FA Cup quarterfinal 1955

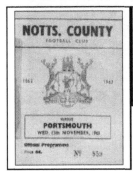

Portsmouth (h), Football League Cup Fourth Round 1964	Notts County v Blackpool ticket from 1997	Nottingham Forest (a), 2000 Nottinghamshire County Final

THE HATTER

FOOTBALL LEAGUE DIVISION ONE
SATURDAY 5th FEBRUARY 1983
LUTON TOWN v LIVERPOOL

TODAY'S MATCH IS SPONSORED BY

BEDFORD TRUCKS

Official Matchday Programme   Price 50p

---

62. Luton Town v Liverpool

Played at **Kenilworth Road** on 5th February 1983

Football League Division One

Luton Town (1)1 [Stein]
Liverpool (2)3 [Rush, Kennedy, Souness]

Attendance 18,434

The three teams promoted at the end of the 1981-82 season had been Luton, Watford and Norwich. Luton's was the only ground out of the three that I hadn't been to, so I decided to make the long trip down to Bedfordshire.

Luton Town's only real moment of glory had come in 1959, when they reached the FA Cup Final, only to lose 2-1 to Nottingham Forest. Thirty years later, the two teams met again at Wembley, this time in the Football league Cup Final, and once again Forest collected the trophy. Luton, though, had achieved success on the same stage a year earlier, when in 1988 they came from 2-1 behind to defeat Arsenal 3-2 to win the league Cup, the turning point coming with a penalty save that would have seen Arsenal go 3-1 in front in the goal had been scored. They had nearly returned to Wembley in the FA Cup in 1985, losing in extra time to Everton in the semi-final after being just minutes away from a victory in ninety minutes. Luton also lost out at this same stage to Wimbledon in 1988 and Chelsea in 1994. Their record victory came on April 13th 1936, when Bristol Rovers were trounced 12-0. This game saw the Luton makeshift striker Joe Payne scoring *ten* goals, the first time that this had been achieved in the English game.

We started off in my car, taking Kevin and dropping Martin off at Newton-le-Willows as he was supposedly travelling down with John, Ron, Paul and Gary. However, Gary didn't turn up as arranged, so they were one short. John was always keen on having a full load as his was a company car and he had to pay back a fixed amount per mile for private mileage, and he wasn't too happy about missing out on a share of the petrol money. Both of our cars set off for Luton, but not far down the M6 John passed us and flashed us to pull onto the hard shoulder, where he suggested we all try and fit into his hatchback Sierra at the next services. We drove on to the services and found that by putting Kevin in the 'boot' we could all fit in reasonably comfortably, so leaving my car at the services we continued on our journey south. One of the things I remember from the journey was hearing that Karen Carpenter of the Carpenters singing duo, had been found dead that morning following a heart attack.

We arrived in Luton at lunchtime, parking on a housing estate with the ground in sight, and then we split up, Kevin and I walking the long way into town and calling at a chip shop. After a pleasant stroll we made our way to the ground, which clearly hadn't changed a great deal since the club's fourth division days. We met up again there with the rest of our party and discussed where to go on the ground. There were no seats available, and the others didn't want to go on the Liverpool end as visiting supporters were locked in at the final whistle - one thing I'd learned from Martin was that these lads were keen on a quick getaway as soon as the final whistle blew.

Eventually we decided to go on the home end (not a decision we would have taken on almost any other first division ground) and found a place on the left of the Luton Kop. Martin became quickly conspicuous by his absence, as he didn't want to be with a group of Liverpool supporters in case any trouble erupted. There was a pre-match display on the pitch, with David Yip (television's "The Chinese Detective") being interviewed and a Karate display taking place. Paul let us know that he was a belted Karate expert - whether the locals near us heard this or not I don't know, but we were able to talk and cheer freely throughout the game without any fear of trouble.

The game began fairly evenly, until the half-hour mark when Luton took the lead through a Stein goal. Rather than deflating Liverpool, the setback spurred us on and within five minutes Rush had equalised and Kennedy had scrambled home a somewhat controversial second goal. The score remained at 2-1 until late in the second half when Graham Souness curled home a superb third goal which was to be included on the BBC's "Goal of the Season" program as a leading contender for the award. With minutes remaining we moved towards the exits, and on the final whistle ran back to the car.

It wasn't a long way up to the housing estate, but it was all uphill and by the time I got there I was totally out of breath and coughed on and off in the car for the next hour or so! We eventually got back to the services and the change of cars - much to Kevin's relief, I should imagine. To avoid having to go south to the next turnoff, which was quite a way off, I took the "No Entry" exit from the services across the bridge and back on to the other side, a route normally reserved for police and delivery vans

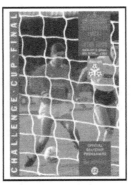

Arsenal, Football League Cup Final 1988

Nottingham Forest, Football League Cup Final 1989

Everton, 1985 FA Cup Semi-Final

Wimbledon, 1988 FA Cup Semi-Final

Chelsea, 1994 FA Cup Semi-Final

Luton v Blackpool ticket from 1996

63. Walsall v Liverpool

Played at **Fellows Park** on 14th February 1984

Milk Cup Semi-Final Second Leg

Walsall 0
Liverpool (1)2 [Rush, Whelan]

Attendance 19,591

63 Walsall – Fellows Park

As Liverpool headed for their fourth consecutive League Cup Final appearance, they were drawn to face Third Division Walsall in the semi-finals. This was a rare moment in the spotlight for Walsall, whose previous claim to fame had come way back in the 1930's when they knocked mighty Arsenal out of the FA Cup. They had eliminated Manchester United from the FA Cup in the Third Round in 1975, but that was at the time that United were a Second Division side themselves. That season had seen them equal their best FA Cup performance, when the Fifth Round was reached – a stage they were to reach, but not better, on a half dozen occasions. During Walsall's progression to the semi-finals of the League Cup, they had defeated Arsenal at Highbury – fifty years after their famous home FA Cup victory.

The first leg at Anfield had seen Walsall more than hold their own in forcing a 2-2 draw. For the second leg I managed to get two tickets and I took Barbara and the children down to Newcastle to visit Barbara's relatives, Brian and Cynthia, before driving Brian the thirty or so miles down the motorway to Walsall. There was a lot of traffic going into the town, and we finally found ourselves a little walk away from the ground in one of the official car parks. Although it was my first visit to Fellows Park, I'd seen the ground on numerous occasions on trips down the motorway. As we queued to get in, Brian suddenly felt somebody pushing against him at the turnstile, and as soon as he got through he found his wallet had been stolen. By now the thief was out of sight on the other side of the gates. Fortunately Brian only had a couple of pounds in the wallet, but he was more concerned about the papers and cards also included - when he finally got his wallet back a couple of weeks later, thankfully all but the money was still present.

After buying programmes we went inside the ground. Liverpool had been allocated all of one end, plus half of the paddock. Behind the goal it was absolute chaos, with people standing on every available vantage point, even on top of the concrete shelter on the running track in front of the terrace. In contrast, there was plenty of room in the paddock, so we stood in comfort there. The chilling similarity of events at Hillsborough five years later reminded me of this game. The rest of the ground was equally full as almost 20,000 waited to see if this would be the biggest night in Walsall's history. After just nine minutes of play, the answer seemed to be 'no' as Ian Rush headed the opening goal from a corner. The next three quarters of an hour produced some fairly indifferent football, with Walsall rarely threatening the kind of upsets they performed at Anfield.

It is often said by over-dramatic reporters that "such-and-such's goal brought the house down". When Ronnie Whelan scored to make it 2-0, that's **exactly** what happened, as the surge behind the Liverpool goal collapsed the small wall containing the advertising hoardings that separated the terrace from the cinder track behind the goals, halting the game for quite a while. The players moved into the crowd to help carry to safety some of the injured. Apart from one girl who suffered a broken pelvis, the other injuries seemed very minor. A lot of credit also had to go to the Liverpool fans at the back of the terracing who remained calm throughout the stoppage. My abiding memory is of Graham Souness carrying one of the injured fans across the pitch and down the players' tunnel. Apparently, during Liverpool's previous visit to Walsall in the 1968 FA Cup, a wall had collapsed, and not surprisingly the home team were now re-named 'Wallfall' by the fans.

After a lengthy delay the game restarted, though what effect the accident had on the players will never be known. Walsall had a few very good chances to reduce the arrears, but wasted them all with bad finishing, and when the game finished we'd triumphed 2-0. By the time we'd returned to the car, driven out of Walsall and reached the motorway it was now quite late, and fog began to be a problem. Consequently we only stayed at Brian's for a few minutes before continuing our journey back to Freckleton. It was now foggy all the time, with visibility down to a few yards. For miles I was following the taillights of the car in front, at one stage being only a few feet from them rather than the yards I thought I was, due to the deceptiveness of the situation. Thankfully, as we entered Lancashire the fog suddenly cleared, and the remainder of the journey was much easier, although I had cramp in my neck after straining forward to see for forty miles and more.

Walsall v Liverpool ticket from 1984 (left) and Walsall Town Swifts v Bootle 1891 (right)

63 Walsall – Fellows Park

Liverpool (a), Football League
Cup Semi-Final 1984

Manchester United (a), FA Cup
Third Round 1975

Manchester United (h), FA Cup
Third Round Replay 1975

Newcastle United (h), FA Cup
Fourth Round 1975

Arsenal (h), FA Cup Third
Round 1933

Arsenal (a), Football League
Cup 1983-84

64. Roma v Liverpool

Played at The Olympic Stadium on 30th May 1984

European Cup Final

Roma (1)(1)(1)1 [Pruzzo]
Liverpool (1)(1)(1)1 [Neal]

Attendance 69,693
{*Liverpool won 4-2 after penalties* - for **Liverpool**, **Nicol** missed, **Neal**, **Souness**, **Rush** and **Kennedy** scored; for **Roma**, **Di Bartolomei** scored, **Conti** missed, **Righetti** scored, **Graziani** missed}

64 AS Roma – The Olympic Stadium

The final game of a great season for Merseyside was the European Cup final in Rome. After Liverpool had won the League Championship and the Milk Cup, defeating Everton in a replayed final, Everton completed Merseyside's domination on the home front by beating Watford in the FA Cup final and also winning the FA Youth Cup. Liverpool reserves won the Central League title to go with their other trophies.

Roma, for all of their worldwide fame, had achieved very little on the European stage, with just a solitary Fairs Cup Final victory over Birmingham City in 1961 to show for their endeavours. They did reach the EUFA Cup final in 1991, but were defeated over two legs by fellow countrymen Inter Milan. Domestically, they had won the Italian title only twice, in 1942 and 1983, so this was their first attempt at winning the European Cup. Roma had to wait until 2001 for their third Italian league success. They had been more successful in the Italian Cup, with seven victories between 1964 and 1991.

As the build-up for the final began, television showed film of riots in the city as Roma fans tried to get tickets for the final. Liverpool had been allocated 18,000 tickets, many less than on our previous visit there, but only 10,000 were sold as fear of trouble swept the city. There were also rumours of match fixing during the semi-final, when Roma overturned a 0-2 first leg deficit to defeat Dundee United 3-2 on aggregate, with similarities to Liverpool's exit against Inter Milan at the same stage of the tournament in 1965.

We had more time in Rome this time than on my previous visit in 1977, and I set off at 3:30 a.m. to collect Kevin and drive to Speke to catch the 6:30 a.m. flight to Rome. There was a touch of early morning fog as I drove to Preston, but nothing to make the journey tricky. It had cost me £169 for the flight and match ticket, which was a little more than I could really afford, so I decided to sell off part of my football and rugby programme collection. As well as bringing in a nice sum, I also saved myself a fortune, as I was regularly spending £20 to £30 a month on adding to my collection.

At Speke I saw Ian Henderson amongst the crowds waiting for flights, just as I had on our previous trip to Rome, and on board the plane Kevin and I were sat with a local lad called Tony who ended up staying with us all day. We arrived in Rome after a two and a half hour flight and prepared for our coach journey to the stadium. At the airport we were having a laugh with the locals, holding up newspaper photographs of Ian Rush at the window, before setting off.

I had as much time as I wanted for sightseeing, so when we were given a street map of the city with notable places marked on it I started to plan what I wanted to do. When the coach pulled up at the ground, there were a few Liverpool fans already there, but further on were hundreds of Roma fans and for the first time I began to feel a little uneasy as the atmosphere began to get a little threatening. Some Scousers playing football near the coach park warned us that there was trouble with the locals, who were "crazy". After leaving the coach we walked on past the locals, making sure we kept our hands on our scarves as it was obvious that they wanted our colours. Crossing the bridge over the Tiber we were still enormously outnumbered, and we decided to head away from the ground and into the city for the day. Carloads of fans, horns blaring, were flashing past all over the place.

We'd been told that the best method of transport was on the trams, but you had to get tickets for them first. We went to the tram stop and tried to find out where we could get tickets from, but had trouble making ourselves understood. Meanwhile, we were being taunted now by a gang of Roma fans, chanting "Eng-land, Bas-t*ds, Eng-land, Bas-t*ds". All we could do was walk away, with them still hurling abuse at us. I managed to get a tram ticket from a stall and we jumped onto the next tram into the city, getting us away from one lot of troublemakers at least.

We didn't go very far on the tram, before continuing on our walk. Some more Italians came up to us, and one of them wanted Kevin's hat. When he wouldn't give it him, the Italian grabbed it and ran off down the street, disappearing into the crowd. Just after this we split up from the main group of Liverpool fans, leaving just Kevin, Tony and myself. We were trying to find the famous Trevi Fountain, and thought we'd got there up some steps, although I was surprised that it wasn't very crowded. I found out later that we'd been to the Fountain of Balcarres, just a short walk away from the Trevi.

It was now approaching lunchtime and we set off further in to the centre towards the Coliseum. I went to a stall to get a drink, and the stall-owner tried to get away with giving me change for a 10,000 Lira note when I gave him 20,000, a difference of about £5, but fortunately I had my wits about me. We then made our way to the Coliseum and sat on a wall across the road from it while we ate our lunch. Suddenly there was a commotion, with three young scruffy girls running down the road chased by a middle-aged Liverpool fan yelling, "Stop them". Kevin jumped up and grabbed the oldest girl, who was about 11. It turned out they'd stolen his wallet, complete with his match tickets, and the girl reluctantly handed them over to him – along with a calculator she had obviously stolen from somebody else. We then carried on with our lunch, and I just turned round in time to see the girls sneaking up through the gardens behind us, otherwise they may well have had our bags complete with everything we had - tickets, passport, money, camera, the lot! I had let go of my bag while I ate my lunch, but I kept a tight grip on it after this incident.

I was happy when we were on the move again, this time heading for St. Peter's Square and the Vatican. I stopped off at some of the stalls on the way, buying what looked like a Roma version of the match programme and a souvenir for Iain. Kevin had already been inside the Vatican back in 1977, so after taking some pictures of it, Tony and I went inside. I'm not sure if I managed to see the Cistein Chapel or not, but there was a lot to see and I was very impressed. I *know* we didn't see the Pope, even though he was in residence.

Although the Vatican was nice, most of the rest of Rome was decidedly shabby, with graffiti prominent nearly everywhere. We set off again on our walk from St. Peter's Square, passing the Swiss guard who look after the Pope and I went into another gift shop and bought a souvenir for my daughter Shelley. Further along the approach road to the Vatican we came upon our first group of Liverpool fans for a while outside one of the bars. Next minute, a police van raced up and started moving them away. They certainly weren't causing any trouble, and it made me wonder where these police were when the Roma fans were harassing us.

The three of us now set off for the walk back towards the ground, again through the seedier parts of the city, stopping to look for something to eat on the way. We finally reached the ground about two hours before kick-off, and walked along the route to the Roma end. I wasn't worried about being in the middle of hundreds of Roma fans on the way to the game, but Kevin was a little concerned so we turned away from the ground and off to the side through the police-controlled barriers. This again showed the absurdity of the policing - the barriers were designed to keep people away from the ground until they'd had their tickets checked, yet we'd walked unheeded with the Roma fans on the other side of the barriers!

Kevin bought himself another hat from one of the many souvenir stalls before we moved round to our end. When we got there, we met some friends who'd come over on a later flight, and they claimed the morning papers were full of rumours about Graham Souness moving to Italy during the close season. This did in fact turn out to be his last game for Liverpool before he signed for Sampdoria. We then made our way towards our turnstiles. I had one worrying moment when a group came behind us chanting "Campioni, Campioni" but when they ended "Campioni Liverpool" I realised that they were Scousers who'd adapted the Italian for 'champions' into their chant.

Once inside the ground, we saw an amazing sight. Apart from our end, the other three sides of the ground were filled to capacity with Roma fans, and the noise they made as they chanted "Roma, Roma" was unbelievable. Without doubt, it was the greatest single atmosphere I had ever experienced. Our end, in contrast, was quite sparse. As we'd left 8,000 tickets unsold, the Italian authorities had wanted to sell them locally, but Liverpool refused. In light of what was to happen a year later in Brussels, it was a very wise decision. We found ourselves some good seats as a schoolboy match progressed on the pitch.

The team came out to walk round, and we went right up to the fence to cheer them, and they in turn clapped us back. Shortly after this, the first trouble began with the fans at the left of our end, who were right up against the section containing Roma fans. Fans from one section began throwing bottles, sticks and things at those in the other section, who retaliated in like manner. Bruce Grobbelaar went over and implored our fans to stop, but they took no notice. Eventually, what seemed like an entire battalion of riot police came in and moved our fans in some fifty yards, creating an empty no-mans land between the groups. The Roma fans were as much to blame for the trouble as Liverpool, but nobody said a word to them.

After a long wait, the teams came out and the match began. Somewhat surprisingly, we took the initiative, the team not being overawed by the volume of support. They may not have been, but I was, especially when Roma's fans unfurled a flag containing a picture of the European Cup, which must have been a hundred yards in length as they passed it along the heads of the crowd. These flags are commonplace now, but that was the first time I had ever seen anything like it.

Grobbelaar made an early save at Graziani's feet, but after quarter of an hour, Liverpool took the lead. Johnston hit a cross to the far post and as Whelan challenged 'keeper Tancredi in the air, the ball fell loose in the box. A defender tried to clear before Rush reached the ball, but he hit it against Tancredi, where it ricocheted back across goal to Phil Neal, who toe-poked it into the net from eight yards. Five minutes later, Ray Kennedy's free kick was met by Neal's head and Johnston jumped to flick it over Tancredi for what ought to have been number two, but as Souness ran in to blast the ball over the line the referee blew for a dubious offside. Grobbelaar made one good near post save from Graziani, but Rush then brought an equally good save from Tancredi, with a rising shot after a poor defensive clearance. Towards half-time Roma began to get on top and with two minutes remaining they equalised. Conti's initial cross was blocked, but he swung the ball in again and Pruzzo rose to flick his header over a diving Grobbelaar and into the net, resulting in a cacophony of noise around three quarters of the Olympic Stadium.

The second half began with Roma still on top, but not looking particularly dangerous. They were able to pick out their men with fifty-yard passes, but despite the influence of people like the Brazilian Falcao, they didn't seem to have the commitment of the Liverpool team. Kenny Dalglish, who had forced Tancredi into making one save, still hadn't fully recovered from a cheek injury he had sustained in January and was generally ineffective. Substitute Nicol added width down the right wing and suddenly we were creating chances again, and five minutes from time he was put through on goal only for Tancredi to rescue Roma with another fine save.

The score was still 1-1 after ninety minutes, but into extra time, we were well on top as it looked like Roma had settled for penalties. The only threat to Liverpool came in the second period when Grobbelaar saved well low-down from a Conti shot. As we couldn't convert our supremacy into goals we had to resign ourselves to that unsatisfactory way of deciding who would be the Champions of Europe.

The penalties were sited at the Roma end, which seemed to give the advantage to them, but we had first shot, which slightly tilted the advantage towards us. At least it seemed that way until Steve Nicol stepped up and blasted his shot high over the bar. Kevin was so disappointed that he turned to me and said we probably wouldn't score with *any* of our penalties. Di Bartolomei scored Roma's first, before Phil Neal sent Tancredi the wrong way to level matters. Next came Bruno Conti, and like Nicol he put his shot over the bar and it was back to all square. Skipper Souness hit our third penalty high into the roof of the net, causing me to have heart flutters as I thought that yet another one was clearing the bar, and Righetti levelled matters again.

Up stepped Ian Rush, and he sent Tancredi the wrong way with a fairly gentle kick to claim his 50th goal of the season in all competitions. Graziani was next to the spot as he prepared to take Roma's fourth kick. Grobbelaar was acting the fool on the line a little, wobbling his legs like a jelly, and I don't know if he intended to put the Roma player off or not, but Graziani's shot clipped the top of the bar and sailed over. We were jumping up and down, unable to keep calm any more, and Alan Kennedy stepped up to see if his goal could win the European Cup for us for a fourth time. Kevin couldn't watch, but 'Barney Rubble' hit his shot perfectly into the left hand corner to give him the claim to fame of scoring the winning goal for Liverpool in two European Cup finals. It was certainly the most dramatic of all victories, and it meant that Joe Fagan had won the treble in his first season as manager, upstaging even Bob Paisley's many achievements.

After the lap of honour we left the ground for the coaches. There was a huge crush from the Liverpool end, which suddenly descended into panic as rocks started flying at us from the trees above. We could do nothing to escape the ambush but just cover our heads and continue to try to get to the coaches. When we reached the line of them, we couldn't find ours at first. We found out later that some did leave empty when the drivers saw that there was trouble. I ran to the front of the line looking for the coach and saw a mob of Italians chasing across the car park, so I hurried back. Luckily we did find our coach and were soon on our way back to the airport. Later reports had forty Liverpool fans injured in the violence, and yet UEFA punished both clubs for the after-match trouble. Our 'crime' must have been to spill blood on foreign pavements!

At the airport it seemed the Italians couldn't wait to see the back of us. I just had time to buy a souvenir for Barbara and say hello to Martin's friend John before we were on our plane. There was a slight delay in take-off because two extra people were on the plane, but once the captain announced that we'd be there all night if they didn't leave they soon got off. Apart from the stench from Kevin's feet when he took his trainers off, it was a pleasant flight home, with plenty of singing. We were filmed leaving the plane, and it was shown on the BBC the next night, but although Kevin saw us, I managed to miss it. I drove Tony back home before we went back to Preston. Again, Kevin took off his shoes, along with his socks this time, wringing the sweat from them out of the window, and I had to drive with my window open to be able to breathe properly. It wasn't the best way of ending another glorious away day in Europe!

As a footnote, Liverpool were to be involved in a series of 'firsts' regarding penalty shoot-outs. Added to this first ever shoot-out in a European Cup Final, they won the Charity Shield against Leeds in 1975, an FA Cup semi-final against Portsmouth in 1992 and the Worthington Cup Final against Birmingham in 2001 all after a shoot-out. In each case, it was the first time each of these matches had been settled in this manner.

Alternate version of the programme

Alternate version of the programme

Alternate version of the programme

Flight details and boarding passes

FOR HOLIDAYS AND TRAVEL

[illegible]

[illegible]

[illegible] [illegible]

Report to Liverpool Airport (Main Building) at 04.30 hrs. for Flight NB 2751

Depart Liverpool at 05.30 hrs.

Arrive Rome Ciampino Airport at 09.00 hrs.

Please note: Time in Rome is one hour in advance of U.K. time, watches should be put forward one hour.

After clearance of Customs and Immigration coaches will transfer you directly to the Stadium, please note where the coaches are parked as it will be dark when the game finishes. Your Coach will be marked "Town's Travel Coach C" – you may board any coach so marked.

After the game board a coach marked "Town's Travel Service Coach C" for return to the Airport at approx. 23.00 hrs. – please note coaches cannot wait longer than 23.15 hrs., passengers arriving after this will be required to take a taxi at their own expense to the Airport.

Depart Ciampino Airport on flight NB 2752 at 01.00 hrs.

Arrive Liverpool 02.30 hrs.

Note: Passengers must be in possession of a valid passport.

Rome is probably the most notorious city in the world for pick pockets, for your own benefit do not carry with you any unnecessary valuables.

Local transport is available from the Stadium to the Town Centre and return for those people wishing to visit the town but note tickets for local buses and trams must be bought from the machines or local selling points before boarding the vehicle, it is a criminal offence to board a bus or tram without a ticket.

PLEASE NOTE – FLIGHT TIMINGS

We regret the flight departure time change but this has become necessary due to the Air Traffic Controllers in Rome working to rule during part of the day of 30th May, it is necessary for the flights to arrive earlier to avoid missing the match.

Should you have a serious problem or experience any real difficulty whilst in Rome please contact our agent or the British Embassy, telephone Rome 396 4755441.

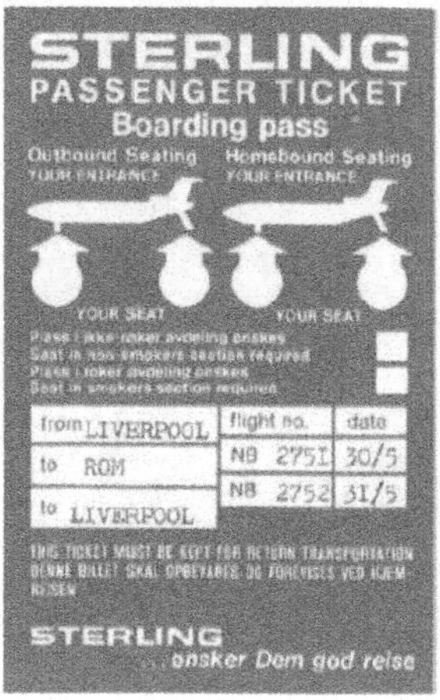

Alternate version of the programme	Alternate version of the programme	Liverpool (h), 2002 Champions League

Birmingham City (a), Inter Cities Fairs Cup Final 1961	Inter Milan (h), 1991 EUFA Cup Final	Inter Milan (h), 1991 EUFA Cup Final

Inter Milan (a), 1991 EUFA Cup Final	Roma v Liverpool tickets from 2001 and 1984 and Rome transport ticket	Inter Milan (a), 1991 EUFA Cup Final

66

65. Stockport County v Liverpool

Played at **Edgeley Park** on 24th September 1984

Milk Cup Second Round

Stockport County 0
Liverpool 0

Attendance 11,169

65 Stockport County – Edgeley Park

After winning the League Cup for four seasons in a row, Liverpool began their defence of the trophy with a tie at lowly Stockport County. The draw brought back memories of the 1965 FA Cup clashes between the clubs, when Liverpool were fortunate to survive at Anfield against Fourth Division County before winning the replay and embarking on the journey which brought them their first Wembley triumph. Stockport also provided the opposition for Liverpool in the Fifth Round of the 1950 campaign, which ended with the reds' first Wembley final appearance. That Fifth Round appearance, along with others in 1935 (against West Bromwich) and 2001 (against Tottenham), represented Stockport's best attempts at landing the major cup in England.

Stockport had a period of near success in the 1990's without ever quite achieving the goal of winning a trophy. They lost in Wembley play-off finals against Peterborough in 1992 and Burnley in 1994, as well as losing 1-0 to Stoke in the 1992 Autoglass final. In 1997, they reached the League Cup semi-finals, only to lose to Middlesbrough over the two legs.

As I'd never been to the Stockport ground before, I got a ticket and took Martin, Kevin and another lad to the match. I had once planned to go to watch Stockport play Southport at Christmas 1968, as I liked County then, but bad weather made me wary of going to that game. So it was some sixteen years after I had originally intended when I finally found my way to Edgeley Park.

After a slight detour in Stockport where I found that I was going away from the stadium, we parked in a street just a few minutes walk from the ground. Not very many Liverpool fans had made the short trip and we had plenty of room in our paddock, especially when I found out that it extended in front of the stand and we hadn't just been allocated the corner. County's fans did turn up in force though, and the final crowd was over 11,000. It seemed that despite the rival passions, everybody inside had one thing in common, as both sets of supporters sang, "We only hate Man United"!

There was little to cheer about in the game, which ended in a disappointing goalless draw. After just two minutes, Coyle robbed Neal as he tried to play his way out of defence, and Osher Williams drove in a twenty-yard effort that just shaved the bar with Grobbelaar beaten. County goalkeeper Mick Salmon made some important saves, beginning by smothering efforts from Robinson and Whelan. In the second half, Walsh clipped an effort past Salmon but missed the target, and Neal attempted to lob the 'keeper but Salmon saved his effort well. In the dying minutes, Whelan unleashed a long-range effort high into the corner but once again Salmon was equal to the challenge.

After the game we were locked in for about fifteen minutes while "the streets were cleared of the Stockport fans". Had there been a larger Liverpool following, or had we been the followers of certain other first division teams, the delay could have started a riot, but the fans took it all very well. They even joked with the mounted police, especially when the horse near us decided to relieve itself where it stood, causing us to hastily retreat. Eventually we were let out (although there was no sign of the streets being cleared!) and we were finally able to set off for home. The second leg was also a struggle for Liverpool, requiring extra time before they achieved a 2-0 victory.

Southport (h) Christmas 1968

68

Stoke City, Autoglass Trophy Final 1992

Tottenham (a), FA Cup Fifth Round 1991

Liverpool (a), Football League Cup Second Round 1984-85

Liverpool (a), FA Cup Fourth Round 1965

Brentford (h), FA Cup Third Round 1951

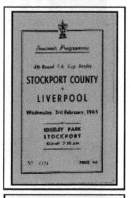

Liverpool (h), FA Cup Fourth Round Replay 1965

Middlesbrough (h), Football League Cup Semi-Final 1997

Stockport v Middlesbrough ticket for the 1997 semi-final

Middlesbrough (a), Football League Cup Semi-Final 1997

66. Sheffield Wednesday v Liverpool

Played at **Hillsborough** on 2nd February 1985

Football League Division One

Sheffield Wednesday (0)1 [Marwood]
Liverpool (0)1 [Lawrenson]

Attendance 48,246

66 Sheffield Wednesday – Hillsborough

Early in 1985, Liverpool made their first league visit to Hillsborough for fifteen years. Kevin and Martin asked me to go with them to make up the numbers in the car, along with Ron and Paul. John, the fifth member of the group who now travelled regularly to games, lived in Wakefield, and it was pointless him going with the others for such a short journey – he didn't actually get to this game anyway, going to a wedding instead. We used my car to pick up Ron at Newton, then left it at Paul's in Rochdale as we drove in his car to Sheffield. He drove across some very narrow and high country passes for quite a way, and we passed the time on the journey answering football quizzes.

Sheffield Wednesday were yet another club with a famous past but a sketchy present. League Champions on four occasions, in 1903, 1904, 1929 and 1930, they were also FA Cup winners in 1896, 1907 and 1935, as well as being runners-up in 1890. Since the Second World War, though, all they had to show was a runners-up position in the league to Tottenham in 1961 and in the cup to Everton in 1966. They did experience a resurgence in the early 1990's, defeating Manchester United at Wembley in 1991 to lift the League Cup, and losing to Arsenal in finals of both the League Cup and the FA Cup two years later – with defeat sweetened to some extent by their semi-final victory at Wembley over city rivals Sheffield United. Wednesday became known as the 'yo-yo' club in the fifties, when they were promoted from the Second Division in 1950, 1952, 1956 and 1959 only to quickly make the return journey after the first three occasions. Hillsborough was their fifth permanent home ground, after Highfield, Myrtle Road, Sheaf House and Olive Grove. They moved to Owlerton in 1899, and in 1912 it was renamed to Hillsborough.

We had stand seats behind the goal at Hillsborough on the Leppings Lane end, and an enormous crowd of over 48,000, many thousands of them from Liverpool, brought back the good old days for Sheffield Wednesday. The football failed to live up to the billing, but after the scoreless opening half (notable only for Shelton volleying a Marwood cross wide) Wednesday took the lead. Three minutes before the hour mark, Hansen overhit a back pass and the ball went out for a corner. Chapman headed on Blair's kick and Marwood scored to put Wednesday ahead, totally against the run of play. The remaining half hour saw Liverpool bearing down on the Sheffield goal in search of the equaliser, and with less than five minutes remaining Mark Lawrenson rose to head home Dalglish's free kick from six yards out. This was no less than we deserved, for we had missed chance after chance during the half. Rush rounded Hodge but the ball took a bobble and the shot went over, and on two occasions Wark missed with headers from Dalglish crosses.

By the time we equalised, Martin had already started to leave and the others were getting ready too. I was determined to stay until the final whistle, and only grudgingly agreed to move towards the gangways. Chapman had a chance for Wednesday, but shot straight at Grobbelaar, and Steve Nicol, put clean through the Wednesday defence, missed a glorious chance in the final minute by hitting the ball just too high with only Hodge to beat. Then the whistle blew and the mad scramble to get out of the packed ground and race to the car began. I ended up going down the wrong way from the ground and had to ask the police for directions to the road where we were parked. Fortunately, I remembered the name of the shop on the corner, and I didn't keep them waiting as Paul was just ambling towards the car as I entered the street. Perhaps it was just as well, for I'm not sure they would have waited for me if I'd been late!

Sheffield Wednesday v
Liverpool ticket from 1985

West Bromwich Albion, 1935
FA Cup Final

Manchester United, 1991
Football League Cup Final

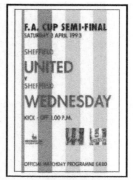

Sheffield United, 1993 FA Cup
Semi-Final

Arsenal, 1993 Football League
Cup Final

Arsenal, 1993 FA Cup Final

Arsenal, 1993 FA Cup Final
replay

Barcelona (h), Fairs Cup
quarterfinal 1962

Blackburn Rovers (h), 1887,
first game at Olive Grove

Kaiserslautern (a), EUFA Cup
1992

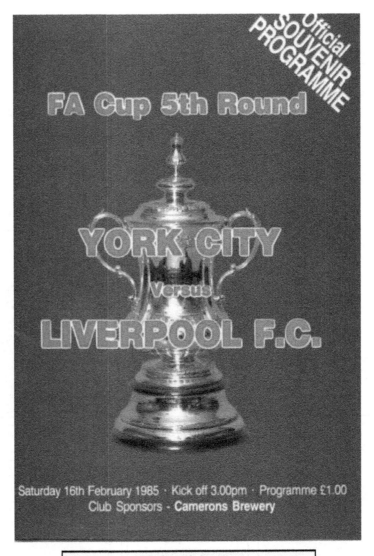

67. York City v Liverpool

Played at Bootham Crescent on 16th February 1985

FA Cup Fifth Round

York City (0)1 [Sbragia]
Liverpool (0)1 [Rush]

Attendance 13,485

67 York City – Bootham Crescent

In round five of the FA Cup Liverpool were drawn away to Third Division York City, conquerors of Arsenal in the previous round. The FA Cup had seen the biggest days in York's history back in 1955, when they took mighty Newcastle United to a replay in their semi-final tie, with a Third Round victory at cup giants Blackpool the highlight of the run. Other than that, York's biggest success was in reaching Wembley in the Third Division play-off final in 1993, when they lost the 'battle of the railway towns' to Crewe. In the League Cup, York were quarterfinalists in 1962, losing 2-1 at Rochdale.

I went to York with the same party as I had been with at the Sheffield Wednesday game. Surprisingly, the game wasn't all-ticket, with only our end requiring tickets. There was some doubt as to whether or not the game would go on, but after York covered the pitch overnight with bails of straw the referee gave the go-ahead. It was a cold but sunny day as we entered the beautiful city of York and headed for Bootham Crescent, where massive queues were already forming for the home end. We walked around the ground and the streets near it, getting some local fish and chips before going into our open end. The chips, with the extra crispy bits, rank as just about the best I have ever had at a football game, and I always try to revisit the shop whenever I'm in York.

Just after we entered the ground there was a commotion outside, as apparently some Leeds fans had come to the ground and they charged at the Scousers still waiting outside. We didn't realise this at the time though, and found ourselves a central position at the back of the old, boarded up, terracing we were on. The match was never a classic, and although York had a goal disallowed somewhat dubiously in the first half, once Ian Rush scored just after the break I was sure that we were through as I couldn't see York equalising. I was wrong though, and with only a few minutes remaining, a move saw them hit the bar twice before Sbragia forced the ball home at the third attempt to draw level. We then went straight down to the other end of the pitch, and Ronnie Whelan volleyed home a magnificent shot only for the referee to again rule no goal, and just after this incident the whistle blew to signal a Tuesday night replay at Anfield. As we left the ground there was a commotion inside it, as York fans invaded the pitch and ran over to the Liverpool end looking for trouble. We had a job to get past the police cordon to reach the cars, having to turn back on our original route to find a way through.

A massive crowd of 43,000, many from York, packed Anfield to watch the replay, and this time there was no second chance for Denis Smith's team. The goals flowed all through the night, Wark hitting three and Whelan two in the 7-0 victory, the only surprise being the absence of Ian Rush and Kenny Dalglish from the scoresheet. A year later, at the same stage York and Liverpool met once more, with Liverpool fortunate to get an equaliser to survive at Bootham Crescent. In the replay, York led at Anfield and it took extra time before Liverpool could progress to the quarterfinals on the way to a League and Cup double.

Southport (h) 1956-57 – record
9-1 victory

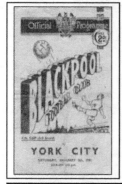

Blackpool (a), FA Cup Third
Round 1955

Newcastle United, 1955 FA Cup
Semi-Final at Hillsborough

Newcastle United, 1955 FA Cup
Semi-Final replay at Roker Park

Tottenham (h), FA Cup Fifth
Round 1955

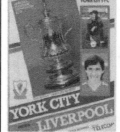

Liverpool (h), FA Cup Fifth
Round 1986

Liverpool (a), FA Cup Fifth
Round Replay 1986

Arsenal (h), 1985 FA Cup
Fourth Round

Ticket for the York v Liverpool
tie in 1985

Liverpool (a), FA Cup Fifth
Round Replay 1985

68. Barnsley v Liverpool

Played at **Oakwell** on 10th March 1985

FA Cup Sixth Round

Barnsley 0
Liverpool (0)4 [Rush 3, Whelan]

Attendance 19,838

68 Barnsley - Oakwell

Liverpool's FA Cup Quarter Final tie was against Barnsley at Oakwell, and ITV chose it as their live televised match. The tie and venue weren't decided until the Monday earlier, when against all the odds Barnsley won 2-1 at Southampton despite going a goal down early on. I really wanted Southampton to win, for I knew that I would *have* to go to Barnsley as I'd never been there before and I really didn't fancy the journey. I was getting more and more fed up of travelling, and even the trip to Liverpool was becoming a chore.

Barnsley had appeared in two FA Cup Finals, but both were before the First World War. Newcastle United had defeated them in 1910, but two years later they lifted the trophy by defeating West Bromwich Albion 1-0 after a goalless draw in the first game. Towards the end of the twentieth century, Barnsley had a brief stay in the Premiership, and in 2000 they almost found their way back again, reaching Wembley for the First Division play-off final against Ipswich only to fall at the final hurdle. In the League Cup, their best performance came with a quarterfinal appearance in 1982, and they came close to a Wembley FA Cup appearance by reaching the quarterfinal stage in 1998.

With the game being shown live, it wasn't made all ticket, and we set off with the same travelling arrangement as for the Sheffield Wednesday and York games. On our way I was told that one of the Liverpool directors, Brian, had got six stand tickets for us, but he wasn't going to show until half-an-hour before kick-off. We arrived in Barnsley in pouring rain a good two hours early. It was a typical mining area, looking very grimy, and while Paul and Martin went off for their usual pre-match drinks, Ron, Kevin and I went for a walk in the neighbourhood of the ground. We tried to find a chip shop, but nothing was open on a Sunday in Barnsley.

After killing as much time as we could we went round to the players' entrance to wait for the minibus containing Brian to arrive. There was a lot of activity around the entrance, which should have been reserved for Barnsley fans as the Liverpool end was cordoned off by the police, but Liverpool fans were getting in and scuffles kept breaking out periodically throughout our wait. The police were pathetic really, because it was blatantly obvious who the troublemakers were but they did nothing to disperse them or move them on. We were talking to some Barnsley fans who'd been to Southampton, and they said there'd been trouble there at the end, with a few of the Barnsley fans being attacked by home supporters after revenge. Some of the scuffles now were taking place round us, with one Liverpool fan in white pants ducking behind Ron and kicking out at a Barnsley fan, and still the police failed to act.

Eventually, the minibus arrived twenty minutes before kick-off. Ron went to see Brian, then came back and said as there'd only been five tickets, they would go to Ron, John, Paul, Kevin and Martin, and I would have to pay and go in the terraces. I wasn't pleased at all with this, for once again I'd been helping them out by filling the car, and John, if anybody, should have been made to pay to get in. I wasn't left with any choice though, and went in the paddock directly under where they were sat in the stand. On reflection, I should have gone round to the Liverpool end with the thousands of other reds even if it meant my being locked in for quarter of an hour after the finish - it would have served the others right having to wait for me! The Liverpool fans were all having a great time taunting Jimmy Greaves of ITV who was in the commentary box on our end. Still, I didn't, and I stood with some ordinary Barnsley folk with quite a lot of room around me to enjoy the game in some comfort. There were a few idiots not too far from me, one wearing a Manchester United hat, but after they were constantly abused and showered with cans by the Liverpool fans in the stand the police took action and moved them on.

In the first half, play was fairly even, and at the interval the tie was still scoreless. Liverpool stepped up a gear after the restart, and a goalkeeping error saw an Ian Rush shot slither through into the net. Minutes later Ronnie Whelan added a second, and after a slight hiccup when Barnsley (as Walsall had the season before in the League Cup semi-final) wasted two great chances to reduce the arrears, Ian Rush poached twice more to complete his second hat trick of the season and comprehensively finish the game at 4-0.

Ipswich, First Division Play-Off Final 2000

Liverpool (a), Football League Cup quarterfinal 1982

Liverpool (h), Football League Cup quarterfinal replay 1982

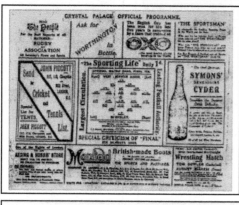

West Bromwich Albion, 1912 FA Cup Final

Arsenal (a), FA Cup Fifth Round 1987

Doncaster Rovers (a), Sheffield County Cup Final 1969

Barnsley v Manchester United ticket 1998 and a draw ticket

Newspaper souvenir of the 1910 FA Cup Final v Newcastle

Birmingham (a), First Division Play-Off Semi-Final 2000

Manchester United (h), FA Cup Fifth Round 1964

Sheffield United (h), County Cup Semi-Final 1956

Santos (h), 1997

Aston Villa (h), FA Youth Cup Semi-Final 2002

Leicester City (h), FA Cup quarterfinal replay 1961

1910 FA Cup Final and Replay, Barnsley v Newcastle United

69 – Heysel Stadium, Brussels

69. Juventus v Liverpool

Played at **The Heysel Stadium, Brussels** on 29th May 1985

European Cup Final

Juventus (0)1 [Platini penalty]
Liverpool 0

Attendance 55,000

The match was played despite the riots beforehand that left 38
supporters dead and hundreds more seriously injured.

69 – Heysel Stadium, Brussels

Defeat in the FA Cup semi-final replay against Manchester United left Liverpool with just the European Cup to chase on the trophy front. They reached the final once again, and this time it was held in Brussels against Juventus. With Everton also reaching a European final, in the Cup Winners Cup, I rang Towns Travel to see about trips to the game and had to tell them which team and which game! I finally booked another one-day trip for Kevin and myself, flying from Liverpool.

Juventus were bidding to become the first team to lift all three European trophies, although on their previous two final appearances at this stage they had been defeated by Ajax in 1973 and Hamburg in 1983. They made three appearances in three seasons in the final in the 1990's, gaining some revenge by defeating Ajax on penalties in 1996, and losing to Borussia Dortmund and Real Madrid in the following two seasons. They also lost in the first all-Italian final in 2003, going down on penalties to AC Milan after a goalless draw at Old Trafford. Their Cup Winners Cup success had come as recently as 1984 against Porto, leading to their victory over Liverpool in Turin in the Super Cup Final. They had appeared most in the Fairs Cup / EUFA Cup, losing in 1965, 1971 and 1995, and winning in 1977, 1990 and 1993. Domestically, they held the record number of league successes, with well over twenty titles by 2000.

Martin wanted us to go to Speke with him, even though his flight left several hours before our 9 a.m. departure, and was due back a couple of hours before ours too, but I wasn't keen and in the end I persuaded Kevin to go later. I drove to his house and parked in his garage before he drove us to the airport. He had a little trouble starting the car, due probably to damp plugs in the cool early morning air. The weather during the week had been glorious during the day, but quite cold overnight.

On our arrival at Speke we had a problem or two finding the car park, as its location had changed since our trip to Rome twelve months earlier, and we eventually parked near Speke Hall before making the short walk to the International Departure lounge. While waiting for our flight I noticed a few familiar faces from the past, including the man with the bad leg from Rome in 1977, some girls I remembered from Paris in 1981 and some other people I recognised from our trip to Rome in 1984. We also found that Ron and a lad called Bob, from Bolton, were on our flight, and we stayed with them for a while, until it was time to board the plane.

As we boarded I noticed a lad taking cine-photos of the fans boarding. I wasn't to realise it at the time, but those pictures were to be in the Friday morning papers after what happened in Brussels. It was a short flight to Brussels, but even so I was a bit annoyed that no refreshments were served, although I suppose that was why we managed to get such a cheap flight. As we approached the airport, we got our first hint that things weren't well in the city, with an announcement from the travel courier for Towns. He said that due to trouble in the city, we were going to be driven straight to the ground, instead of the original plan of dropping us in the centre of Brussels.

By the time we left the 'plane, it was now around noon local time. We had been given clear information about boarding our coaches, and finding the same one to return in as we'd travelled out on, as the coach was driving straight to the runway rather than leaving us in the main airport building. Here at least plans had been made to keep the fans apart. As we streamed towards passport control a plane carrying Juventus supporters arrived, and their fans disembarked on an aisle parallel to ours but separated by a barrier of glass. All was good humoured as we exchanged chants and taunts with each other - we thought we were crazily dressed until we saw what some of the Italian fans were arrayed in!

On leaving the airport we had a lengthy walk to where the coaches were parked, and a long wait there until all the coaches were filled. As we finally drove off, I was really quite glad for the delay as it meant there was less time to be spent hanging around the ground, which I was now getting a little apprehensive about following the courier's warnings and the trouble in Rome a year earlier.

On arrival at the ground we met up again with Ron and Bob, who had travelled on a different coach to us. It was clear from the colours on show that there were ten times as many Liverpool fans around the stadium as Juventus supporters. The main Italian support seemed to have been deposited in the centre of Brussels. After a short walk around the ground we found a chip shop and bought a bag each for our dinner, and that was the only time I spent any Belgian money until we got into the ground. It was also noticeable that all of the stall-owners and shop-owners were selling small bottles of beer to the Liverpool fans as fast as they could. They had to take some share of the blame for helping to set up the conditions for the trouble that occurred later on.

69 – Heysel Stadium, Brussels

The weather was beautiful and hot, and just a short walk away was a small park by a fountain which was full of Liverpool fans sunbathing. As we walked up there a car full of Italians was driving through and had to stop for other traffic. It was immediately surrounded by Scousers, but again everything was very jovial with handshakes between the two nationalities the order of the day. Once in the park we found a patch of unoccupied grass and stretched out for the afternoon. I had a good long chat with Bob, who was a mine of statistics and knew far more than I did about individual games and performances. Even so, he was surprised at how much I knew about games in the early history of the club, and we got along really well.

Every now and then during the afternoon we heard sirens as police cars were in action, so obviously things weren't as calm as they looked from where we were. In addition, a lot of the empty beer bottles were being hurled into the road and smashed, leaving glass everywhere. Just before we were ready to leave the park, a young lad of about nine years of age screamed in pain as he trod on a piece of glass, and suddenly blood was everywhere. It probably looked a lot worse than it actually was, but even so it was totally unnecessary and no doubt ruined the lad's big treat. We left then and walked a couple of hundred yards looking in vain for a toilet, eventually using the side of a building across from some open ground! Such a short distance from the ground there was nobody else in sight.

We walked to the ground, there now being just over two hours to kick-off. It appeared to be well-organised at the Liverpool end, with small gaps between wire-mesh fencing being guarded by police who were checking everybody's ticket before allowing them through. One lad was trying to slide under the fencing to get through this first checkpoint, for once again not enough tickets had gone to the supporters of the two teams contesting the final. We walked further around this fence surround to the Juventus end, and began to notice how things were changing. First of all there were unguarded gaps between the fence, then there were tears and gaps in the fence and finally there was no fence at all by the time we reached their end of the ground. We walked past hundreds of Italians and started back to our own end, this time inside the fence without having undergone any ticket checks. Ron and Bob left us as they had stand tickets on this side of the ground, whilst Kevin and I had seats in section B on the other side. Given the choice, I would rather have stood on our end, but I knew well in advance that we had been issued with stand tickets.

There was nowhere that I could see where programmes were being sold and we decided to go and try inside the ground. This created a bit of a problem for us, as we couldn't seem to find our entrance. The way we thought led to it, past section Z, was a dead end. It also surprised me to find that there were a lot of Juventus fans queuing there. To get to our end we had to go back out, down a road, and then come up to the front entrance of the stadium. To get in our section we just showed our tickets to a chap on the door and climbed the steps. There was a toilet halfway up which we went in, and it had an open window looking on to the terracing. I looked through and was amazed to see thousands of black and white Juventus colours on this third of our end. We went up the steps to our seating and to take a first proper look at the ground. It was abundantly clear that we'd got the rough edge of the ticket deal. The far end was completely filled with Juventus fans, as was three quarters of the stand I was in. The opposite stand was split about half and half, and our terracing was sectioned off so that the near third of it was full of Juventus fans. Apparently, this section Z had been allocated to Belgians but 95% of the tickets found their way to Juventus supporters. The other two thirds of our end were packed solid with Liverpool fans, with only a flimsy-looking fence separating the groups. Kevin, seeing the Juventus supporters, said we were going to have to go through those Italians to get back to the coaches after the game, and he wasn't looking forward to it when we won.

We were confident of victory, even despite the rumours outside the ground that the Swiss referee had been receiving 'special attention' and free gifts from Juventus officials in the period leading up to the final. It wasn't the first time that these kinds of allegations had been made about bribery in games involving Italian sides. A schoolboy game was taking place on the pitch, and we watched that for a while, as well as watching the massive Italian flags being passed over the crowd, just as had occurred in Rome a year earlier. The Liverpool team came out to look at the pitch and sample the atmosphere and they all seemed to be in good spirits, shaking hands with some wheelchair bound fans situated around the edge.

It was now around 7 p.m., 75 minutes before kick-off. In section Z, a gap had now formed between the massed Juventus fans and a hundred or so Liverpool fans who must also have got tickets from the

Belgians and were in that same third of the terracing. A door was opened in the fence surrounding the pitch, and these Liverpool fans were moved out of section Z and round to sections X and Y. The only problem with this was that sections X and Y were already full to capacity.

A lad came and sat down next to me with a programme, which he said he'd got just outside the main entrance, so Kevin and I went back upstairs. We couldn't find the programmes, but stopped for an ice cream before returning to our seats. It was now around 7.15, and section Z had filled so that there were no gaps between the four thousand or so Italians and the few hundred Liverpool fans inside the fence, along with the ten thousand plus more Liverpool supporters just on the other side of the fence. Five minutes later, the trouble began. It literally was a fight involving three people, two Liverpool supporters and an Italian, towards the front of the section. The Liverpool duo attacked the Italian, then ran off, but when they noticed they weren't being chased back a few more Liverpool fans came back to resume the fighting. In a matter of moments it escalated and about a dozen Liverpool fans rushed across at the massed Italians, kicking out at anybody and everybody in their way. The Italians retaliated this time, with about thirty or so of them rushing back at the Liverpool fans, who then in turn retaliated with a charge comprising about fifty people. Kevin was saying they were crazy, and if they didn't stop they'd get us banned from Europe. After this latest assault, the Italians failed to retaliate, choosing instead to cram themselves closer together as they lived up to their Second World War reputation of cowardice.

All attention in the stadium was now fixed on this action instead of on the schoolboy football that was taking place on the pitch. The Liverpool fans were charging across now in greater numbers, and the Italians were retreating in panic. About half a dozen or so police, the only ones on duty in the ground, went into the no-mans land between the two factions, but a minute later, they ran out again, shaking their heads. Had there been adequate policing, the trouble would have ended there and then, as it had in Rome a year earlier, but the Liverpool fans now knew they could get away with anything. They began to wade into the Italians again, battering them with fists, feet, flagpoles and any other objects they could lay their hands on. At the top of the terracing, any Italians now entering were set upon as soon as they came in. The flimsy fence between sections X and Y and section Z had gone during the disturbance, and the Italians were crammed into one corner of section Z trying desperately to clamber onto the pitch surround and reach relative safety. Unbelievably, the police were trying to force them back, even though it was obvious that they were desperate to escape, not invade the pitch. The front of the terracing, which had been bedecked with Juventus flags and banners, was now being stripped by the Scousers and the fencing torn down.

Meanwhile, at the other end the Juventus fans had begun to tear down the fencing that separated them from the pitch and were bombarding the police with their missiles. The trouble at our end was getting worse as Italians clambered desperately onto the pitch, climbing over fellow supporters in their panic. The fencing at the front had been flattened by the crush of people, and all the while the Liverpool fans were indiscriminately battering anybody and everybody on the outside of the group, forcing the crowd further and further into a corner. Such was the crush that a wall at the side collapsed with a sickening thud, spewing fans everywhere. The riot at the other end was growing nasty now as well. Back at our end, the pitch was full now of escaped fans, many of whom had been injured making their escapes. Amazingly, some idiots were on the pitch playing with a football, with total disregard for what was going on. Some of the other Juventus fans had noticed us now, and after vainly trying to clamber up the stand to us they were trying to get the other Italians in the stand to come and attack us. Kevin turned to me and said "we're dead" and I admit I couldn't see any way we could possibly get out of this one in one piece. I still didn't (or wouldn't) realise how serious things were until I looked over at the mass of debris at the front of the terracing. People were still forcing their way out, and I noticed that there was what looked like a man's body on the ground, with everybody just trampling all over it. I shouted "Hey, watch out" in shock, then realised that nobody could take any notice of me anyway.

It wasn't long after this that the last Italian was 'removed' from Z section. I moved in towards my seat as I needed to get away from a Scottish Liverpool fan who had just come in to the ground, and was shouting for the Liverpool fans to 'get stuck in' even more to the Juventus fans. One lad I passed thought I'd just come in and asked "How many are dead now?" I must have looked surprised, for he said, "What do you think those are that they're carrying off on stretchers. There's been twelve dead so far".

69 – Heysel Stadium, Brussels

Up until that moment I had still refused to believe that anybody could be dead. After all, it was only a football match, and fights at soccer grounds had been occurring for years now. But they were carting off limp bodies on sections of broken fencing from the terracing and I suddenly had to believe that it was so. Odd skirmishes were being fought out on the pitch now as injured Liverpool fans, who were being treated by ambulance staff, were attacked by revenge-seeking Italians. A cameraman got too close and was chased and kicked by the furious Juventus crowd. More police were on hand now and they began to move the Juventus fans into the crowd down the sides and towards their end, and they began to congregate around the tunnel. One Liverpool fan I saw was being carried on a stretcher towards the tunnel, but when he saw the anger there he refused to go in range of the Italians until police could restore some order, and even then he only just got down the tunnel unscathed.

At the Juventus end things were now totally out of control as their fans, who had scarves covering their faces to avoid identification, battled in front of the terraces with the police, using missiles from the broken down fencing and shattered lumps of concrete. The police were totally passive during all of this, allowing them to do as they pleased. At one stage the mob ran all the way round the ground to the Liverpool end and hurled rocks into the ranks of the Liverpool fans in the stand and terracing on the far side of me. Things had quietened down now at our end, as if the enormity of what had been done began to sink into the heads of the Liverpool troublemakers. The stretchers were still carrying out lifeless bodies, and the steward for our section went to look over the side, where all of the bodies were apparently being laid side by side, and then came back holding his hands up to indicate thirty were now dead. The tannoy, which had in vain been broadcasting appeals for the fighting to stop, now started reading out name after name, presumably from Italians trying to contact lost friends and relatives. I looked round at the numb faces around me. One woman who was on our trip was crying her eyes out on a man's shoulder. I had already removed my scarf and covered my red colours in shame - a small, but meaningful, gesture on my part.

It was now around 8 o'clock, the scheduled kick-off time, but it was obvious that there was no chance of the game starting because the pitch was still full of people wandering all over the place. Liverpool's manager Joe Fagan had announced before the game that this would be his last game before he retired. He had been out to try and stop the trouble, but he left in tears as he realised that his pleas were having no effect whatsoever, a terrible way to end a career for one of the truly nice people in football.

At long last, an hour after the trouble had started, armed police moved into the ground and formed line after line facing our fans, with mounted police supervising the operation. Once again they showed their total ineptitude, for rioting was still going on unabated at the Juventus end and no extra police had so far moved in there. An hour after the scheduled kick-off time, Phil Neal came out and went to make an announcement to the fans over the loudspeaker to the effect of "Listen, we're sitting there waiting to play a game of football and we're sick and tired of what's going on. Behave and then we can get on with the match". He left the pitch to tremendous applause. The Juventus captain came out a minute later to make a similar appeal to his fans, and was in fact mobbed by his worshipping followers, who now seemed to have forgotten all about the earlier goings on.

There has been a lot of criticism about the fact the 'game' was played. Being there, I knew that it was the one thing that could defuse the situation, providing Juventus won, for make no mistake their fans were the biggest problem now. The very fact that they were covering their faces to avoid identification showed that they were professionals in the violence stakes as against the English amateurs. At just after half-eight the teams took the pitch to an almighty cheer round the ground. Both sets of players were totally aware of what had gone on, and some of them, mainly Italians, had to be persuaded to play in the game. Again, critics have blasted the fact that the fans could 'enjoy' the game after what had gone on. For my part, I was so relieved to have something else to think about that I cheered for that reason alone. What the critics forget is that if the horror became too much for them, sat at home in front of their television sets, they could always turn away and come back to reality - for us the horror **was** the reality.

As soon as the teams had taken the pitch, the police had charged the Juventus rioters and wedged closed the huge gap in the fence, and they remained like that throughout the game. It began badly for Liverpool, as Mark Lawrenson dislocated his shoulder and went off injured after just two minutes. The Italian front three of big names Michel Platini, Paulo Rossi and Sibbi Boniek, all of whom I had been really looking forward to seeing, not surprisingly hardly showed. Wark and Walsh were both just inches away from getting first half goals, before Walsh became our second casualty of the match as he went off injured at half time. The game seemed to have had the desired effect on the supporters, for everything remained calm during the interval.

In the second half Liverpool remained firmly on top, but on a rare Juventus break Gary Gillespie fouled Boniek well outside the box. The Swiss referee immediately pointed for a penalty, which on reflection could have started another riot. Fortunately, there were no protests of note from Liverpool and Platini scored past Grobbelaar, sending the insensitive Italian fans wild with delight. As the game progressed I was more than half hoping we wouldn't score so that I could leave at the final whistle while the Juventus fans were still inside celebrating the trophy award. With a few minutes left came another potential riot-provoking incident as twice within five seconds Liverpool had clear penalties refused. It was obvious to me and everybody else present or watching throughout the world that the referee had been told to let Juventus win for the sake of peace, with only UEFA "officially" denying that this was the instruction after the game. Kevin and I made our way to the exit and the second the final whistle blew we dashed out of the ground.

Outside, a solid line of police met us. Apparently on television it said they were going to be policing the route all of the way back to the coaches. This was a total fabrication, as the instant we turned the corner the line disappeared, and we didn't see another policeman all evening. We hurried through the unlit streets, which would have been full of Juventus fans from section Z had there been no trouble in the ground, and bumped into the limping chap off our flight. He remembered me, and asked about Alex as he tagged along with us towards the coaches. We also saw Brian and Rocky on our way back to the coaches. They had been in section Y, and weren't aware of what had been happening as they were too far away to see clearly.

As we neared the coach park there was a commotion across the road, and not stopping to take chances, we hurried for the railings to the coach park and clambered over them, helping the limping man over as well. On the coaches we relaxed a little, especially once we moved off for the airport. The radio was on and with my limited command of French I could half make out some numbers that were being said, followed by names - possibly the casualty list. One girl near to me said "That's it, we're in the UEFA Cup next year", a reference to the fact that for the previous nine years we had competed in the European Cup. I just turned to her and said "We'll be banned". There could be no doubt about that.

When the coach arrived back at the airport we were left waiting on the tarmac for an age while the driver went to find out what he should do. The other coaches that had been with us gradually moved off, leaving us on our own in a highly vulnerable position if any Italian coaches arrived. We saw Martin outside on the tarmac and he signalled to us through the window. One lad on our coach couldn't wait any longer and got off the coach to have a leak, going by some empty coaches. Typically, as soon as he'd done this our driver returned and started off again, leaving him to run back after us and also to explain to the airport security guards what he was doing outside. Fortunately, we only turned the corner to where all the other coaches were parked, waiting to put the fans back onto the flights.

A passport control had been set up on the approach to the runway and we all queued there waiting to get on to the plane. It was chaotically organised, but I suppose the Belgians just wanted to get rid of us as quickly as possible without the chance of our causing any disruption to anybody else. We met up again with Ron in the queue, but surprisingly nobody seemed in the least bit concerned about the events of a few hours earlier. Ron, in fact, was getting irate with the Towns Travel organiser for having us wait for such a long time, and shouted "Come on, the new season starts on August 17th". Eventually we boarded the plane, and although the stewardess said there were to be no refreshments on the journey home, she let us take some sips from the bottles of water that were in the cabin as we were all so parched. On the flight back we were all given cards to fill in with our names and addresses to hand into the police on our return to Liverpool so that they'd have us in their records as 'safe'.

On landing back at Speke we had another long wait to go through customs, probably because most of the people in front of us hadn't filled their cards in yet. A family in front of me was talking to one of the police, who described what it had been like on the television, and he confirmed that about 40 were dead and nearly 500 injured. As we passed through customs and back into the arrival/departure lounge, scores of television crews were around, including some from Italy, stopping and interviewing odd people about the incidents.

By now it was about 2:30 a.m. We went straight out to the car and Kevin tried to start it, without success. I arranged for some lads in the next car to give us a push, but to no avail as the car still refused to start. I'm sure Kevin would have sat there for the rest of the morning trying to start it and staring looking at it, but after a few minutes I made him get up and do something about it. The people at the car park couldn't help at all, so we went back to the airport again, I phoned directory enquiries for the AA number and Kevin reluctantly phoned them and gave the details. Considering that he was a fully paid up member, I couldn't understand why he was so reluctant to make use of the service. Another plane full of supporters had arrived whilst we were there. I'd seen a morning paper and had seen some of the pages inside detailing the horror. An ITV cameraman and interviewer were talking to a supporter, asking him what he thought of it, holding up the paper, and generally getting him to talk about what had occurred. When asked if he'd go to Europe again, he said "No way". I was also making up my mind never to go to go to an away game again, although at the time I still intended going back to Anfield. The interviewer then went up to another lad and asked him what he thought. "Great" was the reply, "I've had a fantastic time", and he walked on, leaving me feeling utterly disgusted.

We went back to the car to wait for the AA, with dawn now approaching. After a while waiting in the car I went back again to the terminal building to ring Barbara. I asked Kevin if he was coming to ring his parents, but he said they'd be asleep. Barbara answered the phone after just a few rings, and I let her know that we were back okay but waiting for the car to be fixed. She said Harry next door had offered her some sleeping pills to get some rest but she'd turned them down, waiting to see if any phone calls would come through. The phone had apparently been ringing all evening from anxious relatives, but obviously she couldn't tell them anything. I asked her to ring Kevin's parents to let them know we were back. When I eventually arrived home, she told me that they had been up all night waiting for a message and were extremely grateful for her call.

By now we had been waiting for an hour and a half for the AA, and I wondered if their patrol had come and gone again, so I rang them back and they said he should be on his way. As I walked back to the car I saw an AA car driving into the wrong car park, so I hailed him, found out it was the right one and went with him to our car. He diagnosed damp as being the problem, and he was able to restart the car in a matter of minutes. I finally got home at about 5:30, and went straight upstairs to kiss Iain and Shelley and climbed in bed with Barbara, holding her tight for the rest of the night.

The next morning she was going to take Iain and Shelley for a walk in the park, leaving me in bed. Even though I'd only had a little sleep, I didn't want to be left on my own so I got up and went with them, lying down on the grass in the park in the hot sun. After my worries that I'd never see them again I didn't want to be separated from them. When we got back home I put the television on. Every programme was devoted to the events at the stadium, showing the bodies being removed, and tears were rolling down my face. I rang Rocky's wife to let her know I'd seen him after the game, as beforehand she had told me he'd got a ticket off some Italians for the fatal section Z, and I wanted to reassure her that he was okay. Apparently, though, he'd managed to phone her from Ostend after the game so she knew all was well. She also said that one of the victims had been shown with just a soggy mass where the head should have been, and when I asked Barbara she said Iain had also noticed that, saying - 'there's a man without a head', and she'd had to tell him he was wrong.

The true facts now were that thirty-eight people were dead and 454 injured. Another was to die some weeks later, making the final death toll thirty-nine. Twenty-two of the dead were Italians, some just children, most of the rest Belgians and one a Britain who worked in Belgium and had just gone along for the game.

Then the recriminations began, with everybody trying to pass the blame onto the police, UEFA, the stadium organisers - everywhere but onto the real culprits, the Liverpool fans. John Smith, Liverpool chairman, claimed National Front activists and Chelsea supporters were behind it all. Some newspapers blamed Scottish based supporters. It was all becoming even nastier.

On the Friday I went back to work, but apparently I was pale and ghostlike all day. I went to the bank at lunch time and handed my Belgian notes back to exchange them for the equivalent in English currency, but in truth I would gladly have given them back for nothing as I was just glad to see the back of them. Kenny Dalglish was appointed Liverpool's new manager following Joe Fagan's retirement, but with the focus away from football he had a very difficult beginning. He wasn't helped by the conflicting stories that came out of the dressing room as to whether or not the players knew about the tragedy before the game eventually went ahead. Some people, such as Bruce Grobbelaar, claimed that they were aware of the deaths, whereas others, including Dalglish, claimed that they hadn't been told anything at all about it.

Liverpool announced that they were voluntarily pulling out of Europe for the next season, and the Football League announced that they were withdrawing **all** English clubs from Europe for the season. UEFA then made their own decision, which was to ban all English clubs from European competition indefinitely, with a further three-year ban on Liverpool once the ban was lifted. Initially, the ban applied to *any* English side playing *anywhere* in Europe, even in Scotland, and a Blackpool schoolboy's team who were on a tour of France had to be sent home early because of it. To my complete anger and amazement, Liverpool appealed to UEFA about the severity of the ban. I wrote a very critical letter to Liverpool's chairman, John Smith, and he replied some weeks later disagreeing with me but respecting my viewpoint.

Several people were arrested after video pictures were printed of those the police thought most responsible for the riot, but it took years before they were extradited to Belgium to face trial. In the end they were sentenced whilst they were back in England, and told to 'return to Belgium to serve their jail terms'. Needless to say, they remained in England. In contrast, the Italians had very quickly tried and convicted their supporters who were engaged in the trouble, including one who was seen on television firing a starting pistol at the police.

Over the summer, my attitude hardened and I resolved that I would not be going back to watch football, whether at Liverpool or anywhere else. The Heysel tragedy had killed my love of the game.

* * * * *

Twenty years after Heysel, television documentaries revealed some of the hidden truths behind the decisions taken on the evening of the tragedy. Despite the official story, players from both sides now admitted that they had been fully aware of the tragedy and that they had been ordered to play the game against their wishes. For the first time since the disaster I saw some of the match action, including the key penalty incidents. The foul on Boniek was so far outside the area that awarding a penalty for such a trip could have caused a riot under different circumstances. Yet when Platini 'scored' from the spot kick, he celebrated as if it really meant something – as did the entire Juventus team at the end of the game. The foul on Ronnie Whelan, on the other hand, was one of the clearest penalties in the history of the game, but when Liverpool questioned the decision, the referee told Phil Neal that under no circumstances was he going to allow the score to come back to 1-1. As Whelan said in 2005, it didn't matter, the match wasn't real anyway, but it did prove the lies of the authorities when they'd tried to deny that the game had been fixed. The abiding opinion of players of both teams was that the game should *not* have taken place, and playing it was an insult to the memory of those who died.

Above - Liverpool fans sunbathing in
the shadow of the stadium, little
knowing what would soon occur there

Left – Onze magazine photo issue
depicting the scenes

Right – Juventus tribute edition

Trip and flight details

FOR HOLIDAYS AND TRAVEL

FLIGHT '5'
DAY RETURN 29TH MAY

CHECK IN AT LIVERPOOL AIRPORT INTERNATIONAL BUILDING AT
09.30 HOURS.
AER LINGUS FLIGHT DEPARTS   11.10 HRS
ARRIVE BRUSSELS   13.20 HRS
AFTER CUSTOMS AND IMMIGRATION BOARD THE BUSES MARKED '5'
FOR THE JOURNEY TO THE STADIUM.

NOTE: NO ALCOHOL OR OFFENSIVE WEAPONS OF FIREWORKS WILL BE
ALLOWED IN THE STADIUM. THE BELGIAN POLICE MAY INSTITUTE A
SEARCH OF ALL PERSONS ENTERING THE STADIUM, THEREFORE
'DUTY FREE' SHOULD NOT BE BOUGHT ON THE OUTBOUND FLIGHT.
AFTER THE MATCH BOARD THE COACHES MARKED '5' PLEASE NOTE
THE LAST COACH WILL DEPART THE STADIUM 30 MINS AFTER THE
FINAL WHISTLE.
DEPART BRUSSELS ON AER LINGUS FLIGHT
THE AIRCRAFT WILL LEAVE AS SOON AS POSSIBLE AFTER THE
ARRIVAL OF THE COACHES. THE RETURN FLIGHT TAKES 1 HOUR
NOTE: TOWNS TRAVEL SERVICE CANNOT BE RESPONSIBLE FOR ANY
EXPENSE CAUSED BY PASSENGERS MISSING THE APPROPRIATE
TRANSPORT.

DO NOT FORGET YOUR PASSPORT......

Aer Lingus ☘

Charter ticket and baggage check
In conjunction with Master ticket

TOWNS TRAVEL, WIDNES

Issued to _____
(Name of Charteror)

From	LIVERPOOL	Flt. No.	Date
To	BRUSSELS	EI 4956	29 MAY
To	LIVERPOOL	EI 4957	30 MAY

Name of Passenger   MR. S. WILSON

(Passenger inserts name here and in spaces below.)

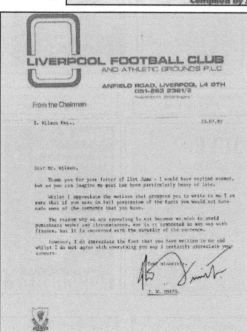

A "Daily Mirror" article on the tragedy from 1999, under the 'Events of the Millennium' heading (above), the letter from Liverpool chairman John Smith (left) and Juventus v Liverpool, Champions League quarterfinal 2005 (below)

Liverpool v Juventus ticket – the back showing stadium sections

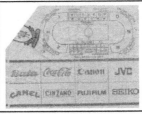

1970, Sheffield Wednesday v Juventus, Anglo-Italian Cup

Juventus v Porto, 1984 Cup Winners Cup Final

Athletic Bilbao v Juventus, 1977 EUFA Cup Final

Paris St Germain v Juventus, 1996 Super Cup Final

Hamburg v Juventus, 1983 European Cup Final

Hamburg v Juventus, 1983 European Cup Final

Borussia Dortmund v Juventus, 1997 European Cup Final

Borussia Dortmund v Juventus,
1997 European Cup Final

Juventus v Borussia Dortmund,
1993 EUFA Cup Final

Borussia Dortmund v Juventus,
1993 EUFA Cup Final

Juventus v Fiorentina, 1990
EUFA Cup Final

Fioreutina v Juventus, 1990
EUFA Cup Final

Bruges v Juventus, 1978
European Cup Semi-Final

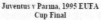

Juventus v Parma, 1995 EUFA
Cup Final

Liverpool v Juventus, European
Cup Winners Cup 1965

Parma v Juventus, 1995 EUFA
Cup Final

69 – Heysel Stadium, Brussels

It took another tragedy – Hillsborough in 1989 – to get me to return to a football ground. Almost a hundred Liverpool supporters were crushed to death at the FA Cup semi-final against Nottingham Forest. I chillingly recalled my own visits to Hillsborough and the Leppings Lane end earlier in the decade as I listened to the tragedy occurring.

It was decided that every football game in Britain would kick-off at 3:07 on the following Saturday as a mark of respect, with a minute's silence immediately beforehand. The cities of Liverpool, Sheffield and Nottingham had already decided that all traffic lights would be switched to red for one minute at 3:06, and the city bells would ring out, with cars being allowed to stop anywhere. They appealed for traffic, shops and everybody who could do so to come to a stop and observe the silence at 3:06. In Europe, too, a minute's silence was being observed, and apparently this was particularly poignant at the AC Milan v Real Madrid European Cup semi-final, with the fans singing, "You'll never walk alone" after the silence. Everybody seemed to realise that such a tragedy could happen to *any* football fans *anywhere*. Manchester United offered a lot of very welcome support, perhaps somewhat surprisingly in view of the hatred between the two sets of supporters.

I decided to take Iain to Anfield on the Saturday, where a special ceremony was being planned. We drove straight to Liverpool after Iain had played his morning junior football match, arriving at around 1:30 and parking as close to Goodison Park as we could reasonably get. Iain was wearing his Everton scarf and I wore my Liverpool one for the first time since the Heysel disaster nearly four years earlier. After that awful night, I had put all of my red attire into a bottom drawer and left them untouched.

As we walked past Goodison, we passed several people who were wearing football scarves, and when we reached Stanley Park we saw hundreds of others. They were in the process of making a special link of intertwined scarves from Goodison right across the park to Anfield, with alternate blue and white and red and white favours tied together to indicate how the city was united over the tragedy. It was a very emotional journey through the park, viewing the thousands of scarves that lined the way. The crowds at Anfield filled the road outside the Shankly Gates as further queues of people waited to enter the ground to pay their own tribute. I took Iain towards the end of the queue with the intention of joining in there. I soon saw that the queue stretched all the way from the entrance to the ground in Anfield Road, down Lothair Road, round the front of the Kop, up and down Kemlyn Road and just about every other street we could see. There was no end to it in sight.

I realised that we'd never get in to the ground at all if I went right to the end, so we walked back past the front of the Kop and up the narrow alley that led to the gates at the Kop end of the main stand. These gates were strewn with scarves and flowers, so Iain and I gently moved through the crowds and I left my two red-and-white hats at the foot of the gates amongst the pile of tributes. We stood there a moment in silence, and then just turned and joined the queue that went right past this spot as it made its way towards Anfield Road. I still feel guilty now about queue jumping on such an occasion as this, but try and excuse my actions by telling myself that it was my only opportunity to pay my respects and heal my own four-year old wound.

The time was around 2:30 p.m. by now, and the queue was gradually moving towards the entrance gates. The skies were grey, in sympathy with the mood, and most of the people there held bouquets of flowers, ready to leave them on the pitch alongside the millions of other floral tributes that were already there. We reached Anfield Road again shortly before 3 o'clock, and saw that around the Shankly Gates hundreds of scarves, programmes and other tributes had been left there. We slowly went inside these gates and towards the open gate that led into the ground, passing by the new souvenir shop. Less than a month earlier we had visited that shop on our way to visit my sister in Wales, and Iain had gone in wearing his Everton scarf, receiving some strange looks from the Liverpool people. In contrast Evertonians were now being welcomed into Anfield with open arms as the club made it clear how it valued the warmth and neighbourliness shown by its friends across the park. Only the day before, the Everton team had called at Anfield prior to making the journey to London for the game against Tottenham, and they had received a heroes' welcome from the thousands who were there waiting to pay their own tributes to the disaster victims.

As we entered the ground and walked along the touchline towards the Kop, the true magnificence of the floral tribute met our eyes. The entire pitch from the Kop goalmouth to just short of the half way line was covered with flowers, scarves, hats, umbrellas and flags. The Anfield Road end goalmouth was similarly covered, and on the Kop itself every inch of every barrier had a scarf, flag or banner

97

draped over it. We paused for a moment to put some money in one of the huge collecting bins that were in place around the ground, and I noticed that in the 'home' trainer's dugout somebody had placed a copy of the programme from the fateful match.

We crossed the pitch via the matting that had been placed over the grass to protect it, and took the opportunity to take a closer look at the sea of flowers that stretched to the Kop, before going to take our seats in the rapidly filling Kemlyn Road Stand. One lad who was sat directly in front of me told us that he had been in the crush at Hillsborough, receiving a bruised head before he managed to get on to the pitch. The crowds were still entering and walking round the pitch, and the Salvation Army band played solemn music in the centre circle, with a band of Scots Guards in the Anfield Road stand waiting to play 'The Last Post'. At just before five past three, the gates were closed and everybody still inside the ground was asked to go and sit in any of the three stands surrounding the pitch.

To huge applause, a party came out of the players tunnel, consisting of some Liverpool players and wives, other officials including Gordon Taylor, secretary of the Professional Footballers Association, and the two Archbishops of Liverpool, the Protestant Reverend David Shepherd and the Catholic Reverend Derek Warlock. At 3:06, we all stood to observe a minute's silence, which was broken only by the sound of some heart-rending sobs. The heavens opened as if in sympathy with the feeling of desolation that everybody involved must have had. The two Archbishops then led a short service, followed by the Salvation Army band playing "You'll Never Walk Alone". There were some half-hearted attempts by the people in the stands to join in, before Gordon Taylor laid another wreath on the pitch to further great applause, and the players and officials went back inside.

Iain and I made our way to the front of the Kemlyn Road stand as people began to leave. There were some chaotic scenes as people leaving the stands met up with those walking around the pitch now that the gates had been opened again, and the stewards were naturally concerned to avoid even the remotest possibility of any crushing. Fortunately, things quickly sorted themselves out and everything settled down again. I decided to leave my one remaining and treasured scarf as my own tribute, for leaving the hats hadn't really been a sacrifice as far as I was concerned. I handed my scarf to the stewardess, who laid it gently on to the pitch, and after taking one last photograph of it we made our way back up the stairs of the stand and out of the back. People at the doors were handing out leaflets offering counselling advice to all who needed it. We edged our way along Anfield Road through the throngs, and then back down the side of the ground where queues of people were still waiting to enter to pay their own tributes.

We walked through the rain back towards Goodison, taking the route on the outside of the park this time. There was one especially poignant poster at Goodison, depicting a composite-badge, the right half of which came from the blue Everton badge and the left half from the red Liverpool badge, with the message 'Merseyside Unites' written above the badge and '95 RIP - A Blues Fan' underneath.

The moving sight at Anfield – my scarf is circled, centre-left

Celtic (a), First match after Hillsborough

Everton (a), First competitive game after Hillsborough

Nottingham Forest (h), First game at Anfield post-Hillsborough

Nottingham Forest (h) 1990, First anniversary of Hillsborough – and my return to football after an absence of almost five years

season
nineteen ninety one
ninety two

£1.00

LINCOLN CITY
football club

**BARCLAYS LEAGUE
DIVISION FOUR**

Saturday 2nd May 1992

kick off 3.00 p.m.

versus
BLACKPOOL

main club sponsor
FLINDALLS LTD

---

70. Lincoln City v Blackpool

Played at **Sincil Bank** on 2nd May 1992

Football League Division Four

**Lincoln City (1)2 [Carmichael 2 penalties]
Blackpool 0**

Attendance 7,884

With the exception of the Hillsborough memorial and anniversary, I had nothing to do with football for close to six years following the Heysel disaster. It was only when my eldest son Iain asked if I would take him to a Blackpool match for his tenth birthday that I returned to the game. We began to be regular followers of Blackpool starting with the attempts at promotion in seasons 1990-91 and 1991-92, although I didn't go to a game without one of the children for another seven or so years.

In May 1991, we saw Blackpool miss out on promotion as they lost in the play-off final at Wembley, on penalties to Torquay. Twelve months later, Blackpool were again well placed for going up, and with one game remaining, we knew that a point at Lincoln would mean automatic promotion. This was irrespective of how Mansfield, our only challengers for the promotion place, were to do. The only cautionary note was that Blackpool had been in an identical position a year earlier, but a 2-0 defeat at Walsall combined with the results from elsewhere had consigned 'Pool to the lottery of the play-offs.

Lincoln hadn't had much to cheer about in their history. Formed in 1883, their highest league position was fifth in the Second Division in 1902. They reached the equivalent of the FA Cup Fifth Round on a few occasions, the last also being in 1902, but they made headlines for the wrong reasons in the 1980's. First of all, they were the visitors at Bradford City in May 1985 when the fire in the main stand killed more than fifty people. That game was abandoned and never played. They were also the visitors at York when the game was abandoned at half time after the death of one of the York players. They were Fourth Division champions in 1976 when Graham Taylor was manager, amassing a record points total of seventy-four, but eleven years later they became the first club to be automatically relegated from the Football League to the Conference – although they did bounce straight back a year later as champions. They were defeated 3-2 by Millwall in the Football League Trophy Final of 1983, reached the Millennium Stadium in Cardiff in 2003 for the Third Division play-off final, only to lose 5-2 to Bournemouth, and their best performance in the League Cup saw them reach the Fourth Round in 1968, going out after a replay to Derby County.

Barbara went and bought us two tickets for the game on the Monday. I had wanted us to have seats in the stand, but those few tickets had already been sold, so we took terracing places instead. During the week we heard that Dave Bamber was a doubtful starter. As he had been an ever present so far, scoring 35 goals, it would be a big blow if he were missing.

The game at Lincoln was never going to be easy, as the home side had won their last six matches, the last three results being 5-1 at Chesterfield, 3-0 at home to Hereford and 4-1 at Halifax. We did have some good news on the eve of the game, though, as Dave Bamber had recovered from his virus and was fit to play.

I had printed my route to Lincoln after using the 'Autoroute' software, and we set off at about 10:45 a.m. for the trip to the east coast. On the journey, we saw plenty of cars and coaches decked out in tangerine, the only other colours on view being those of Leeds fans as we entered Yorkshire. Leeds were about to receive the Championship Trophy before their final home match, following Manchester United's defeat at Anfield six days earlier.

Leaving the M62 motorway to join the M1, both the road and service station were full to the brim of Blackpool fans, with an estimated 5,000 making the journey. We were making good time until just a few miles outside Lincoln, when we were held up for about half an hour by the volume of traffic waiting to cross a toll bridge. We arrived in heavy rain about ninety minutes before kick-off, and parked close to the ground. I even parked outside house number 37, our own house number, hoping that would be a lucky omen! We walked up to the ground, and queued in our appointed queue at gate 17 – another omen, I hoped, as the 17th was both Iain's and my daughter Shelley's birthday.

It was obvious from the outside that the Blackpool fans had been allocated more than just the visitors section of the terrace, and after getting inside we saw that one side of the ground was completely given over to our supporters. The stand to our right was in the process of being rebuilt, otherwise we would probably have been located there. The programme had an article in it which was quite scathing in its attack on the decrepit state of our Bloomfield Road ground, and I said to Iain that it was a little unfair seeing that Blackpool were on the verge of having a new stadium built. Clearly, the programme editor knew more than I did about how long it would be before anything happened on that front! In fact it was nine years before anything began to happen at Bloomfield Road!

We moved towards a wall at the front, and after a few minutes I realised that the chap next to me, who was 'grease-painting' his daughter's face in tangerine, blue and white, was Robert Frowen, and I chatted to him as we waited for kick-off. It was the first time I'd seen him at a game in many a long year. The Lincoln stewards and police were being extremely friendly towards us, allowing a few lads in fancy dress to join in the pre-match kick-in for the Blackpool team. Nearer kick-off, a lot of children were allowed to climb over the wall and sit on the running track as the pressure grew with the fans continuing to come in. Blackpool fans were looking for every vantage point, even climbing on to the pre-fabricated buildings at the top of the terrace. There were also a hundred or so Blackpool fans in the seats directly opposite us, but with no roof on our side there wasn't the atmosphere you'd expect for such a big game. The outnumbered home fans probably hadn't seen this many visiting supporters in years - if ever.

We played into the wind in the first half, Mitch Cook going close with one shot from the edge of the box, but neither side were threatening until a clumsy challenge in the box gave Lincoln a penalty. McIlhargey got his hand to Carmichael's shot, but it crept in off the post. At half time, with the wind due to be behind us for the second period, Robert said you must favour Blackpool to score at least once in the half. With Mansfield drawing 0-0 at home to Rochdale at the interval, hopes were still high even if we were unable to equalise.

Blackpool controlled most of the second half, without looking too dangerous until near the mid-way point, when a concerted spell of attacking got the crowd roaring, "Come on you Poo-el". One goalbound shot was just turned aside and Groves picked up the loose ball, but his shot from a narrow angle hit the side of the post.

Rumours came through of the score at Mansfield, and as often happens in these cases each rumour gave a totally different score. However, with only a few minutes left it seemed that Mansfield were 2-0 ahead, and it looked like a last-day disappointment for the second year in a row. A man stood next to us was trying without success to tune his radio into a local station that might have given more accurate news of the score in the Mansfield match.

Robert, clearly having given up on 'Pool, left with his daughter Hannah, and in injury time a trip on the edge of the area gave Lincoln a second penalty, which Carmichael blasted into the roof of the net. We were all silenced, but suddenly the Blackpool fans opposite in the stand began leaping up and down and hugging each other, and it seemed that news must have come through of a Rochdale equaliser. Hundreds of Blackpool fans on our side clambered over the wall and invaded the pitch, as chants of "Going up, Going up, Going up" rang round Sincil Bark. The people with the transistors couldn't confirm anything, and the chap stood next to me with the radio said the local reporter was accusing Blackpool fans of invading the pitch to try and get the match abandoned!

Things did appear to be getting a bit nasty as Blackpool fans went over to the home end, and the groups seemed to be taunting each other – seven years after my visit to the Heysel, and nobody seemed to have learnt a thing! Manager Billy Ayre and the players came over to try and get the fans off the pitch, and after about eight minutes the game was able to complete it's final thirty seconds. There was still no confirmation of the Mansfield score, but it now looked like they had won, as there were no longer any celebrations. We went back to the car and found out that though Rochdale *had* scored, it was only to reduce the arrears to 2-1, and that was the final score. The false hope from the score rumourmongers and the atmosphere as we left the ground reminded me of the similar gloomy feeling on leaving Huddersfield way back in 1968.

After a wrong turn going out of Lincoln, I finally found the right road and we set off for home, stopping at the McDonalds restaurant on the A57 roundabout for some tea. There were a lot of dejected Blackpool fans there, but at least some began to look with hope to the play-offs. To complete a disappointing day, I decided to take the "town" route home, across the A57 through Sheffield, the Snake Pass and Manchester (all through city centres) before reaching the motorway. I started to suffer from cramp and had to stop for a walk in a seedy area of Manchester before we finally got home in four hours - an hour longer than it took us to get there.

There was a happy ending, though, three weeks later, when Blackpool returned to Wembley and defeated Scunthorpe after penalties to gain that elusive promotion place.

Millwall (h), 1983 Football League Trophy Final

Bohemians Prague (h), 1969

Telford United (h), Conference 1988

Tulsa roughnecks (h), 1979

Lincoln v Blackpool ticket from 1992

Derby County (h), Football League Cup Fourth Round replay 1968

71. Wigan Athletic v Colchester United

Played at Springfield Park on 5th February 1994

Football League Division Three

Wigan Athletic 0
Colchester United (0)1 [Dickens]

Attendance 1,695

71 Wigan Athletic – Springfield Park

I decided during the 1993-94 season that I would go to see the league clubs who I hadn't seen before, when they were in action in the North West. One of the first such visits took me to Springfield Park, home of Wigan Athletic, and Iain came with me to the game against Colchester. The only previous time I had been to a game in Wigan was for the New Year's Day Rugby League game between Wigan and Blackpool Borough in 1981. On that occasion, I had found my way to the football ground and had to be directed to the rugby ground - this time the reverse happened.

Wigan had joined the league in the mid-1970's after a long and successful spell as one of the leading non-league sides in the country, where they reached Wembley in the 1973 FA Trophy competition, only to lose 2-1 to Scarborough. As a non-league side, they gave Manchester City a scare before losing 1-0 in the FA Cup Third Round in 1971. They found success at league level more difficult than expected, although they did achieve Wembley glory when Brentford were defeated in the Freight Rover final of 1985 – a trophy that was won again in 1999 against Millwall. Wembley was tantalisingly close in a bigger competition in 1987, when Leeds eventually saw off the Latics in an FA Cup quarterfinal tie, and the Fourth Round of the League Cup was reached in 1982.

We arrived at the ground a few minutes before kick-off, yet it was very quiet there. Iain went in the juniors' entrance and was given £1 back by a steward, and then we were both given tickets (as was every body else) to get into the 'members enclosure' - the covered terracing. As it was about to rain heavily, and I was full of a cold, it was a welcome move.

The first half was played in a very silent atmosphere - there was nothing for the small crowd to chant about, the most notable happenings being when Colchester kicked two balls out of the ground in the space of sixty seconds. Iain had brought his radio, and I listened to some of the Scotland v England Rugby Union fixture, where Scotland finally took the lead in injury time only to concede a penalty immediately, which England kicked to win the match.

There was more action and noise after the break, with both sides coming close to breaking the deadlock. From one free kick, United's Cawley hit the bar, and then Watts made a hash of it when clear with only the goalkeeper to beat. With just ten minutes left, the visitors made it third time lucky after Dickens collected a poor back-pass by ex-Evertonian Kevin Langley and rounded Farnworth to score the only goal of the game. His own 'supporters' had barracked Langley throughout the game and it was hardly a surprise that his confidence was so low that he made the error. The Wigan fans immediately started to leave, hardly supporting their side in its fight to remain in the league as they were lying towards the foot of the table. They were to struggle until the end of the season, a win two games from the end finally securing their safety. The final minutes saw Wigan pressing for an equaliser, and as we moved behind the goal on our way out, we managed to get ourselves on the television coverage of the highlights from one corner, when the ball was in the Colchester goalmouth.

Wigan v Blackpool ticket from 1998 (above) and Wigan Borough v Stoke, FA Cup, 1926 (below)

Newport County (h), first league
season 1978-79

Manchester City (a), FA Cup
Third Round 1971

Leeds United (h), FA Cup
quarterfinal 1987

Tranmere (h), League Cup
1978-79 – first as a league club

Aston Villa (h), Football League
Cup Fourth Round 1981-82

Grimsby Town (h) 1978-79 –
first home league game

Peterborough United (h), FA
Cup Second Round 1970-1

East Fife and CWKS Legia (h),
1980

Hereford United (a),
Herefordshire Cup Final 1972

N.P.L. CHAMPIONSHIP WINNING SQUAD 1992-93

GM VAUXHALL CONFERENCE

MARSDEN CUP

v. **BLACKPOOL**

SATURDAY 23rd JULY 1994

Kick-off 3.00 p.m.

---

72. Southport v Blackpool

Played at **Haig Avenue** on 23rd July 1994

Marsden Lancashire Cup

Southport (0)1 [Quinlon]
Blackpool (1)4 [Sheedy, Rodwell, Goulding own goal, Brown penalty]

Attendance 1,287

109

The 1994-95 season began with Blackpool defending the Marsden's Lancashire Cup, and GM Vauxhall Conference side Southport were in our qualifying group. Southport had been a Football League side until the late 1970's, but they had lost their place and had languished outside the league ever since. As the century drew to an end, they became one of the leading lights in the Conference, reaching Wembley in the FA Trophy final of 1998, only to lose to Cheltenham. Their best run in the FA Cup came in 1931, when they reached the quarterfinals, only to crash out *9-1* at Everton!

In the close season, Billy Ayre had resigned as manager following one run-in too many with the Oyston's, and new boss Sam Allardyce had immediately been given a small fortune to spend on strengthening the team. His signings included defender Phil Brown from Bolton, goalkeeper Les Sealey from Manchester United, and striker Tony Ellis from Preston.

We decided to go to the game at Southport that opened the group, and Iain, Craig and I set out on a scorching hot Saturday afternoon in July to cover the short distance between the seaside towns. On the way we saw a lot of cars with Blackpool scarves hanging out of the window, with the fans obviously all keen to see the new players. When we parked and passed the pub near to the ground all we could see were Blackpool fans in their tangerine or dark-blue and light-blue shirts, the new away kit being a copy of the old home kit of the 1930's.

We queued along with a long line of other Blackpool supporters, and just managed to get in before kick-off time. We met up with Rob Frowen inside the ground, but couldn't find any programmes on sale. Apparently Southport had expected about 300 away fans, not the thousand or so who completely filled the terrace behind the goal and to the side. All of our new signings were named in the starting line-up, but with the heat I was a little concerned about the effect on Iain and Craig. All of the players were having constant liquid intakes from the numerous water bottles that were thrown onto the pitch, a welcome innovation from the summer's World Cup in the United States, but there was no such relief for the fans.

Blackpool almost opened the scoring when a close-range Bamber effort squirmed out of the Southport goalkeeper's grasp and hit the post, bouncing back into the grateful custodian's arms, and at the other end Sealey acrobatically turned one shot aside. After almost half an hour of play, Sheedy found himself with the ball in the box to the left of the goal and he slotted his shot into the net by the far post for the opening goal. Shortly after this, Sheedy received a knock and was replaced by Cook - throughout his career, Sheedy had been one of those players who was injury prone, and as a result he never quite managed to live up to his enormous potential.

Just before half time, we went with Rob and his son to queue up for a drink and it was *twenty-five minutes* before we managed to get served. Fortunately, the drinks kiosk was adjacent to the terracing so we could still watch the game while we queued, and the ice-cold colas were **very** welcome when they finally arrived. While I was waiting in the queue, I spotted a door near to the turnstiles that looked as if it was an entrance to a shop, and I left Iain with Craig in the queue while I went to investigate. Sure enough, it was a programme shop, and they still had some of the match programmes left. They were possibly those returned from the almost-empty Southport end, so I was able to get some for us before going back to queue for our refreshments.

We stayed behind the goal for the second half, as Blackpool were now attacking this end of the ground. Rodwell turned in the penalty area and shot low past Moore for the second goal after nearly an hour's play, and with just over fifteen minutes left a low cross hit Goulding and bounced into the net for the third goal. Melvin Capleton came on as a substitute for Les Sealey, who had shone on his debut by making three or four excellent saves, and was temporarily making me take back my claim that he was over the hill and a poor signing for Blackpool. Within a minute it was 4-0 as Ellis was fouled in the area and Brown struck home the spot kick, with me taking a photograph of this goal from the side.

In the final ten minutes Southport deservedly pulled a goal back with a low shot from the edge of the area by substitute Quinlon. They almost scored a second as they pressed strongly towards the finish, but at the final whistle it was a comprehensive 4-1 victory for Blackpool, which earned us four points - three for the victory, plus an additional one for scoring at least three goals. We chatted amicably with a home steward during the game about the good behaviour of the Blackpool support, and then left the ground in a procession of tangerine and blue-shirted fans - I was very impressed with the away kit, on the first occasion that I had seen it.

Brown scores his penalty

Cheltenham, FA Trophy Final
1998

Everton (a), FA Cup
quarterfinal 1931

Hull City (a), FA Cup Fifth
Round 1966

Everton (h), FA Cup Third
Round 1968

Huddersfield Town (h), Last
League Fixture 1978

Liverpool (h), Liverpool Senior
Cup Semi-Final 1998

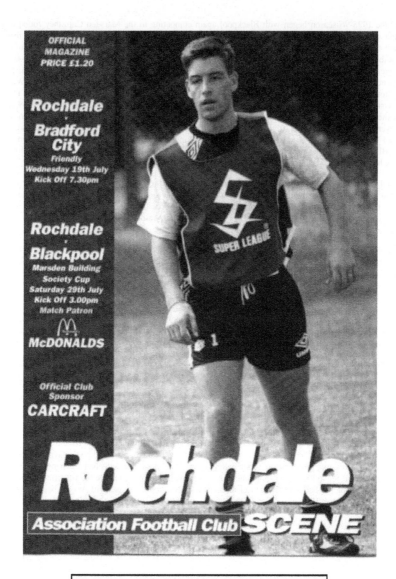

73. **Rochdale** v Blackpool

Played at Spotland on 29th July 1995

Marsden Lancashire Cup

Rochdale 0
Blackpool (0)1 [Ellis]

Attendance 1,265

73 Rochdale - Spotland

As the 1995-96 season began with Blackpool again competing in the Marsden Cup, they found that after defeating Preston 1-0 at home they only required a draw at Spotland against Rochdale to reach their third consecutive final. Although Rochdale were always associated with the lower reaches of the Football League, they did contest the second ever final of the Football League Cup, losing 4-0 on aggregate to Norwich City in 1962. This was in the pre-Wembley days of the competition, and Rochdale never managed to reach the national stadium. They almost managed to get to the Welsh National Stadium in 2002, losing narrowly on aggregate to Rushden and Diamonds in the Third Division play-off semi-final. Throughout their history, they only achieved promotion once, in 1969, but in the FA Cup they hit the headlines in 2003. After defeating First Division sides in Preston and Coventry, they reached the Fifth Round before losing narrowly at Wolverhampton 3-1, the second and third Wolves goals in the last twenty minutes both looking suspiciously offside. The tie was shown live on BBC, and Rochdale won many friends and admirers by their approach. This was the second time they had reached the last sixteen, the first being in 1990.

I took Iain for my first visit to the ground on another sweltering hot day. It was soon too hot for us to stand by the wall, so we had to move back under cover of the stand, but despite the heat this game was infinitely better than the Preston match a few days earlier. We all thought that in-dispute striker Andy Watson had decided to play after all, but it was a coloured look-alike called Richard Brown who turned out for the 'Pool.

In the early exchanges Quinn was put clean through but hit the ball against the goalkeepers legs, and co-strikers Ellis and Preece were both just wide with shots. New right back Brown linked up well with the attack, and one fan said he was no good for Blackpool as his passes didn't keep going out of play! This became a standing joke through the years as almost without exception new loan players and signings quickly descended into the Blackpool way of being unable to find a colleague with a pass. Blackpool totally dominated proceedings, with Ellis and Quinn going close again, but we were unable to break the deadlock in the first half. Almost all of the noise had come from the Blackpool fans, who made up around half of the small crowd. It was so hot that the paint on the crush barriers was melting, and we had to take great care to avoid leaning on them and getting covered in a sticky, silvery mess.

At half time, ex-Oldham player Andy Barlow replaced Scott Darton to make his Blackpool debut. Blackpool carried on where they had left off, in total control, going close on several more occasions, before Ellis took the ball in mid-field, advanced to the edge of the box and hit home a glorious shot on fifty-five minutes. Blackpool didn't ease up at all, and from an Ellis cross, Preece's downward header was handled in the box. Ellis took just two steps for the penalty, and hit a woefully weak shot that Gray saved easily. With under twenty minutes remaining, this seemed to lift both the Rochdale team and their supporters, who were chanting for the first time in the entire game, and Blackpool were forced backwards as Rochdale applied some pressure. Even so, Mel Capleton didn't have a shot to save, although Rochdale did have an appeal for a penalty turned down - ex-Blackpool player Deary was booked for protesting this decision, to the delight of the Blackpool fans. Ellis had another typical run at goal and cut inside to let loose a shot which just curled wide before the referee blew the final whistle to signal that Capleton had kept his first clean sheet as a Blackpool player. With Wigan being defeated shortly afterwards at Bloomfield Road, Blackpool clinched a hat trick of victories in the competition.

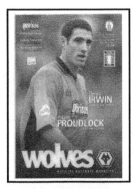

Norwich City (h), Football
League Cup Final 1962

Norwich City (a), Football
League Cup Final 1962

Wolverhampton Wanderers (a),
2003 FA Cup Fifth Round

Rushden and Diamonds (a),
2002 Division 3 Play-Off S/Final

Blackburn Rovers (a), 1961-2
Football League Cup Semi-Final

Notts County (h), FA Cup 2
1949 – Record Crowd 24,231

Rochdale draw ticket

Manchester United (a), 1986 FA
Cup Third Round

Rochdale v Blackpool ticket
from 2000

MORECAMBE F.C.

OFFICIAL MATCH DAY PROGRAMME

PRE-SEASON FOOTBALL AT CHRISTIE PARK

A Warm Welcome to this afternoon's visitors

BLACKPOOL F.C.

who play here today in the

• MARSDEN LANCASHIRE CUP •

Saturday 27th July 1996
Kick-Off 3.00 p.m.

SHRIMPLINE 0891 227319

• £1.00 •

---

74. Morecambe v Blackpool

Played at Christie Park on 27th July 1996

Marsden Lancashire Cup

Morecambe (2)2 [Ceraelo 2]
Blackpool (1)3 [Bradshaw, Quinn, Thorpe]

Attendance 1,692

Blackpool's 1996-97 season began with their annual defence of the Marsden Lancashire Cup, less than four weeks after the final of 'Euro-96' had officially ended the 1995-96 football season. Blackpool were drawn in a group including Morecambe and Rochdale, with the other group comprising Preston, Wigan and Southport, and the opening fixture was at Morecambe.

Despite being a non-league side, Morecambe had achieved Wembley glory with a 1974 FA Trophy Final victory over Dartford by two goals to one. They also had a few successful forays in the FA Cup, twice in the new century reaching the Third Round before succumbing to Ipswich Town. Their biggest disappointment, though, came in 2003, when they lost a penalty shootout to Dagenham in the semi-final of the Conference play-offs, with Dagenham scoring an eighty-ninth minute goal to take the game towards its climactic shoot-out.

On the morning of the game we all went to Stanley Park where my daughter Shelley was competing in the North of England Sprint Triathlon there, and I watched her first event before leaving at about half one with Iain, Craig and Claire for Morecambe. We made good progress until we reached Lancaster, where we were held up for an age through the old city centre, and I said to Iain that we'd no chance of being there in time for the kick-off. No sooner had I said that than the traffic cleared and, more by luck than judgement, I found myself on the right road into Morecambe with the ground just a couple of hundred yards away. There were a large number of Blackpool fans making their way to the game, although there didn't seem to be as many as in the Southport game a couple of years earlier. It was Gary Megson's first match as manager, and we got in the ground just before kick-off. I managed to get a spot right at the front so Craig and Claire could see easily enough. Blackpool wore their new away kit of Blue-and-White stripes with a Tangerine collar.

After twelve minutes of mainly Blackpool pressure, Morecambe split the 'Pool defence for Ceraelo to score past Banks with a low shot into the far corner. Blackpool put more effort into the game now, and an Ellis shot was turned for a corner, Lydiate headed the cross onto the bar, and then Ellis hit the post. Completely against the run of play, Morecambe broke again on twenty-one minutes and Ceraelo scored again. Things just wouldn't go right for Blackpool, and when Preece pulled a cross back which evaded the goalkeeper, Philpott failed to make contact with the ball from five yards out in front of a gaping goal. Just when it seemed that it wasn't going to be our day, Bradshaw hit a speculative thirty-five yard shot which flew into the net with Morecambe's ex-Preston 'keeper rooted to the ground. Two minutes later, Quinn was tripped in the box and he got up to take the penalty himself, but it was a weak affair which the 'keeper blocked. Quinn even failed to put the loose ball home as the 'keeper managed to get in the way of his shot to deflect the ball for a corner. Banks made a good save just before the interval from Morecambe's third shot of the game, and although we were 2-1 behind at the interval, the performance had been reasonable enough.

At the start of the second half, a small group of Morecambe fans came round from the opposite goal to stand in the paddock close to the Blackpool fans. Preece curled a free-kick inches wide of the goal, but everyone's attention now was on the taunting home fans, and it was no surprise when the Blackpool element moved over to confront them. The remainder of the afternoon was filled with hostility, and the police had to move dogs and horses into the ground.

Morecambe missed a near-open goal on the hour as Blackpool struggled to get any flow going at all, but very few people noticed as the action off the pitch was now dominating the afternoon. Morecambe fans continued to taunt Blackpool with chants about Owen Oyston's jail sentence ("Where's your rapist now" to the tune of "Chirpy-chirpy-cheep-cheep"), and the Bradford play-off defeat ("2-0 up and f****d it up" - that chant was going to rebound on them shortly).

Morecambe missed another great chance to seal the game, and they were to rue this miss as with seven minutes to go, new signing Ben Dixon (who had come on as substitute) fed Ellis on the wing. Ellis turned brilliantly to lose his marker and crossed for Quinn to side-foot volley the ball home for the equaliser. With two minutes to go, a Mellon shot took a wicked deflection and wrong-footed the goalkeeper. Substitute Thorpe won the race for the loose ball to turn it into the net for the winning goal. Ellis almost got a fourth in injury time, bringing a good save from the 'keeper, as Morecambe's heads dropped, and Blackpool 'got out of jail' to record a winning start to Gary Megson's reign.

74 Morecambe – Christie Park

Ticket for the Morecambe v Ipswich FA
Cup Third Round tie in 2001, and Craig
and Claire at the Blackpool game

Dartford, 1974 FA Trophy Final

Dagenham & Redbridge (a) 2003 Conference Play-Off s/f

Dagenham & Redbridge (h) 2003 Conference Play-Off s/f

Ipswich Town (a), 2003 FA Cup Third Round

Rotherham United (h), 1979 FA Cup First Round

Hull City (h), FA Cup First Round 1992

75. **Squires Gate** v Tranmere Rovers

Played at **School Road** on 29th July 1996

Friendly Match

Squires Gate (1)3 [Barnes 2, Arnold]
Tranmere Rovers XI (3)3 [Walker 3]

Attendance 80

75 Squires Gate – School Road

The day after the Morecambe game, I was at my mother's reading the local papers, and saw that Squires Gate had arranged a pre-season friendly with a Tranmere Rovers side for the next night. Squires Gate were managed by ex-Rovers player Mark Hughes, and he had arranged the prestigious friendly through his connections with John Aldridge.

Squires Gate were one of three North West Counties teams within a hundred yards of each other at the southern end of Blackpool. Founded in 1948, they hadn't achieved any success of note until the present time, but good days were just around the corner. In the Second Division of the league, they defeated Formby on aggregate in the Division Two Cup semi-final in 1998 to celebrate their fiftieth year by reaching the final at Skelmersdale. Although defeated on the night, they reached the final again in 2001, defeating Bacup Borough 1-0 in another game held at Skelmersdale. In 2002, they attained promotion to the First Division, the high point in their short history. Prior to joining the North West Counties League, they had been runners-up in the West Lancashire League in 1980-81, and Richardson Cup winners in 1986-87.

According to the paper, it was expected that Eric Nixon and million-pound valued striker Ian Moore would be playing for Rovers. I took Iain and Claire to the game, and Eric Nixon was about the first person we saw when we got in. I asked him if he was playing, but he said he was just there to watch tonight. The Tranmere players were mainly youngsters - the only name I recognised was Kenworthy, and he could have been another player of the same name, although some of their squad did go on to become well known in the future.

Rovers began well and were 2-0 up in less than quarter of an hour, as Robbie Walker first of all headed a cross home, then hit a low shot under the diving Gate 'keeper. Squires Gate didn't have a chance until the half hour mark, and that one was hit over the bar from inside the box, but with five minutes of the first half to go Kevin Barnes pulled a goal back with a low shot. We had just walked behind the goal to go and get Nixon's autograph, but when the goal went in he headed back to the changing room before we reached him. Almost immediately, Rovers were two in front again as Walker completed his hat trick with a shot which went in off the post.

Squires Gate competed well after the break, hitting the post with a header ten minutes into the half and then bringing a good save from the visitors' 'keeper. Tranmere responded by putting a header from a corner just over the bar, where it rolled down the netting to land at Iain's feet. We had gone right behind the goal (literally inches away from it) and Iain had said that the best thing about being there was that the ball couldn't hit you!

Just about every Tranmere attack was being pulled up for offside as all their first-half fluency disappeared, and Gate deservedly pulled a goal back when Barnes hit his second from a low shot midway through the half. Kenworthy looked to have made it four for Tranmere with fifteen minutes left, hitting a tremendous shot against the post. The effort looked like it was going straight for us, as we had moved to just alongside the netting, and we instinctively ducked to avoid it - the Squires Gate 'keeper Woodcock turned to me and said (tongue in cheek) "I had it covered". Squires Gate sensed they could still salvage a draw from the game, and almost levelled matters when Paul Arnold met a cross to head the ball across the 'keeper but just over the bar. Two minutes later, Arnold met another header and this time put it into the net for the equaliser. In the last five minutes, Kenworthy had a shot blocked and Tynan tried to work his way through the home defence, but Gate were the side who looked most likely to get the winner. The game finished in a 3-3 draw and it was an excellent night's entertainment.

75 Squires Gate – School Road

Formby (h), 1998 NW Counties
Division Two Cup Semi-Final

East Fife (h), 1999

Bedlington Terriers (h), FA Cup
Second Qualifying Round 2001

Bacup Borough at Skelmersdale,
Second Division Cup Final 2001

Squires Gate v Manchester
United Youth ticket, 2003

Manchester United Under 19's
(h) 2003

First Footing Volume 04
Steve Wilson

First Footing
Volume Four
By: Steve Wilson

Barbara, Claire, Craig and Shelley at Blackpool v Stockport in December 1994

Contents – Volume IV

No.	Date	Match Details	Comp	Crowd
		Season 1996-97		
76	310796	Blackpool Mechanics 0 Blackpool XI (0)1 [Symons]	Frndly	50
77	010896	Blackpool Wren Rovers (1)1 [Baron] Bury XI 0	Frndly	40
78	010197	Shrewsbury Town (0)1 [Ward] Blackpool (3)3 [Preece 2, Mellon]	Div 2	2787
79	180397	Walsall (0)1 [Hodge] Blackpool (0)1 [Clarkson]	Div 2	3459
80	290397	Chesterfield 0 Blackpool 0	Div 2	4974
		Season 1997-98		
81	221197	Freckleton 0 Blackrod Town 0 *{after extra time}*	LAS3	30
82	100198	Lytham St Annes (2)3 [Southern, Parry, Lean] Milnthorpe Corinthians 0	WL2	40
83	240198	Kirkham & Wesham (1)4 [Mendonca 2, Whipp, Hornby penalty] Padiham 0	WL1	40
84	170298	Grimsby Town (0)1 [Burnett] Blackpool 0 *{Northern area semi-final}*	AWS	8027
85	230298	Kirkham and Wesham (0)1 [Mendonca] Alexander Drew 0 *{ Semi-final at Lancashire FA Headquarters, Leyland }*	LAS	200
86	140398	Northampton Town (1)2 [Freestone, Heggs] Blackpool 0	Div 2	6586
87	090498	Squires Gate 0 Tetley Walker (2)3 [Dack 2, Tandy] *{Final at Skelmersdale United F.C.}*	NWC2 Cup	300
		Season 1998-99		
88	180898	Scunthorpe United (1)1 [Forrester] Blackpool (1)1 [Bent]	WC1	2211
89	260998	Stoke City (0)1 [Crowe penalty] Blackpool (2)3 [Carlisle, Aldridge 2]	Div 2	15002
90	281298	Macclesfield Town 0 Blackpool (0)1 [Howarth own goal]	Div 2	3919
91	130299	Chester City (1)1 [Murphy] Peterborough United 0	Div 3	2087
92	270299	Halifax Town 0 Hull City (0)1 [Brown]	Div 3	4455
93	200399	Rotherham United (0)2 [Whelan, Thompson penalty] Peterborough United (2) 2 [Grazioli, Davies]	Div 3	3979
94	270399	Lancaster City 0 Gainsborough Trinity (0)1 [Price]	UniPr	205
95	050499	Scarborough (1)3 [Tate 3] Carlisle United 0	Div 3	3604
96	080499	Fleetwood Freeport (1)2 [Johnstone penalty, Maindes] Warrington Town (0)1 [Whitehead] *{Final at Darwen FC}*	NWC2 Cup	350
97	010599	Port Vale (1)2 [Gardner, Griffiths] Queens Park Rangers 0	Div 1	9851
		Season 1999-2000		
98	140899	Darlington (0)3 [Gabbiadini, Duffield] Macclesfield Town 0	Div 3	5117
99	170899	Ayr United (0)2 [Reynolds, Bone] Hamilton Academical (0)1 [D Henderson]	CIS2	1789
100	110999	Queen of the South 0 Stenhousemuir (1)3 [Hamilton, Graham 2]	SDiv2	928

North West Counties Football League
Division Two

Blackpool Mechanics Football Club

‥v‥

BLACKPOOL FC
Pre-Season Friendly
Wednesday 31st July 1996
Kick Off 7-30pm

Official Match Programme 50p

Main Sponsor 1996-97:
AZTEC TRAVEL
Match Programme Sponsor 1996-97:
MECHANICS CLUB SHOP

---

76. Blackpool Mechanics v Blackpool

Played at Marton Stadium on 31st July 1996

Friendly Match

Blackpool Mechanics 0
Blackpool (0)1 [Symons]

Attendance 50

4

In another couple of nights it was a visit to Blackpool Mechanics for their friendly against a Blackpool XI, and both Iain and Craig came with me to this game. I was already a regular visitor to the ground, for Blackpool Gladiators Rugby League club played their matches at the same venue. Mechanics were the second of the three close North West Counties clubs, currently undergoing a transitional period that saw them rooted to the bottom of the Second Division. They did have a bright future in prospect, though, with their youth side defeating Accrington to win the Lancashire Youth Cup in 1998, and they had previously won the West Lancashire League title and Richardson Cup double in both 1960-61 and 1961-62.

We arrived at the ground at ten to seven, as it was advertised as a 7 p.m. kick-off, but the game didn't actually start until twenty past seven for some reason. Blackpool's side contained Andy Watson and Craig Allardyce from the brink of the first team, plus Austrian trialist Eric Orie, who had done well for the first team in an earlier friendly outing against Grimsby. Mechanics included Kevin Barnes, two-goal hero for Squires Gate two nights earlier, and later to play for Fleetwood, Lancaster City and then Blackpool themselves. I worked with Kevin's brother, Steve, and always kept a close eye on his career, which culminated in an appearance for Blackpool at Fulham, managed by the England manager Kevin Keegan.

In the early exchanges, Blackpool's Carden rounded the Mechanics' keeper but hit the outside of the post, and Watson laid the ball off for Allardyce to hit the top of the bar. Mechanics themselves came close to scoring twice before the break when Heighton saved a low shot and a header from a corner beat Heighton but also cleared the bar by inches. I'd spent the first half talking with Rob Frowen (who was mockingly chanting "In the net" every time Blackpool got a corner), but he left with his daughter Hannah at half time - in truth, they didn't miss much of a spectacle.

The second half was also fairly devoid of excitement, but Blackpool took the lead when they were awarded a rather fortunate penalty for a defender handling the ball after a corner had been crossed in. Symons scored from the spot with some ease. Gardner brought out a good save from Mechanics 'keeper Baldwin, but the game was still fairly ordinary in the strong, cool wind. Allardyce ought to have made it 2-0, but his low shot was weak and a defender managed to clear the ball off the line. Blackpool were struggling against the North West Counties League team, although they still had most of the chances, with Carden blasting one well over the bar, then just failing to get his foot to a low cross. Symons was put clear after a rare good move in mid-field but he only managed to put the ball into the side netting, and he then missed an easy chance when in an offside position. In the last minute, Allardyce put a header wide to bring to an end to a rather unsatisfactory game.

Blackpool Gladiators v Workington Town, first Rugby League match at Marton Stadium 1992

Bacup Borough (h), Floodlit Trophy 1994

Accrington Stanley (h), Lancashire Floodlit Youth League Final 1998

77. Blackpool Wren Rovers v Bury

Played at **Brew's Park** 1st August 1996

Friendly Match

Blackpool Wren Rovers (1)1 [D. Baron]
Bury 0

Attendance 40

No programmes issued for this game

77 Blackpool Wren Rovers – Brew's Park

I completed my visits to see all three local North West Counties League sides by going to a third friendly, between Blackpool Wren Rovers and a Bury XI.

Blackpool Rovers played on a ground adjoining that of Squires Gate. Whereas Gate and Mechanics were in the Second Division of the North West Counties League, Rovers were one of the leading sides in the First Division, making appearances in the FA Vase and FA Trophy and having ambitions of gaining promotion to the Unibond Northern Premier League. Prior to their elevation to the North West Counties League, they had twice won the Lancashire Amateur Shield, in 1969 and 1971, had been crowned West Lancashire League Champions in 1969-70 and 1970-71, and had won the Richardson Cup in 1970-71 and 1971-72.

And yet their manager, Brian Wilson, was fully aware of the fact that it made no sense to have three sides in such a short proximity in the same league. He recommended that the clubs should merge, but fell foul of the self-interest that meant each club wanted to retain its own individuality. It was ironic, therefore, that when Wilson left to become manager at Fleetwood, most of the Rovers players went with him and the club had to resign from the league, joining instead the Third Division of the league below, the West Lancashire League.

At the game, I was a little surprised when there was no admission charge, although a club representative did come round with a bucket taking a collection to pay for the officials' expenses. There was also no programme, as "Bury didn't send us details of who was in their team" - Squires Gate's programme for the Tranmere game had showed "to be announced" under the Tranmere side, and the issue was a complete sell-out. Rovers had produced a programme for their friendly against a Blackpool XI a week earlier, and that did refer to the Bury match, but that was the only documentation to hand for this match.

It was another cold and windy evening, and Iain was the only one who wanted to come with me to this game. 'Next door', Squires Gate were playing a friendly against Poulton, and we looked over the wall on a couple of occasions - there was a 'crowd' there in single figures. When our game began, Wren took the lead in the first minute with a shot from Dave Baron that was too powerful for Bury 'keeper Phillips. It should have been 2-0 on eight minutes, but Nolan hit the ball wide when in a good position in the box, and soon after Walsh volleyed over from a right wing cross when in the area. Wren were well in control as the game continued, although it did get a bit patchy towards half-time. I asked one of the Bury officials for their team, although I had managed to 'guess' most of them as their coach spent the entire game shouting 'instructions' to his players - and leaving them in a position where they were too frightened to use their own initiative during the play.

The second half continued with Wren well on top, substitute Dave Windridge doing particularly well, along with Walsh. It was on the hour before Bury managed their first shot of the half, but Watson's effort was well over the bar. Bury did raise the tempo for a short period, but it was soon back to Wren pressure and Windridge was on the end of a move to almost force home a second, the ball being turned behind for a corner. Nolan was playing well, but his finishing from good positions was letting him down. The tackling from Wren was particularly strong, and the Bury lads were finding it difficult to deal with. With twenty minutes remaining, Forrest was just over with a shot on the turn for Bury, and Swales was also just wide with a twenty yard effort, but Wren still came closest to scoring, forcing a good save from the visiting goalkeeper. It had been a very impressive performance from the Blackpool side.

After having watched all three local sides in a few days, I reflected on their differences. It was strange that the 'lowest' placed of the three, Squires Gate, were involved in the best game, with the largest crowd, and the most informative tannoy, giving details of each goal-scorer and the time of the goal. In contrast, the highest of the three, Blackpool Wren Rovers, attracted the lowest crowd and had no tannoy announcements whatsoever.

8

Left - Burscough (h), FA Vase 1997

Blackpool (h), 1983 – ticket (above) and programme (right)

78. **Shrewsbury Town** v Blackpool

Played at **Gay Meadow** on 1ˢᵗ January 1997

Football League Division Two

Shrewsbury Town (0)1 [Ward]
Blackpool (3)3 [Preece 2, Mellon]

Attendance 2,787

The snow around Christmas caused the postponement of Blackpool's trip to Walsall, which I was planning to take Iain and Craig to, and seemed likely to put paid to my first trip to Shrewsbury on New Year's Day. However, a morning pitch inspection left it as the only Second Division fixture to take place.

Shrewsbury were one of those sides bordering Wales who achieved more success in the Welsh Cup than they did in their native England. Before the war, they had Welsh Cup victories in 1891 and 1938, following those with four more victories in 1977, 1979, 1984 and 1985. They reached Wembley in the 1996 Auto Windscreen Shield competition, only to lose 2-1 to Rotherham, the same side who defeated them in the semi-final of the inaugural League Cup competition in 1961. They reached the FA Cup quarterfinals twice in three seasons, in 1979 and 1982, and the 2002-2003 season saw them defeat Everton in the Third Round of the FA Cup, yet four months later they were relegated to the Conference. It only took them a year to return to the league, though, after defeating Aldershot on penalties in the Conference play-off final.

The journey down to Shrewsbury was fine until I left the motorway, when it was a little tricky manoeuvring some of the snow-covered roads, but all in all the driving conditions were acceptable. We arrived ninety minutes before kick-off, and lunched in one of the cafés recommended in the 'Football Fans Guide' before entering our end. The pitch was covered in snow, and it seemed surprising to me that the game was going ahead. Shrewsbury were kicking in at our end, and their greying 'keeper Edwards was having a joke with the Blackpool fans, who pelted him with snowballs at every opportunity. Because of the snow-covered pitch, the referee brought an orange ball on in stead of the normal white one, and this delighted the Blackpool fans, whose chants of 'Tangerine Ball, Tangerine Ball, Tangerine Ball' seemed to indicate some initiative had passed to us through this choice of colour.

Blackpool started with a very attacking formation, with Philpott, Quinn, Preece and Ellis all going forwards. They soon made inroads into the home defence, and it was no surprise after eight minutes when Preece found space on the left-hand side of the box and cut in to drive the ball low into the net. Shortly afterwards, he was free again on the left but his cross to the unmarked Ellis was too low, then he hit a shot over the bar, before Philpott again found room down the left to cross to Quinn at the far post. With the entire goal at his mercy, Quinn headed straight at Edwards. Blackpool continued pushing forwards, and after twenty-eight minutes, Ellis found space on the left and pulled the ball back for Preece to score the second. Just before half time, Preece again made inroads on the left, pulled the ball back for Quinn, and he turned it to Mellon. Mellon's shot seemed weak, but it bobbled over the diving Edwards' arm and we were 3-0 ahead at the break.

The second half saw us in even more dominant form, with Quinn fluffing a chance to make it 4-0. Ward pulled a goal back for Shrewsbury with a quarter of an hour to go, but this just prompted Blackpool to take even more control, and but for some poor finishing, a much larger win would have resulted. Brabin missed the best chance, side footing the ball wide of the post when he had been put clear, and Preece almost got a hat trick with a shot that landed on the roof of the net. Quinn too was just over with one shot as we recorded our first away win in four months. At the back, Blackpool were very solid, with Tony Butler in outstanding form.

We came home via the motorway, as I didn't relish the thought of driving back through the icy unlit country roads now that it was dark, and even though it made for a longer journey, it was a safer one. The weather was still causing problems all over the country, and Blackpool suffered with the re-arranged game at Walsall being called off once again on the Friday morning.

Aldershot Town, Conference Play-Off Final 2004

Lovells Athletic, Welsh Cup
Final 1948

Cardiff City (a), Welsh Cup
Final 1977

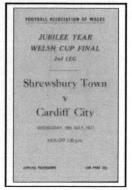

Cardiff City (h), Welsh Cup
Final 1977

Wrexham (a), Welsh Cup Final
1979

Crewe (a) 1951 – First League
Season

Newport (a), Welsh Cup Final
1980

Newport (h), Welsh Cup Final 1980

Rotherham (h), Football League
Cup Semi-Final 1961

Wolverhampton (a), FA Cup quarterfinal, 1979

Leicester City (a), FA Cup quarterfinal, 1982

Everton (h), FA Cup Third Round 2003

Shrewsbury v Arsenal ticket, FA Cup Fifth Round, 1991

Spartak (h), 1964

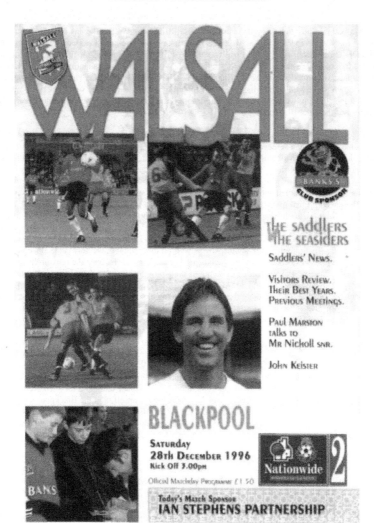

79. **Walsall** v Blackpool

Played at **The Bescot Stadium** on 18th March 1997

Football League Division Two

Walsall (0)1 [Hodge]
Blackpool (0)1 [Clarkson]

Attendance 3,459

Blackpool's thrice-postponed league match at Walsall finally took place the day after Iain's sixteenth birthday in March, and I finished work early to take both Iain and Craig on the Tango Junior Supporters Club coach. All I had to pay was the cost of the coach seats, for the match tickets were included free of charge as part of a reciprocal agreement between the two supporters' clubs. The coach was equipped with a video and we watched Blackpool's 4-0 1995-96-season victory over Swansea on the way down to the Midlands, which meant that the journey seemed to take very little time. When we arrived at the stadium, we went into the family room prior to kick-off, before going into the ground to sit with all of the other Blackpool fans.

Walsall were one of the first sides to move from their old ground to a modern more-accessible stadium. Once in the Bescot, they achieved success on the big stage by being the second side to gain promotion via the play-offs at the Millennium Stadium, defeating Reading 3-2 at Cardiff the day after Blackpool had disposed of Leyton Orient.

Their new ground was small and the away end had a low roof which generated an incredible amount of noise - there weren't that many Blackpool fans at the game but the noise level was exceptional. Most of the singing referred to the previous Saturday's home defeat of Preston, when recent signing Phil Clarkson scored both the goals in the 2-1 victory.

The first twenty-five minutes of the game saw us well on top, although we only came close to scoring once when a cross was headed over the goalkeeper but just cleared the bar. The remainder of the half became fairly scrappy, and Walsall failed to put us under any pressure at all until first-half injury time, when a high ball hung in the wind and was headed against the inside of the post with Banks beaten. Fortunately for us, the ball ran along the line before being cleared for a corner. The corner also posed problems, with Banks having to stretch to palm the ball behind for a second corner, and in the remaining moments of the half we were put under some intense aerial pressure by Walsall's tall attack.

During half-time there was a penalty shoot-out between the Junior Seasiders and Walsall's Junior Saddlers. Craig and Iain had declined the chance of taking part in this, but most of the rest of the people taking the kicks for Blackpool were those we knew. Walsall had a goalkeeper called 'Sumo', who was rather overweight, but he played very well and after eight kicks had been taken Blackpool still hadn't scored. The last six Blackpool supporters, though, were older ones, and they scored to give our side a 6-4 win. The final Walsall penalty was taken by Sumo himself, and the Blackpool fans chanted 'Sumo, Sumo' as he ran upfield to take it - and miss! The Blackpool fans were chanting '6-4 to the Seasiders' as the thirty young supporters did a lap of honour around the pitch to great applause after an entertaining few minutes, and Sumo received a special cheer as he came down to our end.

Shortly after the second half had begun, there was a huge roar from the previously silent home fans as news came through that Stoke had taken the lead against their rivals Wolves. They were silenced again almost immediately, though, as Marvin Bryan broke down the wing, reached the by-line and cut the ball back for Clarkson to score with a shot into the top-left of the net. In the celebrations following the goal, I got knocked over onto Craig and my glasses flew off, but luckily Iain was on hand to catch them. Walsall's response saw Banks make a fine save from Kevin Wilson's shot, and then the home side wasted a good chance when Wilson shot wide, but generally they weren't causing us too many problems as they persisted in putting high balls into the Blackpool penalty area. This all changed, though, mid-way through the half when Walsall played their first football of the game, taking the ball from their own penalty area and cutting through the Blackpool defence. It left Blackpool's Tony Butler with no option but to pull down Walsall striker Martin Butler - and left the referee with no option but to send *our* Butler off.

The situation had now changed totally, and after Banks had made yet another brilliant save from the free-kick, Walsall put us under an aerial bombardment for the remainder of the game and we were reduced to clearing the ball anywhere. It seemed like it was going to be our day, for when Banks could only parry a shot to Walsall's Butler, the shot was ballooned over the bar with the net inviting. Most of the Walsall fans were on their way out, and the Blackpool fans were in tremendous voice, when in the *fourth* minute of injury time Walsall equalised. Hodge ran thirty yards at the retreating Blackpool defence and put in a low shot that even Banks couldn't save to give the home side a draw that they probably deserved on reflection - although it was a sickening blow at the time.

Our coach journey home was somewhat muted after this, and we were almost silent as we watched the film 'Phenomenon' with John Travolta - or at least most of it, as we arrived back in Blackpool just as it was coming to its climax! It was a few years later before I finally saw the end!

| Reading, Second Division Play-Off Final 2001 | Insert for the Blackpool game | Sheffield United (a), FA Cup Fifth Round 2003 |

| Walsall v Blackpool ticket from 1991 | Aston Villa (h), opening of Bescot Stadium 1993 | Walsall draw ticket |

CHESTERFIELD

CHESTERFIELD F.C.   Official Matchday Magazine

BLACKPOOL FC

SATURDAY 29th MARCH 1997   KICK OFF 3.00pm   £1.50

80. Chesterfield v Blackpool

Played at **Saltergate** on 29th March 1997

Football League Division Two

Chesterfield 0
Blackpool 0

Attendance 4,974

19

On Easter Saturday, Iain and I caught the 'Tango' coach once again for the away match at Chesterfield. As we entered the Derbyshire town, we saw the famous crooked spire at the St Mary's and All Saints church, before we went to a playing field where the young Blackpool fans played football against their counterparts from Chesterfield for an hour or so. We passed shop windows on the way that were bedecked in Chesterfield blue as the town prepared for their forthcoming FA Cup semi-final against Middlesbrough at Old Trafford. Blackpool were without Jim Quinn, who was once again on World Cup International duty for Northern Ireland.

There was a little confusion when we arrived at the ground, as it seemed that only the children had been allocated free match tickets, but the Tango officials soon sorted it all out so that we were all together. We sat in a small section of the main stand that was reserved for visiting supporters, and the roof helped to generate quite a good atmosphere. In contrast, the main Blackpool contingent were stood on the open terracing, where practically no sound at all carried as far as the pitch. Huddersfield's ex-Blackpool defender Andy Morrison was sat on our row with his son, keeping in touch with his old team and chatting with the supporters. The strong wind made control difficult, and the ball seemed to be over-inflated as it bounced up and over players throughout the game, which didn't help in producing flowing football.

Despite this, Blackpool began very brightly, and put on almost all of the pressure during the first half. Mellon had a shot from outside the box that thudded into goalkeeper Mercer's midriff, and Preece ran to meet a cross but put his header wide. That miss was unfortunate as far as I was concerned, as I had picked his number out on the coach and if he had scored the first goal I would have won £5! Clarkson, who seemed to be able to find more time on the ball than the rest of the players, was just over with an overhead kick and Ellis was even closer with a powerful header that just cleared the bar. Not long after this, Ellis turned in the box and hooked a ball over his shoulder that beat Mercer, but unfortunately it beat his right hand post as well. Chesterfield were tending to play high balls in to their tall coloured striker Morris, but Butler and Linighan dealt comfortably with everything that was put their way, and with Bryan also performing well both in defence and attack, we remained the better and more positive side throughout the half.

During the half-time break, many of the Chesterfield supporters who had been behind the far goal moved round the ground to the terracing next to the Blackpool section, as their team would be attacking that end in the forthcoming forty-five minutes. Rather than watch the game, the two sets of fans spent a considerable time hurling abuse at one another.

At the start of the second half, Barlow blasted a shot that flew inches wide of the right hand post, although the game tended now to become a little dull. Chesterfield had their first real chance after around an hour, when Banks had to save with his feet from a close-range downward header following a corner, and seconds later he had to be out quickly to dive at Morris' feet as the striker chased a through ball. Action soon returned to the opposite penalty area where Ellis once again turned in the box and sent a typical cross-shot just past the top right angle. Little was seen of Chesterfield's 'wonder' striker Kevin Davies or old-stager Beaumont, and the mood of the game was clear for all to see as the Blackpool fans called on Gary Megson to bring on new signing Brett Ormerod as "we need to win this game". Ormerod had been signed from non-league Accrington Stanley, and Megson eventually brought him on for the disappointing Darton for the closing ten minutes. He had barely been on the pitch before Ellis had another shot in the box, and this one was goal-bound until a defender rather fortuitously stuck out his foot backwards to deflect it away from goal. Ormerod showed a nice turn of pace, but once he had beaten his defender he stumbled on the ball as perhaps nerves got the better of him. Ellis turned once more in the box, but this time his shot went over, and it was clearly not going to be his day. It took a low shot by Hewitt, well held by Banks, to register Chesterfield's first shot on goal, and that came in the dying moments of this rather disappointing game, and soon afterwards the referee blew his whistle to severely disrupt the play-off hopes of both sides.

Chesterfield went on to give Middlesbrough the fright of their lives in the semi-final, with only a controversial disallowed goal when a shot hit the bar and clearly crossed the line preventing the Spireites from winning. The game was eventually drawn 3-3, but Middlesbrough ensured that there was to be no fairytale ending by winning the replay. Any sympathy that Chesterfield might have had evaporated in 2001 when they effectively bought promotion from the Third Division by making illegal payments to their playing staff. They had previously made two Wembley appearances in the play-offs, losing to Cambridge in 1990 and defeating Bury in 1995. Their best League Cup performance saw them reach the Fourth Round in 1965, losing 4-1 at Northampton, and they won the Anglo-Scottish Cup in 1981, beating Notts County in the final.

Middlesbrough, FA Cup Semi-Final 1997

Middlesbrough, FA Cup Semi-Final replay 1997

Bury, Division Three Play-Off Final, 1995

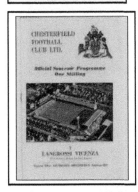

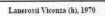

Lanerossi Vicenza (h), 1970

Notts County (h), Anglo-Scottish Final 1981

Notts County (a), Anglo-Scottish Final 1981

Chesterfield v Blackpool ticket from 1997

FRECKLETON
FOOTBALL CLUB

Hodgson Memorial Ground
Bush Lane
Freckleton
Lancashire

Founded 1904-5

SGL CARS
**West Lancashire Football League
Division One**

FRECKLETON Versus BLACKROD TOWN
Hollands Lancashire Amateur Shield 3rd Round
Saturday 22nd November 1997
Kick Off 1-30pm

---

81. Freckleton v Blackrod Town

Played at **Bush Lane** on 22nd November 1997

Lancashire Amateur Shield Round Three

Freckleton 0
Blackrod Town 0

Attendance 30

81 Freckleton – Bush Lane

Having lived in Freckleton for twenty years, I had still never been to see their side play, so I decided to include the three local West Lancashire League sides (Freckleton, Kirkham & Wesham and Lytham St Annes) in my 'to visit' list. It was towards the end of November when I was able to go and see my first game involving Freckleton. I had checked the fixtures on the Saturday morning at the library, and found that they were playing Blackrod Town of their division in the Lancashire Amateur Shield Third Round, with a 1:30 kick-off, to allow for the possibility of extra-time as there were no floodlights at the ground. In fact, it could barely be called a ground, being just a pitch on the local backfields.

Freckleton's glory years came two decades earlier, when they achieved a hat trick of West Lancashire League titles between 1979-80 and 1981-82. They also won the Richardson Cup in 1979-80, and were West Lancashire league Challenge Cup winners in 1980-81.

Barbara took Iain and Craig into Blackpool to go to the Seasiders game against York City, and she was then going shopping with Shelley, so I took Claire along with me for the local match. When we arrived, one of the first things I noticed was that there was a girl selling programmes, which was a big surprise to me. Apparently, this was the first **ever** match in their ninety-year history in which Freckleton had produced a programme, so I had chosen the perfect day to make my 'debut'. Unfortunately, the programme didn't appear to have **any** of the players in the shirt numbers that they actually wore on the afternoon, mainly because Freckleton had over half of the side cry off at the last minute, but the intentions were still admirable. The only player I knew was Iain's school colleague Kevin Whitsey, down in the programme at number 3 but wearing the number 5 shirt, and I listened to the shouts from the side to decipher the Christian names of most of the rest of the players.

The game began in bright sunshine, in front of around fifteen spectators (one or two of them having come with the visitors), and Blackrod tended to control the play during the opening half-hour. Even so, the best chances fell to Freckleton with number ten (Ian) hitting a shot which beat the Blackrod goalkeeper and thumped into the side netting, and Bobby Donaldson just wide of the post with a good, low shot. The last fifteen minutes of the half saw Freck on top, and Donaldson had an injury time chance to open the scoring, but his close range header just went past the post. Kevin Whitsey, who I had initially thought would be out of his depth amongst so many older players, had impressed me. At half time, Claire and I went into the Sports Centre – the first time I had been inside there, too, despite living in the village for all of that time.

When the second half began, Blackrod's Andy Morris went close on a couple of occasions and he was generally proving a handful for the Freckleton defence. He was put through again, but this time Todhunter made an excellent low save, as Blackrod began to dominate the match. Whitsey was gradually becoming more and more influential, but a lot of the Freck attacks were floundering when the ball reached the lanky number 10, Ian. Apparently, he had replaced the club's leading goalscorer after approaching Freckleton to say he wanted to join them from Darwen. Although undoubtedly a skilful player, he was far too greedy, never better illustrated than when he tried (and failed) to beat three Blackrod defenders in the penalty area with Whitsey screaming for the ball and totally unmarked only five yards away. Donaldson also wasted another chance to give Freckleton the lead and at ninety minutes the game was still awaiting its first goal. For Town, fullback Elliot Simm was fortunate to stay on the field after one horrendous challenge on Kevin Whitsey.

During extra time, Claire went into the Sports Centre as she was tired and cold outside. The first period saw the stalemate continuing, but the last fifteen minutes provided several scoring opportunities in front of a crowd that had now doubled to around thirty spectators. Donaldson had a shot for Freck from the edge of the box, but although in the middle of the area he still managed to screw his shot so wide it went for a Blackrod throw. Freckleton began to get on top once more, and Ian headed forward a good ball down the wing, beat his defender and brought a brave save from the visiting goalkeeper's legs.

Town thought that they had scored five minutes from time, when an *indirect* free kick was allowed to go *directly* into the net by the alert Todhunter. In the last seconds of the game, Ian had a final chance to seal the game when the ball reached him on the edge of the box, but the visitors' goalkeeper blocked his shot. It's just as well, really, for the linesman had flagged for offside and the goal wouldn't have counted. This linesman had been involved in controversy throughout the afternoon, having stepped in after one of the officials failed to show. He was with the Blackrod team, and was blatantly biased towards his side. He had spent most of the game shouting instructions and encouragement to his players, and the referee never once spoke to him about it, yet whenever he overruled the referee (to give a decision in Blackrod's favour) the referee *always* took his word as being correct. Frank Towers, who was involved with the Freckleton side, had a row with the linesman over this latest offside, for the 'official' said that the Freck player was level with the last defender – and that is **not** offside under the current regulations. To show how sporting Blackrod were, one of their players shouted at the linesman "Go and tell him to f**k off".

Thankfully, the final whistle blew seconds later to defuse any tensions, and to take a thoroughly entertaining match to a replay (which was won by Blackrod). As we left the field, the players were already in the process of taking the goal nets down, and barely a minute after the final whistle, the posts had gone as well to leave anybody walking past unaware that a match had taken place that afternoon.

Although always in the shadow of near-neighbours Kirkham, Freckleton had their own success in 2004 when they defeated Blackrod 4-1 in the Richardson Cup Semi-Final to set up a Final against Charnock Richard. Although they were defeated after extra-time in the final at Leyland, they also had a good run in the league, only just missing out on the runners-up position to runaway-champions Kirkham.

Kirkham (h), 2001, West Lancashire League
Division One

Poster for the Richardson Cup Final – no
programmes were printed for the game

82. **Lytham St Annes** v Milnthorpe Corinthians

Played at **Church Road** on 10th January 1998

West Lancashire League Division Two

Lytham St Annes (2)3 [Southern, Parry, Lean]
Milnthorpe Corinthians 0

Attendance 40

It was very wet as 1998 began, and football matches were postponed all over the country. I was hoping to make my first trip to see Lytham St Annes play in the second week in January, but further heavy rain during the week meant that all local games were in doubt for the weekend. However, a dry Friday and Saturday rekindled hopes of the games taking place. I set off with Craig, with the intention of going to watch Blackpool Mechanics play Skelmersdale if the game was off, but when we arrived at Church Road the pitch was perfectly playable. In fact, when I checked the results that evening, I found that all of the local games were played as the fears about the weather proved to be incorrect.

Lytham had limited success in the West Lancashire League, finishing runners-up in 1972-73 and winning the Second Division in 1966-67 (when they were also Presidents' Cup finalists) and 2004-05. At the end of this latter promotion season, by which time home games had been moved to the YMCA grounds at Mythop Road, the club surrendered their identity as they merged with Blackpool Mechanics of the North West Counties League

It was a very mild January afternoon, with temperatures the highest that had ever been recorded during the month. The attendance at the kick-off was a miserly twelve, but by the time the game finished some forty locals were watching the play. I checked with the manager, and the two players I had heard of (goalkeeper John Crystal, featured in the Gazette the day before, and Paul Parry, a noted goalscorer) were playing – I never thought to ask if there was a team-sheet of any description.

After early Milnthorpe pressure, Lytham took the lead with their first attack. From a corner, the goalkeeper got down well to save the first shot, but full back Mickey Southern lashed the loose ball into the net via a defender. I leant over to catch the name of the scorer from the manager, who was dictating his own match report into a small tape recorder, and I heard him shout to his assistant to 'get the programmes'. The next thing I knew they brought out some excellent match programmes, which cost "as much as I wanted to give for one", so I bought two for £1. The only criticism I could make of them was that they hadn't managed to get any details of the opposition players. Milnthorpe came close to equalising when a great shot from the edge of the box by their number 2 was superbly tipped over by Crystal. Shortly afterwards, when their number 11 hit another goalbound shot, Crystal again leapt to tip the ball on to the bar and over, although a goal kick was awarded in this case. Lytham were barely in the match as an attacking force, yet two minutes from half-time (and from only their third real attack of the game) Lean put in a cross which went behind a defender for Parry to slide home the second goal.

Milnthorpe forced the pace throughout most of the second half, without being able to make their chances tell. Their number seven hit a shot just wide, and number eight hit the outside of the post. In a rare Lytham attack, Parry tried a long-range shot that went over. Lytham could have had a third when two Milnthorpe players went for the same ball and clashed heads, the ball falling to Lytham's left-winger in the box, but the referee immediately blew for attention to the players, apologising profusely to the Lytham player for stopping the game. The winger then gave Parry a clear chance in the box, which the striker failed to control, as at last Lytham began to look an attacking force. Even so, most of the chances were at the other end, with one being flicked over the goalkeeper but just clearing the goal.

Seven minutes from time, Parry picked up a loose ball and played a beautiful reverse ball for Lean to slide home number three. Milnthorpe wilted somewhat now, and most of the play was at our end, but even so, Milnthorpe should have scored when a ball flashed across goal, just eluding the lunging player at the far post. The referee added six minutes of injury time on, and in that period Parry put a shot wide, Southern hit a free kick just wide and Parry hit a great shot on the turn against the bar, before lofting a further chance over. Any further goals, though, would have been cruel on Milnthorpe, who could certainly count themselves unlucky to lose the game 3-0.

Kirkham and Wesham Football Club

Coronation Road, Kirkham

Versus Padiham F.C.

West Lancashire League Division One

Saturday January 24th 1998, Kick-Off 2:15 p.m.

Sponsors: Hen House Wholesale Poultry

West Lancashire League Division One

---

83. Kirkham and Wesham v Padiham

Played at Coronation Road on 24th January 1998

West Lancashire League Division One

Kirkham and Wesham (1)4 [Mendonca 2, Whipp, Hornby penalty]
Padiham 0

Attendance 40

No programmes were issued for this game

83 Kirkham and Wesham – Coronation Road

I broke new ground yet again a fortnight later, when I took Craig with me to see Kirkham and Wesham play Padiham in the West Lancashire League First Division. Kirkham were having an excellent season, for as well as being Semi-Finalists in the Lancashire Amateur Shield they were on a good league run that had taken them to within four points of the league leadership. They finished as runners-up in the Shield at the end of the season, but subsequent years saw them dominate the West Lancashire League, as well as lifting the Shield trophy on a couple of occasions. The 2003-2004 season was an especially good one for the club, as they were undefeated league champions and Shield winners. To illustrate their domination, they finished as West Lancashire League Champions five times between 1999-2000 and 2004-05, 2002-03 being the only season they missed out on the title. In addition, they lifted a hat trick of Richardson Cups in 1998-99, 1999-2000 and 2000-01. All that they now required was a move to a better ground, for then they would be able to attain promotion to the North West Counties League.

I suppose in some respects this *wasn't* a new ground for me, as it was played at Coronation Road, where Iain used to play his home games for Kirkham Juniors years earlier, but this counted as the first 'official' game I had been to at the venue. I had hoped that programmes would be on sale, especially as Lytham seemed to produce them on a regular basis and they were a division below Kirkham, but I asked and was told that Kirkham never produced them. I later found out that a couple *had* been produced in the past, but only in very special circumstances.

Padiham took to the field wearing Newcastle United jerseys, complete with the Newcastle badge, and Kirkham included in their side at least two ex-Blackpool players. One was the ever-popular Colin Methven, who was nearing the end of his career, and at the other end of the scale winger Chris Best, who had been one of the YTS lads who helped out at the Tango five-a-side tournament that Craig played in two years earlier.

Kirkham took just six minutes to take the lead, the goal coming as a result of an appalling goal kick by the Padiham goalkeeper. The ball went straight to Best on the right, and the tall Mendonca turned in his cross to the far post. Wallace spectacularly volleyed another chance just over mid-way through the half, but overall Padiham had most of the pressure without ever really looking likely to score. Towards half time, Craig began to lose interest a little and took to trying out the 'trim trail' instead of watching the game.

Six minutes into the second half, the game was effectively all over as Kirkham scored their second goal. It came from a corner on the right, with Whipp's kick going directly into goal as it eluded both Best's diving header and the goalkeeper's attempt to keep the ball out of the net. The goal followed another Whipp corner that had just been scrambled behind, and later in the half he swung in another flag kick that the 'keeper had to desperately clutch on the line to prevent another goal. Best and Mendonca linked up well to give Best a glorious chance to put Kirkham 3-0 ahead, but the ex-Blackpool player put his shot wide of a gaping goal.

Padiham were showing signs of losing their self-control, and their young inside forward spoke back to the referee once too often after being fouled and was yellow carded. The youngster kept his head to put in a goal-bound shot that Kirkham's goalkeeper Atkinson just managed to tip for a corner, but despite Padiham's continued territorial advantage, Kirkham were now growing in confidence. When Hornby was crudely barged over in the penalty area as he easily eluded his defender, the referee pointed to the spot, and after a few moments delay while Hornby received treatment, the player got up to sweetly stroke the third goal into the corner of the net.

Five minutes later, it should have been 4-0 as Best was hacked down in the box, but on this occasion the referee waved play on. Padiham were struggling to keep their tempers, and the character of their side was demonstrated as one of their player's dummied Mendonca into making a challenge, and yelled 'sucker' at him – hardly the approach you would expect from a professional, but apparently what was the norm at this level. It didn't take long, though, for one of the crowd to 'remind' the Padiham defender of who were leading 3-0! After the referee had awarded another free kick to Kirkham, and had to call yet another visiting player over while he had words with him, one of the offending Padiham defenders shouted at the official "Get on with it". The referee immediately replied, "I'd love to" – leaving no doubt in anybody's mind as to who was responsible for the delay in play. One of the advantages of watching games at this level was that you were much more aware of the backchat and humour that goes on in a game between players and officials.

Kirkham's centre half Dave Haydock had a free kick tipped round for a corner, before the goal of the game arrived seven minutes from time. Substitute Adam Procter flicked the ball through to Mendonca, and the forward didn't need to alter his stride as he volleyed the ball gloriously into the roof of the net. The only disappointing aspect was that Craig missed the goal as he had just turned away from the pitch! Mendonca was nearly through to complete his hat-trick minutes later, only to see the referee ignore what seemed to be another blatant foul as he advanced on goal, but at 4-0 there were no complaints from players or supporters over the way the game had gone.

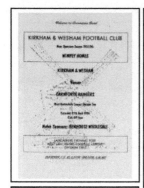

Carnforth Rangers (h), West Lancashire League Division Two, 1996

Burscough Richmond, Lancashire Amateur Shield Final 2004

Dalton United, Lancashire Amateur Shield Final 2001

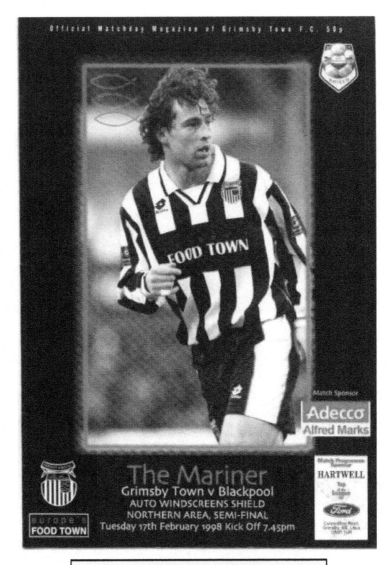

84. Grimsby Town v Blackpool

Played at **Blundell Park** on 17th February 1998

Auto Windscreens Shield Northern Area Semi-Final

Grimsby Town (0)1 [Burnett]
Blackpool 0

Attendance 8,027

It looked as if Blackpool could be on their way to Wembley in the Auto Windscreen Shield, provided they could get past a tricky Northern Area semi-final tie at Grimsby, but unfortunately Blackpool's interest in the competition ended rather disappointingly on the east coast.

I left work early to take Iain and Craig to get the supporters' coach from Bloomfield Road and we set off on the three-hour journey. It didn't seem a long journey, though, as the video of 'Fever Pitch' was shown on the coach. Even though it was about an Arsenal fan watching as the club went for the 1989 League Championship, climaxing with Michael Thomas' injury time title-winning goal at Anfield, I still enjoyed it. We got in the ground just under half an hour from kick-off, and once again there was a very good Blackpool following, with non-playing Jason Lydiate and Phil Barnes sitting in the same section as the fans. It was an excellent near-capacity crowd, no doubt helped by the fact that admission was halved to £6 for adults and £3 for children, and programmes were on sale at just 50p. In fact, such was the demand that I only just managed to get hold of a programme before they had all sold out.

Ex-Blackpool star Paul Groves was captain of a Grimsby side that had most of the play, although the only real scoring chance in a dull first half came when we had a free kick that zipped along the floor and reared up in front of goal. Grimsby goalkeeper Davison was forced to make a diving save to tip the 'shooter' over for a corner. The most interesting part of the half was when we noticed the linesman wearing what looked like ordinary shoes, and despite the full stadium, there was absolutely no atmosphere at all.

Five minutes after half time, we almost took the lead with a bizarre goal, as Davison went to kick a back-pass clear and the ball hit Junior Bent and flew back over the startled goalkeeper and also just over the bar. Banks made a superb save from a point-blank effort a quarter of an hour from time, but he was helpless two minutes later as Burnett was totally unmarked at the far post to head what proved to be the only goal of the night. I had been hoping by now that the tie would go to extra time, giving me the opportunity to see the 'sudden death' golden goal for the first time. But Blackpool never threatened an equaliser, and it ought to have been 2-0 three minutes from time when a Grimsby player somehow lost control of the ball right in front of goal when it seemed easier to score. At the final whistle, it was the Mariners' fans who were celebrating their forthcoming Northern Area final date against Burnley, conquerors of Preston by the same 1-0 margin at Turf Moor. The video on the way home was 'Con Air', starring Nicholas Cage, and in truth the videos were the only entertainment I witnessed all evening.

Grimsby went on to enjoy a season of unprecedented success, visiting Wembley twice. They won the Auto Windshields Trophy, defeating Bournemouth in the final, and for good measure attained promotion with a play-off final victory over Northampton Town. Prior to this, their best seasons had been just before the Second World War, when they reached the semi-finals of the FA Cup in both 1936 and 1939, losing narrowly 1-0 to eventual winners Arsenal in 1936. Thirty years later, it was another London side in West Ham who ended their progress in the League Cup after a quarterfinal replay, a round that was also reached in 1979-80 and 1984-5. They also lifted the inaugural Football league Group Trophy Final, forerunner of the Auto Windshields Trophy, defeating Wimbledon 3-2 in 1982.

Grimsby v Blackpool ticket and coach ticket

Wolverhampton, 1939 FA Cup Semi-Final

Northampton, 1998 Division Two Play-Off Final

Bournemouth, 1998 Auto Windscreens Final

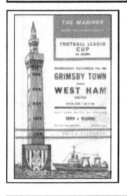

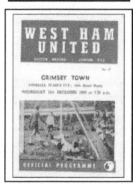

West Ham (h), Football League Cup quarterfinal 1966

West Ham (a), Football League Cup quarterfinal 1966

Wolverhampton (h), Football League Cup quarterfinal 1979

Norwich (h), Football League Cup quarterfinal 1985

Wimbledon (h), Football League Group Trophy Final 1982

Wolverhampton, League Cup quarterfinal second replay 1979

LANCASHIRE FOOTBALL ASSOCIATION
(Established 1878)

HOLLANDS AMATEUR CHALLENGE SHIELD

SEMI-FINAL TIE

SEASON 1997/98

SPONSORED BY HOLLANDS

MONDAY 23RD FEBRUARY, 1998 - KICK-OFF 7.30 P.M.
AT THE COUNTY GROUND, THURSTON ROAD, LEYLAND

ALEXANDER DREW A.F.C.

-V-

KIRKHAM & WESHAM F.C.

---

85. Kirkham and Wesham v Alexander Drew

Played at **The County Ground, Leyland** on 23rd February 1998

Lancashire Amateur Shield Semi-Final

Kirkham and Wesham (0)1 [Mendonca]
Alexander Drew 0

Attendance 200

85 – The County Ground, Leyland

On a Monday evening in late February, I set off with Craig for Kirkham's Lancashire Amateur Shield Semi-Final tie at the Lancashire FA Headquarters in Leyland against Alexander Drew. We arrived about half an hour before kick-off, and it was already apparent that there was going to be a big crowd for a game of this nature – the final attendance numbered around two hundred, of whom just over half had travelled from Rochdale with the Alexander Drew side.

The game hadn't been in progress for more than thirty seconds when Drew demonstrated their approach to it, with the first of their bookings for crude challenges on Kirkham players. Kirkham won a couple of early corners, which Whipp took, and both caused problems in the Drew defence, Best diving to put a near post header just wide from one of them. Nearly all of the play was at the Drew end of the pitch, and Mendonca had a shot blocked which resulted in chaos in the Rochdale side's defence as the ball squirmed around just out of touch of the on-rushing Kirkham attackers. Whipp needlessly lashed one ball into touch when he heard the roars of the opposing fans, wrongly assuming that there was a player on him when in truth he was in acres of space, but the half ended with Kirkham having done everything but score. It was a cold evening, so Craig and I shared a cone of chips at half-time and he had a cup of hot chocolate while I had a chicken soup – I think that this interlude made almost as much impression on Craig as the game.

Kirkham began the second half even more in control, and just seven minutes after the restart they took the lead. A ball across the box reached Mendonca, who had time to stop the ball and carefully pick his spot before driving it low into the net past Dunford. The ground was a construction site in parts, and behind us there was a high fence separating the fans from the building work. On several occasions during the first half, the ball had gone into this area and a new ball had to be used, but the first time this happened in the second half, the ball bounced out again to one of the Kirkham fans. The supporter went to throw the ball back on the pitch for the throw-in, only to see it hit a floodlight and bounce back over the fence!

As Kirkham increased the pressure, a Best cross-shot was almost turned in at the far post by Mendonca, with a defender just getting there first to put the ball behind for a corner. Shortly afterwards, Hornby had Best and Mendonca totally unmarked inside the box but chose to go on his own and the chance was wasted. Best had shown that he was a very good player, but he also had some character defects. During the first half he had kicked the ball away at a free kick, earning a harsh stare from the referee, and after he had ignored the referee's offside whistle for the second time he was correctly booked, even though Drew's Mann shouted to the referee to "just talk to him, don't book him".

Kirkham really were playing some delightful football, using both flanks to full effect, and Hornby had a header well saved before Best put in a curling shot that Dunford just managed to touch behind for a corner. As the game entered injury time, Mendonca totally mis-kicked at the far post with the goal gaping, volleying Best's cross wide, and I began to wonder if Drew were going to get a last minute reprieve due to Kirkham's inability to finish them off. As the referee somehow conjured up an amazing *ten* minutes of injury time it seemed Drew might still be in with a chance, but the final whistle blew as their last shot on goal flew wide of the post, leaving Atkinson in the Kirkham goal having not needed to make a save of note all evening. I came away from the ground having enjoyed this game more than practically any other match all season, and it certainly put the Auto Windscreen Shield semi-final at Grimsby well in the shade.

The County Ground was also the venue for the final, with Fulwood Amateurs defeating Kirkham 2-0, and also that same season the Women's Lancashire Cup Final was played there with Blackpool Wren Rovers Ladies losing 1-3 to Oldham Athletic Ladies. Kirkham went on to have success at the ground as they became regular visitors in a variety of tournaments until they made the move up from West Lancashire League football in 2007.

Leyland Motors played their West Lancashire League fixtures at the ground until the club folded four years later, and Craig eventually appeared as a player there, representing Lancashire Schools FA against a Lancashire FA side at Under 18 Level in 2007.

Lancashire Schools FA v Lancashire FA, 2007

Kirkham v Fulwood, Lancashire Shield Final 1998

Leyland Motors match programme

Blackpool v Oldham, Women's Lancashire Cup Final 1998

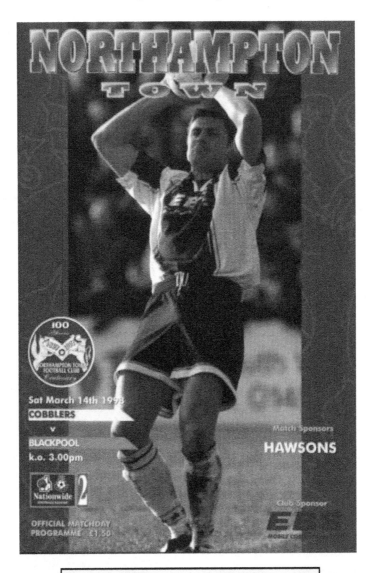

86. Northampton Town v Blackpool

Played at Sixfields Stadium on 14th March 1998

Football League Division Two

Northampton Town (1)2 [Freestone, Heggs]
Blackpool 0

Attendance 6,586

Northampton were one of the first sides to move to a new stadium in this era, leaving behind the County Ground for the purpose-built Sixfields Stadium. Town had hit the headlines in the 1960's when they surged from Division Four to Division One in five seasons, before completing the reverse journey just as quickly. They had a good FA Cup run in 1970, reaching the Fifth Round for the third time in their history before having the misfortune to come up against a George Best-inspired Manchester United. The Irish genius scored six times as United demolished their hosts **8-2**! Twenty years earlier, they had gone out 4-2 to Derby at the same stage. Town were quarterfinalists in the League Cup in both 1965 and 1967, the latter season seeing them eliminate Brighton **8-0** in a Fourth Round replay. In 1998, Northampton were on a high, having won promotion from Division Three at Wembley via the play-offs, and were on their way to a second consecutive play-off final, although this time they would lose out to Grimsby at the National Stadium.

That was still in the future, though, as Iain, Craig and myself travelled on the coach again for Blackpool's fixture at Northampton Town. Unfortunately, despite being the first people to buy tickets for the coach, we were just about the last people to get on it, and weren't able to sit together. Craig and I were on the back seat, Craig sitting next to Emma Clarke who used to run with Shelley for Blackpool and Fylde, while I was sat next to a fat smoker, and Iain was sat a few rows in front of us. We watched a short video of "Alistair McGowan's Football Backchat" before listening to commentary on the top-of-the-table clash between Manchester United and Arsenal. We stopped at Watford Gap services just as Overmars gave Arsenal a well-deserved lead, and the three of us waited on the coach listening to the final ten minutes of play. Arsenal's victory left them six points behind United but with three games in hand, and as at the end of the season they won the championship by a single point, this game was instrumental in deciding the title race. It also caused acute embarrassment for a Manchester bookmaker, who had paid out on Manchester United winning the title a month earlier! I believe he was called Done, and he well and truly was!

We arrived at Northampton an hour and a half before kick-off and walked round the compact ground, looking at the athletics track adjacent to the west stand and also browsing through the programmes that were on sale. I was interested to see a copy of Romford v Southend from 1965 that seemed very like the one I once owned which had got me interested in Romford – I considered buying it until I saw it was priced at £2.50! At a more reasonable price were several Scottish programmes, from clubs like Alloa, Albion, Berwick and Clydebank, which were for sale at seven for £1. In the end, I didn't buy any, though, and we went into the ground to be deafened by the noise from the tannoy in the pre-match build-up.

The early play was encouraging for Blackpool, with on-loan Greenacre looking good up front, but gradually we allowed Northampton to get more in control. This was assisted by our persistence in playing the long ball game – something we weren't very good at as our defenders didn't have the ability to kick the ball accurately over a long distance, and Preece seemed reluctant to take his feet off the floor when challenging for a header. On twenty-seven minutes we fell behind to a goal resulting from a Northampton long-ball, which saw Freestone get past Lydiate and run through to slide the ball under Banks. Bryan immediately had a chance to equalise, but sliced his shot well wide of Woodman's goal. Preece had a shot that was so far off target it almost went for a throw, but Bryan was alert enough to stop the ball crossing the touchline and lay it off for Brabin, who fired in a tremendous low shot that was superbly turned round the post by Woodman.

As Blackpool went through a period when we seemed able to do nothing right, the crowd spotted the suspended John Hills and injured Lee Philpott sitting near us in the stand – how we could have done with the flair that they would have brought to the side. Just before the break, Heggs was clean through on goal in a position several yards offside. Even the forward stopped, expecting the whistle, and by the time he carried on Banks was able to get down to stop his shot from twelve yards out. We ended the half with Greenacre hitting the bar from an acute angle on the left, but in truth it had been a desperately poor away performance against one of the leading sides in the table. I couldn't help feeling that Northampton were yet another team who were just there for the taking if we were to show any initiative whatsoever.

This game saw the innovation of a new league rule, whereby the *minimum* amount of injury time to be played was announced at the end of both forty-five and ninety minutes. Despite this being intended to inform the crowd, some of those round me were complaining that it was a stupid idea – doubtless these same people were in a frenzy at Walsall as the referee added on an interminable amount of stoppage time.

The second half had barely started when there was an incident that could have led to an outbreak of crowd trouble, and which served to fire up both the large Blackpool support and the team. It centred around one of the Blackpool regulars, a man in his mid forties called Dave Hall. For some reason, he started gesturing at the Northampton fans and was asked to refrain by the police. Moments later, the home fans began chanting "1-0 to Northampton Town" and he immediately stood up and gestured obscenely at them, then turned to the backs of the retreating police officers to repeat the gesture to them. Immediately two stewards walked up to him and asked him to leave, but he refused and he eventually had to be forcibly led away by police. This whole incident incensed me, for the supporter was totally in the wrong and the police and stewards had done everything possible to defuse the situation.

The increase in tempo certainly seemed to be felt on the pitch, and during the second half Blackpool won the shot count 11-1. Brabin had half of those shots, though none were on target, but at least he was prepared to have a go. Despite our dominating play, Town went 2-0 ahead just seventeen minutes from time with their sole attempt on goal during the half as Heggs was left totally unmarked six yards out and he placed his header with ease into the corner of the net. Malkin replaced the limping Greenacre and his first involvement was to head a cross goalwards, troubling Woodman more than he had been all half. Malkin also had a goalbound effort inadvertently turned over the bar by Preece, but at the final whistle it was yet another away defeat for the tangerines.

On the coach journey home we watched the video of 'The Full Monty', an excellent and very funny film, before listening to the test match action from Barbados. At least the coach journeys were proving interesting as the number of Blackpool away defeats increased.

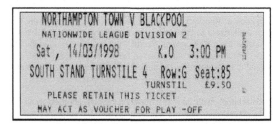

Northampton v Blackpool match ticket (above) and coach ticket (below)

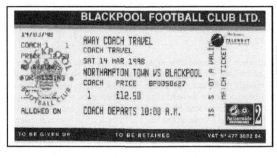

Fulham (h) Division 1, 1966 – record attendance of 24523

46

| Mansfield (h), last game at County Ground, 1994 | Swansea City, Third Division Play-Off Final, 1997 | Barnet (h), first game at Sixfields, 1994 |

| Liverpool (h), 1965-6 in Division One | Manchester United (h), FA Cup Fifth Round, 1970 | Derby County (a), FA Cup Fifth Round 1950 (pirate programme) |

| Brighton (h), Football League Cup Fourth Round, 1966 | Manchester United (h), FA Cup Fourth Round 2004 | Liverpool (a), 1965-6 in Division One |

The
North West Counties
Football League

SECOND DIVISION TROPHY
FINAL 1997-98

SQUIRES GATE
v
TETLEY WALKER

At
Skelmersdale United Football Club

Thursday 9th April 1998
Kick Off 7.30pm

---

87. Squires Gate v Tetley Walker

Played at **White Moss Park, Skelmersdale** on 9th April 1998

North West Counties Second Division Cup Final

Squires Gate 0
Tetley Walker (2)3 [Dack 2, Tandy]

Attendance 300

During a very hectic Easter period, I went to see Squires Gate play Warrington's Tetley Walker at Skelmersdale's White Moss Park ground in the final of the North West Counties Second Division Cup. The name of the ground would hopefully turn out to be a good omen for Gate, who had both a White and a Moss in their team.

A few days earlier, Craig and I had been to see a Gate home match, and when I discussed the final with one of their travel organisers, he persuaded us to go on the official coach instead of making our own way to Skelmersdale. We got on the coach at Kirkham, but I heard a few moans from some of the others on the coach about the number of stops it was making to collect people. It also called at Bamber Bridge and Leyland, with quite a long wait at each stop, but at least Craig and I were there on time. Even with the delays, we arrived at the ground with nearly half an hour to go to kick-off.

I was disappointed with the state of the ground, especially considering that Skelmersdale used to be one of the major sides in the Northern Premier League. We sat in the big stand at the side of the pitch, but could do nothing about the strong, near-arctic wind that blew across us. Nor, it appears, could Squires Gate, as they made an appalling start to this game, which was possibly the biggest in their 50-year history. After only two minutes, a cross from the left by Plant was headed in at the far post by the unmarked Dack, and seconds later Gray had to be quick to get down at the feet of one of the Tetley forwards. On five minutes, Rushton made a break for Gate and had a glorious chance to equalise, but he tried to lift the ball over the advancing Medland, failed to get sufficient height on the ball and only succeeded in lobbing the ball gently into the 'keepers outstretched arms. Gate were to pay dearly for this missed opportunity, for on eight minutes skipper Tandy hit a forty yard effort that the wind accelerated, and the ball zipped past Gray to go into the net off the underside of the crossbar. A through ball bisected the Gate defence on seventeen minutes, giving Dack the chance to make it 3-0, but he shot wide, and Gray was tested with another long-range shot, making an elaborate-looking push-over save. At the other end, Baxter forced Medland to save on a rare Gate attack as Tetley remained generally well in control. Denny put Gallagher in for a chance just before half time, but the shot was sliced well wide of the target.

With the wind behind them in the second half, Gate made more of a fight of it, although they failed to hit the target with any of their efforts. Ten minutes into the half, any hopes of a comeback were ended when Dack cut through the Squires Gate defence and slipped the ball under Gray to make it 3-0. Gate, to their credit, didn't drop their heads, and Moss stretched full-length to attempt unsuccessfully to meet a low Denny cross-come-shot. Substitute Mairs shaved the bar with a volley from the edge of the box with his first touch of the ball, but Tetley were still a danger and wasted a chance to go 4-0 ahead. Gray put a poor goal kick straight into an opponent, but he took too much time trying to lay the ball off and the chance disappeared. Dack thought he'd scored to complete his hat trick, but the 'goal' was disallowed for offside. With a quarter of an hour left, Gate's final chance went when Denny hit the foot of the post from a free kick, and they were even denied a consolation goal when Medland saved at Tomes' feet in the last minute. As the tannoy hadn't announced who was playing for each side, I asked the Tetley supporters sat in front of me who their goalscorers were. They didn't know who'd got the middle goal but they certainly knew Dack – he was their brother!

After seeing the trophy presented, I hoped we'd be back home for around ten thirty, but realised with a sinking feeling that this wasn't going to happen when I saw the others from the coach going into the social club. To make matters worse, most of them had special tickets that gave them admission to the lounge, where some sort of special evening had been organised. I had no option but to take Craig into the smoky public bar after finding out from the trip organiser that they planned to be there until closing time. It didn't turn out to be as bad as I feared, for Craig enjoyed watching people playing snooker and pool, and there was golf from the US Masters on the television. Both sets of players eventually came into the bar after their lounge function ended, and again Craig enjoyed seeing who he could recognise. At half ten, the daughter of John, one of the fans I knew from other Gate games, told us we were ready for going now, but it was another forty minutes before everyone was on the coach and we were able to set off for home. Even the second coach, which had the team and their other halves on it, left before ours did! I decided after this experience that perhaps coach travel *wasn't* always the best option.

88. Scunthorpe United v Blackpool

Played at **Glanford Park** on 18th August 1998

Worthington Cup First Round, Second Leg

Scunthorpe United (1)1 [Forrester]
Blackpool (1)1 [Bent]

Attendance 2,211

88 Scunthorpe United – Glanford Park

With Scunthorpe being one of those grounds I had yet to visit, I decided to go to the second leg of their Worthington Cup First Round tie against Blackpool at the beginning of the 1998-99 season. Scunthorpe were another of those sides who had changed grounds, moving from the Old Show Ground to a purpose-built arena out of town. A perennial lower league club, Scunthorpe did have some measure of success during the eighties and nineties via the play-offs. Their first Wembley visit in 1992 saw them lose on penalties to Blackpool, the same side who had eliminated them at the semi-final stage a year earlier, but in 1999 they defeated Leyton Orient to attain promotion to the Second Division. The Fifth Round of the FA Cup was reached in 1958 and 1970, Liverpool and Swindon respectively ending their dreams of glory.

The new Glanford Park must be one of the easiest grounds in the league to find, being just yards off the end of the motorway, and we were there in time to get a parking spot on the front row of the club's car park. Inside the ground there was very little atmosphere – it was almost like watching a pre-season friendly. A Mike Conroy goal had left Blackpool 1-0 ahead after the first leg game at Bloomfield Road a week earlier.

Blackpool took the lead on ten minutes, Malkin flicking a ball through and Brabin laying it off to Bent, who took the ball across the face of the goal before turning it back into the vacant net. We stayed comfortably in control throughout the half, and Clarkson missed a great chance for 2-0 when he deflected a goal-bound Malkin effort well wide of the post. Just as half time was due, ex-Blackpool youngster Jamie Forrester curled a beauty from the edge of the box over the diving Banks and under the bar for the equaliser. Literally seconds after the game restarted, the referee blew for the interval. During half time, the substitutes warmed up on the pitch and as I was walking back to my seat after taking Craig to the toilet, I heard a shout of 'look out' – followed a fraction of a second later by the ball parting my hair as it zipped past me from a misplaced Clark Carlisle effort!

Forrester's goal had changed the face of the game, and led to a much more interesting second half. Malkin created space and put in a shot that was turned for a corner by Clark as we continued to press, but Scunthorpe had their opportunities as well. Butler was lucky not to be sent off after pulling Gayle back when the latter had a clear run on goal with twenty minutes left, and seconds later Eyre had a goal disallowed for a foul as we started to lose our way. Conroy had time and space from a corner to settle it for us, but he continued his generally mediocre start to his Blackpool career by heading well wide. In contrast, his striking partner Malkin had possibly his best game for Blackpool since his arrival almost two years earlier.

Scunthorpe car park ticket

Blackpool, Division Four Play-Off Final, 1992

Leyton Orient, Division Three Play-Off Final, 1999

Football League XI (h), opening of Glanford Park, 1988

Torquay United(h), Play-Off Semi-Final 1988

Wrexham (h), Play-Off Semi-Final 1989

Blackpool (h), Play-Off Semi-Final 1991

Blackpool (a), Play-Off Semi-Final 1991

Scunthorpe v Blackpool ticket from 1990

Liverpool (h), FA Cup Fifth Round 1958

89. **Stoke City** v Blackpool

Played at **The Britannia Stadium** on 26th September 1998

Football League Division Two

Stoke City (0)1 [Crowe penalty]
Blackpool (2)3 [Carlisle, Aldridge 2]

Attendance 15,002

89 Stoke City – Britannia Stadium

Early in the 1998-99 season, I got the chance to visit the new home of Stoke City at the Britannia Stadium. Blackpool were in the middle of a successful league run, and had narrowly gone out of the Worthington Cup in mid-week despite heroics in goal from Steve Banks.

After Banks' superb performance at Tranmere, it was perhaps fitting that his next game would be at Stoke, home of that *other* goalkeeper called Banks for so many years. On the morning of the game, Craig played football again for Kirkham Juniors, and we set off for Stoke immediately after he had finished playing and got changed. We had a smooth journey down to Staffordshire, and parked easily at the official club car park at the Michelin factory – surprisingly, there was no charge to park there. It was a 20-minute uphill trek to the ground from there, along the banks of the canal complete with its barges and fisherman, presenting a picture postcard image of country life in England. The superb Britannia Stadium, built seemingly at the highest point in the surrounding area, was visible from a distance, and the closer we came to it, the more impressive it looked. It was a truly breathtaking sight – more so as we were out of breath after the climb to reach it! We took time to walk round the ground, looking at the 'Wall of Fame', which contained bricks inscribed with the names of Stoke supporters, and couldn't help but marvel at it. Inside, everything was just as good, and there was another superb Blackpool away following to help add to what was already a memorable day. The only thing that let the ground down was a barely audible tannoy system.

Stoke were well clear at the top of the table, and hadn't conceded a goal at home all season – that is until six minutes into this game, when Clark Carlisle dived low to head superbly past Muggleton. This was perhaps the worst thing that Blackpool could have done, for Stoke lay siege to the Blackpool goal for the next half hour, with Banks saving brilliantly from Lightbourne and also seeing further shots from Lightbourne come back off both post and bar. Bardsley, who was playing well in defence, cleared one shot off the line, before being injured and replaced by Brabin.

Brabin's first act was to slice a ball into the crowd, and this mis-control even made the referee laugh, but other than that he had a superb game, proving virtually unbeatable alongside Carlisle at the back. He showed his class on thirty-four minutes, finding Malkin on the wing, receiving the ball back from the striker, and threading his pass back through to him again on the half-way line. Malkin hurdled the sole defender who was near him and raced down the wing, before cutting back a perfect ball, which Aldridge touched home for a superb second goal. Stoke were clearly stunned at this blow, and although the scoreboard reverted back to 0-0, in actuality it was almost 3-0 when Bushell found himself clear of the defence and only a superb one-handed Muggleton save kept the ball out. (The scoreboard wasn't always biased in favour of the home side – a couple of years later, when Liverpool won **8-0** at the Britannia Stadium in the Worthington Cup, it actually showed the score as **0-9**!) The half ended with Blackpool playing with total confidence and the supporters totally outsinging their Stoke counterparts in City's biggest attendance of the season so far.

Banks began the second half with another fine save from a header, and the pattern reverted to that of the first half, with constant Stoke pressure but Blackpool working tremendously to keep them at bay. 'Pool seemed to be coping comfortably until twenty minutes from time, when the referee awarded Stoke a penalty against Hughes, and Crowe scored from the spot-kick to make it 1-2. Even so, Blackpool didn't seem particularly under pressure, and with four minutes remaining they settled matters when Aldridge rose to head the third goal and send the Stoke fans home in their thousands. To cap a fine afternoon, the crowd even got a well-deserved wave off boss Nigel Worthington! It was without doubt one of the best Blackpool away victories that I can remember seeing. The game is also regularly mentioned as Martin Aldridge's finest in a Blackpool shirt, and it brings a smile to the face to remember this action from a player who was so untimely killed in a road accident just over a year later.

As for Stoke, success wasn't too long delayed, with a Wembley success in the Auto Windscreens final in 2000 followed by promotion via the play-off finals at Cardiff two years later.

Bristol City, Auto Windscreen Shield Final 2000 at Wembley

Brentford, 2002 Division Two Play-Off Final at Cardiff

Swindon Town (h), First Game at Britannia Stadium

West Bromwich (h) – Last Game at Victoria Ground – red issue

Stoke v Blackpool ticket from 2000

West Bromwich (h) – Last Game at Victoria Ground – gold issue

90. **Macclesfield Town v Blackpool**

Played at Moss Rose on 28th December 1998

Football League Division Two

Macclesfield Town 0
Blackpool (0)1 [Howarth own goal]

Attendance 3,919

The next new ground I visited was for Blackpool's first league visit to Macclesfield at the end of 1998. Town were one of the sides who had been promoted to the Football League from the Conference, and they had been promoted instantly to the Second Division. As a non-league side, Macclesfield had been the first winners of the FA Trophy back in 1970, defeating Telford in the final. Although Telford reversed that result in 1989, Macclesfield defeated Northwich 3-1 to capture the trophy for a second time in 1996. They had come to prominence in 1968, when they reached the FA Cup Third Round as a non-league side, giving First Division Fulham a few scares before succumbing eventually 4-2. Macclesfield had won the Conference once before, but their ground was deemed 'not up to standard' and they were refused entry to the Football League. The irony of this was that while Chester's new stadium was being built, Chester City were allowed to play their home league games at Moss Rose!

We had a lengthy trip to the ground, with traffic congestion on both the motorway and during the twenty-mile journey through the Cheshire countryside. I couldn't help feeling sorry for the Chester supporters who regularly had to make this journey when their side were playing home matches at Moss Rose while the Deva Stadium was being built. We parked at the 'Three Crowns' pub, and had a good ten-minute walk from there to the ground. After being searched by the police, though for what I don't know, we finally took our places in the ground with a quarter of an hour to go until kick off.

After the delights of the Britannia Stadium, Moss Rose demonstrated a ground that was *worse* than Blackpool's. Our end was uncovered, but thankfully it wasn't raining – unfortunately, though, the sun was out and shining directly into our eyes throughout the opening half of the game. It reminded me a lot of Blackpool's New Year's Day visit to Shrewsbury in 1997, and the similarities continued with the rapport between the Blackpool fans and the home goalkeeper, which began on this occasion midway through the first half. Just before kick-off, an 'Oyston out' chant came from the Blackpool fans, who were getting sick and tired of the lack of progress at any level in the club under the chairmanship of that family. Following the heights of the Stoke victory, when Blackpool were thinking of a promotion challenge, we were now faced with a long fight to avoid relegation.

In an end-to-end opening on a quagmire of a pitch, both sides created chances, and Nowland was unlucky when he seemed to be through on goal only to have his shot blocked at the vital moment. After such a bright start, with Iain saying that there were bound to be plenty of goals in the game, the match rapidly deteriorated. Banks got down well to save one-handed midway through the first half, and Nowland just failed to get on the end of an Ormerod cross that whipped across goal, but most of the entertainment during the half came from the Macclesfield goalkeeper Ryan Price. The Blackpool fans quickly noticed that he was a look-alike for 'Rodney Trotter' off 'Only Fools and Horses' and spent much of the time chanting 'Rodney give us a dance', 'Rodney is a plonker' and other such songs. Price responded by joining in the fun, even doing a little dance, and helping liven up what was rapidly becoming an awful game.

Blackpool took the lead in bizarre fashion six minutes into the second half. The ball came across from a corner, and the next thing we knew Ormerod was turning away celebrating the goal. According to the radio, Howarth turned the ball into his own goal, although Nigel Worthington claimed Nowland had got a final touch to it. Macclesfield put some pressure on for a few minutes, but Nowland ought to have made it 2-0 on the break when he rose unchallenged at the far post but headed powerfully into the ground and for once the ball bounced up off the sodden pitch and over the bar. Malkin returned from injury to replace Garvey, and for the rest of the game Blackpool were comfortably in control. Banks got a kick in the head late in the game, and Hills was stretchered off after a dreadful challenge by Sodje, but after seven minutes injury time the referee blew his whistle to signal a successful playing end to 1998.

Telford United, 1970 FA Trophy
Final

Telford United, 1989 FA Trophy
Final

Northwich Victoria, 1996 FA
Trophy Final

Fulham (a), 1968 FA Cup Third
Round

Macclesfield v Blackpool ticket
from 1998

Hyde United, Cheshire Senior
Cup Final 1990

Dartford (a), FA Trophy Semi-
Final, 1989

Colchester United (a), FA
Trophy Semi-Final, 1992

Dartford (h), FA Trophy Semi-
Final, 1989

91. Chester City v Peterborough United

Played at **The Deva Stadium** on 13th February 1999

Football League Division Three

Chester City (1)1 [Murphy]
Peterborough United 0

Attendance 2,087

With Blackpool now embarking on a run of away games that were out of our 'travel to' area, I started to make the trips to some of the other grounds in the North that I had yet to visit. The first of these was to the Deva Stadium with Craig to watch Chester City play host to Peterborough United. Chester had moved from their Sealand Road ground in 1992, the Deva being built with one corner in Wales to make it eligible for hosting International matches. Chester's main successes had come in the Welsh Cup, with victories in 1908, 1933 and 1947, though they did have their moments in the English competitions. I first took note of them in 1965, when they led champions-elect Manchester United 1-0 at Old Trafford in the FA Cup, before two late goals saw United overturn the tables. 1975, though, was Chester's finest season. In the League Cup, they eliminated champions Leeds United 3-0 at Sealand Road in the Fourth Round, before seeing off Newcastle after a replay in the quarterfinal. In the semi-final, they drew at home with Aston Villa before losing by the odd goal in the second leg to end their hopes of a trip to Wembley.

It took just over an hour to get to Chester, and that was despite my missing the turnoff for the M56 and having to go an extra ten miles or so to get back to it! We walked round the compact ground, before going in the stand for a very good-value combined price of £11. We were hoping to see Mike Conroy in the Chester line-up, for he had been on loan there for the last couple of months, but unfortunately he had picked up a back injury and had returned to Blackpool. It was a shame, as Conroy had scored three times at Chester, and was seemingly coming back to the form that prompted Blackpool to sign him at the end of the previous season.

From our front-row stand seat, we watched an exciting spectacle unfold before us. In the first minute, Gill took advantage of hesitation in the Chester defence to put in a shot that Cutler somehow managed to get a hand to and turn away. Seconds later, at the other end, Beckett missed a glorious chance to give Chester the lead, shooting wide with only Griemink to beat. He may have had a good reason for the miss, though, for the referee immediately ordered that the ball be changed. In an action-packed opening, Andrews was through for Peterborough only to see Cutler get down to save, and with Aiston for Chester putting over some deadly crosses, a goal at one end or the other seemed only a matter of moments away. Cutler again saved well from Andrews on eight minutes, Chester's Priest volleyed just wide of the Posh goal three minutes later, and Murphy forced Griemink to save mid-way through the half, although his finish seemed weak to me. After a Peterborough penalty appeal was turned down, Andrews reacted quickest to win the ball back and put in a goalbound low shot that hit the feet of one of the players rushing back before being deflected out of danger.

As the action continued to swing from one end to the other, Chester took the lead on twenty-six minutes, a nice move ending with Murphy shooting low under Griemink. Andrews wasted the chance of an equaliser a minute later, but then came the incident which somewhat spoiled the remainder of the game. Shaun Reid (brother of Sunderland manager Peter) and Hooper clashed, with Hooper appearing to commit the initial foul, but Reid clearly elbowed Hooper in the face, and the referee had no alternative but to send him off. Hooper was yellow-carded, and ever afterwards he was booed relentlessly whenever the ball came near him. The game threatened to boil over for a while until Alsford hit a shot that was tipped for a Chester corner by Griemink and reminded everybody that there was a game of football going on.

During half time, I gave a little money to the 'Chester Fighting Fund', which was trying to keep the club afloat. The tannoy announced the crowd, a lowest of the season 2,087, and the announcer said "This really isn't good enough, you need to bring more fans into the ground". All I thought was that the people he should be having a go at were the ones sat at home watching television, *not* those fans who had made the effort to go to the match!

As the second half began, it immediately became clear that Chester were intent on wasting time. Their captain Crosby first told a ball boy off for retrieving the ball, instead of letting it run, and soon afterwards he even had a go at the linesman for the same thing. Griemink again had to get down well to save a long shot, but Chester were relying more and more on breaks as they were forced further and further backwards by the Peterborough forwards. Edwards could have equalised, but put his header over the bar with Cutler off his line, and Cutler saved well from a Butler chip. At the other end, after good work by Aiston, Griemink made an excellent diving save. Despite their numerical advantage, Peterborough rarely threatened the Chester goal, until Rennie all-but equalised on eighty-two minutes with a thirty-five yard effort that beat Cutler and hit the inside of the post, rebounding out to safety. Substitute Grazioli headed over from six yards out on eighty-five minutes, when it seemed easier to score, and there was further cause for celebration amongst the Chester fans two minutes later. Hooper lost the ball in a tackle but left his foot in on the tackler, and the ground erupted as the referee blew for the free kick. It was clear that Hooper had to go, and when the referee showed him the yellow card, followed by a red one, all of the Chester supporters cheered as if they had just won promotion. There was still time for Grazioli to put the ball into the Chester net, but he was given offside and City hung on to record their first win of 1999. The game also saw me attend my 1050th match – of which 800 had resulted in victories for one side or the other, and the other 250 had been drawn, giving a nice symmetry to the figures!

Leeds United (h), League Cup Fourth Round 1974-75

Newcastle United (h), League Cup quarterfinal replay 1974-75

Aston Villa (h), League Cup Semi-Final 1974-75

Cardiff City, Welsh Cup Semi-Final 1971

Cardiff City, Welsh Cup Semi-Final 1973

Wrexham, Welsh Cup Semi-Final 1979

Chester v Leeds League Cup ticket
from 1974 (left) and Rotherham (h)
1990 – last league fixture at
Sealand Road

Barry Town, Welsh Cup Final
1955

Cardiff City, Welsh Cup Final
1970

Cardiff City (h), Welsh Cup
Semi-Final 1969

Aston Villa (a), Football League
Cup Semi-Final 1975

Port Vale, Debenham's Cup
Final 1977

Manchester United (h), opening
of Deva Stadium 1992

Manchester United (a), FA Cup
Third Round 1965

Flint Town, 1954 Welsh Cup
Final pirate issue

Newcastle United (a), Football
League Cup quarterfinal 1974

68

92. **Halifax Town** v Hull City

Played at **The Shay** on 27th February 1999

Football League Division Three

Halifax Town 0
Hull City (0)1 [Brown]

Attendance 4,455

92 Halifax Town – The Shay

At the end of February, with Blackpool at Luton, Halifax's Shay ground became the next one I visited. Halifax made unwanted history when they became the first side to be relegated from the Football League to the Conference *twice,* following their demotion in 2001. Throughout their career, they made headlines more for their exploits towards the bottom of the table rather than for any successes, although they did pull off a major shock when they defeated Manchester City 1-0 in the FA Cup on a mud-patch Shay pitch in 1980. They reached the FA Cup Fifth round in 1933 and 1953, losing to Luton and Tottenham respectively and reached the Fourth Round of the League Cup in 1964, only to lose 7-1 to Norwich. They also reached the semi-finals of the pre-season Watney Cup competition in 1971, eliminating Manchester United along the way.

I set off with Craig after lunch for their game against Gary Brabin's Hull City, and I was a little concerned about this game as Hull fans had been involved in a lot of trouble at their recent away match at Rochdale. It seemed quiet enough around the ground though when we arrived, following a bit of a struggle to find a parking space.

After walking round the ground in the bright sunshine, Craig decided he wanted to sit in the Halifax section, and we took our seats near the half way line – with posts partially obscuring both goal areas! There was a very big Hull following on the new open terracing behind the goal to our right, and as well as Brabin another ex-Blackpool player was on show, for Halifax played Lee Martin in goal. Another ex-Blackpool player, Paul Stoneman, was named in the programme for Halifax, but was missing from the team. Just before kick-off there was a very heavy shower, and we were both glad that we'd chosen the covered section of the ground.

Since Brabin's arrival, Hull had begun to climb away from the foot of the Third Division, and they opened this game as much the better side. Alcide headed just wide from a free kick, and then Brown beat Martin to a ball that had been put across the area, seeing his shot deflected for a corner. Martin had earlier needed to punch another inswinging corner off the goal line, whereas at the other end Wilson had barely touched the ball. Brabin was involved in practically every Hull move – Blackpool sold him because manager Nigel Worthington didn't rate him, but he was in a minority at the club who felt that way. The home fans resorted to booing their own team before the game was even forty minutes old, and for me the Town tactic of hitting aimless long balls was unfortunately too reminiscent of an afternoon at Bloomfield Road to be amusing. Just before half time, a very heavy wintery shower left the pitch covered in white hailstones, and the soaked Hull fans responded brilliantly by increasing their vocal support as the deluge drove everyone else as far under cover as they could get.

During half time, I looked straight ahead over the far stand, and enjoyed the superb panoramic view of the hills surrounding the town – set off superbly by a now cloudless sky! The biggest cheer of the half from the home fans was not, surprisingly, for near neighbours Huddersfield being 1-0 behind at Wolverhampton, but instead for hated rivals Burnley being 4-0 down at *home* to Gillingham. They were to lose the game eventually 5-0, with Robert Taylor of Gillingham scoring all five goals.

The second half saw a resumption of the hailstorm, and also a resumption of Hull dominance. On fifty-three minutes they finally took the lead, with a free kick crossed into the box, which Brabin headed back across goal for Brown to head on and past Martin. The Hull fans really were 'singing in the rain' now. When Town's Thackeray went down injured, we had the ludicrous sight of two stretcher-bearers being called on by the referee and ambling slowly across the pitch to the injured defender. By the time they reached him, he was up and able to hobble the couple of yards to the touchline, at which point the two began to turn and walk back across the pitch until the referee stopped them and made them walk to the nearer touchline. It was a good job, otherwise we'd probably still have been waiting for them to get off the pitch when it was time for the match to finish! Laughable as that was, there was nothing on the pitch, though, to amuse home fans, and Brown ought to have made it 2-0 to Hull after some poor defending, but Martin got down well to save with his legs. A minute later, Brabin looked to have been wrestled to the ground in the box, yet even falling he still put in a shot that Martin was able to save. Alcide was the next to bring a save from Martin, and as the booing rang out again for Halifax's performance, fans were leaving in droves with a good quarter of an hour remaining. There were even some fathers forcing their children to leave with them, clearly against their wishes. At least they'd seen the majority of the match, unlike the Burnley fan who rang in to the 'Radio Lancashire' phone-in that night to say he had left Turf Moor in disgust at half time.

Those who left missed nothing, and for Hull Steve Wilson didn't have a serious shot to save all afternoon, although he dealt more than competently with any crosses into the box, showing superb handling skills. At the final whistle, the travelling support saluted their team, and vice-versa – it was good to see 'Brabs' in full rapport with the fans yet again.

West Bromwich Albion (h), 1971 Watney Cup Semi-Final

Manchester United (h), 1971 Watney Cup First Round

Leeds United (a), West Riding Cup Final 1972

Tottenham Hotspur (h), FA Cup Fifth Round 1953

Orgryte (h), 1976

Stoke City (h), FA Cup Fourth Round Replay 1969

Manchester United (a), League Cup Second Round 1990

Newcastle United (a), League Cup Second Round 1971

Burnley (a), Sherpa Van Trophy Northern Semi-Final, 1988

| Manchester City (h), FA Cup Third Round 1980 | Halifax v Blackpool ticket from 1989, and a draw ticket | Blackpool (a), LDV Northern Semi-Final 2004 |

93. Rotherham United v Peterborough United

Played at Millmoor on 20th March 1999

Football League Division Three

Rotherham United (0)2[Whelan, Thompson penalty]
Peterborough United (2)2 [Grazioli, Davies]

Attendance 3,979

93 Rotherham United - Millmoor

With Blackpool away at Fulham, where they crashed to a 4-0 defeat, I decided to go to another 'new' ground with Craig. However, his Saturday morning fixture with Kirkham Juniors at Poulton was put back to an 11 a.m. kick-off, so I decided to see what time he finished before choosing whether to try and get to Rotherham v Peterborough or to opt for the closer journey of Huddersfield v Birmingham. Craig finished at around noon, and as we were on the motorway at just after half twelve, I decided to go to Rotherham after all. We made the trip easily, and parked near the ground at just after 2 p.m. We sat in a nice centre-line position in the ground, at a combined cost of £10.50. The two managers were both stood in front of their dugouts just either side of us – Barry Fry of Peterborough and Ronnie Moore of Rotherham.

Rotherham had appeared in the very first final of the Football League Cup in 1961, winning 2-0 at home but losing the second leg at Aston Villa 3-0 to lose the trophy 3-2 on aggregate. That was in the tournament's pre-Wembley days, but they did have success at the National Stadium when they defeated Shrewsbury 2-1 in the 1996 Auto Windscreen Shield Final. The closest they came to top-flight football was in 1982, under the captaincy of Emlyn Hughes. They set a Football League record by winning eight league matches in one calendar month – in February 1982 – but tailed off towards the end of the season and so missed out on promotion. In the FA Cup, they twice reached the Fifth Round, in 1953 and 1968.

Rotherham made the better start to the game, but Peterborough soon began to take control with their small strikers playing some neat link-up football. It was no surprise when Giuliano Grazioli beat the offside trap on eighteen minutes and slipped the ball under Pollitt for the opening goal, but it *was* a surprise to me thirty seconds later when a bad back pass allowed Simon Davies to get to the ball first and take it round Pollitt before turning the ball into an empty net to make it 2-0. There were several clashes going off all over the pitch, with Peterborough's Hooper, the villain of the recent game at Chester, and Rotherham's Leo Fortune-West having quite a tussle. Rotherham fans were infuriated at some strange refereeing decisions, with two penalty claims being turned down – one, when Warne went flying to the ground, was either a penalty or a booking for 'diving', yet neither decision was given. The referee even gave a throw to Peterborough when both sides were lining up for a Rotherham throw-in. One fan sat near me hurled his dinner, a part-eaten sandwich wrapped in grease-proof paper, inches past Barry Fry's head and onto the pitch as he expressed his disgust.

During half time the talk in the stand around us was of the game at Peterborough earlier in the season, when Rotherham trailed 2-0 at the interval and came back to win 4-2. Further 'evidence' for this comeback came with the preceding match, when they had beaten Scarborough 4-0 at home, and as they had just completed the double by winning by the same score at Scarborough, they were hopeful that history would repeat itself with respect to the Peterborough second half performance.

Such a comeback didn't appear to be likely, though, as the half restarted with Peterborough again comfortably in control. It wasn't until ten minutes into the half that Rotherham threatened the Peterborough goal, Garner putting a header wide when well placed. The closeness of the attempt seemed to spur Rotherham on a little, and Sedgwick had a low shot superbly tipped round the post by Tyler, but on seventy minutes Grazioli thought he'd made it 3-0 only to see his 'goal' disallowed for hand ball. This proved to be a key moment in the game, for on seventy-eight minutes Rotherham at last got a goal back when Whelan headed in a cross – prompting the inaugural playing of the club's new musical accompaniment of a home goal.

Even though they were now only one goal behind, Rotherham still looked second best to Peterborough, but with just three minutes left Sedgwick went tumbling in the box and the referee awarded Rotherham a penalty. The Peterborough fans and players hotly disputed this award, but to no avail, and Steve Thompson stepped up hit the equaliser. As soon as the ball was in the net, Rotherham's substitute Roscoe tussled with Tyler for the ball in his haste to restart the game. Tempers were clearly running high on both sides, and after a foul by a Peterborough player a mass brawl erupted in the centre circle, with the Rotherham goalkeeper Pollitt racing fifty yards to get involved. Punches were clearly thrown, yet the referee took no action at all.

As tempers calmed a little and the players got back to the business of playing football, Davies almost scored the winner for Peterborough, only to stare in disbelief as Thompson somehow got back to block his shot as it was about to cross the line. The full time whistle blew on an entertaining 2-2 draw, but as the players were leaving the pitch there were more scuffles on both sides. Clearly, there was no love lost between these two sides.

Aston Villa (h), Football League
Cup Final 1961

Aston Villa (a), Football League
Cup Final 1961

Shrewsbury Town, Auto
Windscreens Shield Final 1996

Leicester City (h), FA Cup Fifth
Round 1968

Rotherham v Blackpool ticket
from 1995

Leicester City (a), FA Cup Fifth
Round Replay 1968

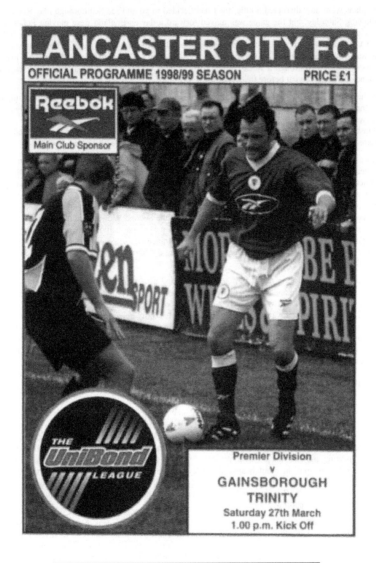

94. **Lancaster City** v Gainsborough Trinity

Played at **Giant Axe** on 27th March 1999

Unibond League Premier Division

Lancaster City 0
Gainsborough Trinity (0)1 [Price]

Attendance 205

My plans were now disrupted a little, for I had decided to go and see Scarborough play Rochdale the following Saturday, but the game was moved forward a day as England were playing Poland on the same afternoon. This change of fixtures also affected my other possible matches, at Huddersfield and Port Vale, so I was left with a blank afternoon to ponder. Ironically, one game I **could** have still gone too was Rotherham against Scunthorpe. Had I opted to go to see Huddersfield v Birmingham instead of Rotherham v Peterborough a week earlier, I would have been able to keep to my initial schedule of grounds I wanted to visit before the end of the season.

By the weekend, my desire to go to a match got the better of me. After briefly considering going to see the 'new' look Blackpool at Chesterfield in one of the few surviving 3 p.m. kick-offs, I finally opted to renew acquaintances with two of Stafford Rangers' foes from my college days, Lancaster City and Gainsborough Trinity. They were playing in a 1 p.m. kick-off at Lancaster in the Unibond League Premier Division – the equivalent of the old Northern Premier League.

Lancaster were formed in 1905, and had their most successful period in the first twenty years of their existence, including a *17-2* FA Cup victory over Appleby just before World War One. Their application to join the Football League Third Division North was rejected in 1921, but they proved their worth via the FA Cup by eliminating Third Division sides Barrow and Stockport, the eventual champions, before losing by the only goal to Northampton. Further appearances in the FA Cup competition proper became regular until the advent of the Second World War, but from 1945 onwards success became more ephemeral. City's more recent cup exploits included a Second Round tie against Notts County in 1973, a First Round FA Cup appearance in 1998 (when they led at Northampton before succumbing 2-1) and a heartbreaking last-minute 2-1 home defeat against Cambridge in the First Round in 2003.

I spent the morning trying to get through to the ground to get directions, but without success. In the end, I set off with Craig and after asking a couple of people in the city itself, we arrived twenty minutes before the kick-off time. It was a lovely sunny afternoon, and we sat in the stand looking at the castle over the far side, high above the nearby railway station. Trinity appeared to be the more dangerous side early on in the game, and worried City with corners and crosses. City goalkeeper Thornley had to be alert on more than one occasion to make smart low saves in amongst a forest of feet. Gainsborough's coloured winger Dexter was proving to be quite a handful, and on the other side Lancaster's right winger Taylor also looked a good player. As Lancaster began to get on top towards half time, one mazy run from Taylor almost produced a shot on goal, only a last ditch block by a Trinity defender keeping the ball out. At half time, though, I was quite disappointed with the fare in a goalless first forty-five minutes.

The second half began in a much brighter fashion, and a Taylor cross to Kennedy saw the striker hit the ball with the outside of his foot. The shot beat Curry quite comprehensively but hit the underside of the bar and bounced out. Relived by this let-off, Trinity took the lead on fifty-two minutes. They were awarded a free kick on the edge of the box, in a central position. Instead of shooting, as the City players were expecting, the ball was played to the left of the wall to Price, who was totally unmarked. Price had time to pick his spot, his shot beating Thornley comfortably and nestling in the corner of the net. Norbury wasted a chance for 2-0 almost immediately afterwards, lashing the ball wide when well placed inside the box. The remainder of the game saw mainly Lancaster pressure, and dangerous breakaways by Gainsborough.

Some nice footwork by Taylor created room, and his cross reached Evans in an unmarked position, but the striker finished weakly and although Curry fumbled the ball he was able to dive on it before a Lancaster player could take advantage of the slip. Norbury again missed a chance for 2-0 when he bobbled his shot wide on seventy minutes, but at the other end Taylor had another chance to equalise, only to see his shot deflected over the bar. Taylor was more and more in control on the wing, and a cross to Evans saw him put in a header that Curry somehow managed to get to and miraculously tip the ball over the bar. It was definitely a far more entertaining second half!

Thornley had to make a good save to stop a Dexter break with three minutes to go, and Taylor blasted well over at the other end in the last minute to waste another chance. In injury time, Thornley made a hash of an attempted clearance, but instead of capitalising on the chance, a poor Gainsborough cross produced a Lancaster break and Kennedy again had a shot that he put over. I was impressed with the performance of Lancaster's 'Frank le Boeuf' lookalike Jimmy Graham, and all in all I felt well entertained at the end of this game. Lancaster could count themselves a little unfortunate to have been beaten.

94 Lancaster City – Giant Axe

Celtic (h), 1995

Cambridge United (h), FA Cup
First Round 2003

Manchester City (h), 1976

Queens Park (h), 2001

Wigan Athletic (h), FA Trophy
Third Round 1975

Notts County (a), FA Cup
Second Round 1972-73

95. Scarborough v Carlisle United

Played at **The McCain Stadium** on 5th April 1999

Football League Division Three

Scarborough (1)3 [Tate 3]
Carlisle United 0

Attendance 3,604

I still wanted to go to Scarborough before the end of the season, especially as they were in danger of losing their league status. So on Easter Monday, while Blackpool were about to suffer another goalless afternoon in their 1-0 defeat at Millwall, Craig and I set off for the relegation dogfight at the foot of Division Three to see the Scarborough v Carlisle United match. Scarborough were second bottom of the table, a point ahead of bottom side Hartlepool, with Carlisle the side immediately above Scarborough. Being in trouble was something of a novelty for the Yorkshire side, for they had been regular visitors to Wembley in the 70's for FA Trophy finals. They won the competition in 1973, against Wigan, in 1976, against Stafford and in 1977, when Dagenham were defeated 2-1. They were also beaten finalists in 1975, when Matlock won the Trophy. They were promoted from the Conference to the Football League at the end of the 1980's, but a decade later they were facing the possibility of making the return journey.

We set off early, well before noon, in case there was a lot of holiday traffic around, but apart from hold-ups around York both going and returning, it wasn't as bad as I feared. On the journey we listened to Preston's 1-1 draw with Manchester City in the noon kick-off. We got to the ground at around 2:15, and I asked a stewardess where the nearest chip shop was. After a walk of some five minutes, we reached it – and found it was shut! We headed back to the ground, and once inside found that the main foodstuff on sale was chips! I should have realised this, as Scarborough play at the McCain stadium, with the 'McCain' in question being the well-known manufacturer of oven-ready chips. Even so, the chips they served us were cold!

Despite being a side fairly recently elected to the league, Scarborough still shamed sides like Blackpool with brand new stands behind each goal, and we went in the home one at a combined cost of £10.50. There was a good atmosphere in the compact ground, and a large Carlisle following contributed towards Scarborough's largest home attendance of the season. Scarborough's veteran ex-Blackpool goalkeeper Tony Parks had to get down to save a Bass shot in the first minute as the game got off to an end-to-end beginning. Carlisle fans were still entering the ground ten minutes into the game, when Parks had to go down well to save at Hopper's feet. United were creating the better chances and Tracey blazed well wide on eighteen minutes when clear on his own in the box. Five minutes later, Bass reacted angrily to a challenge and charged the Scarborough player in the back, in full view of the linesman. Despite this, he only received the yellow card.

Minutes later, 'Boro had strong appeals for a penalty turned down when Jones was felled in the box, and as the home side turned up the pressure, Roberts had a chance but shot wide. On thirty-two minutes, Scarborough took the lead when Tate turned the ball in from close range following some good work on the left. Boro were a little fortunate to retain the lead when Tracey diverted a cross straight into the midriff of Parks. The goalkeeper had the crowd and linesman laughing a few minutes later when he wagged his finger at the official, claiming he should have flagged for offside. Parks was again involved in matters when he appeared to bring Bagshaw down after an error in defence, but the referee booked the Carlisle player for diving. Parks walked back to the goal, and from the way he sniggered behind his hand to the home fans, I judged that he knew that he had got away with the offence. Carlisle were well on top as the half drew to a close, and Hopper almost equalised on the stroke of half time with a header that passed inches wide of the post.

During the interval, boxing champion Paul Ingle from Scarborough was introduced to the crowd, to great cheers - Ingle was due to meet Sheffield's World Featherweight champion Prince Naseem Hamed in a few days time. The second half began with Tracey again shooting just wide in the first minute as United carried on where they had left off. Scarborough, though, were playing well on the break, and on one such occasion Roberts brought a superb one-handed save out of Knight. The same pair were again involved a minute later, Knight again pulling off the save, and as Scarborough now began to assert their control, it was Tate who put them 2-0 in front on sixty-two minutes. Following good work between Roberts and Atkinson, the latter crossed for Tate to head powerfully past Knight.

Within a minute, Clark volleyed over for Carlisle, and they paid the penalty for this miss almost immediately when another move involving Roberts finished with Tate shooting his hat-trick goal low inside Knight's post. Further good work by Roberts almost saw Atkinson score with an overhead kick, and a header by McCauley after a Tate flick-on thumped back off the crossbar as Carlisle wilted under the onslaught of a supremely confident Scarborough side. One amusing moment saw Jones kick the corner flag before the ball as he took a corner kick, the ball barely rolling out of the quadrant.

Tate was close to a fourth goal with an opportunist long-range lob after he spotted Knight had advanced off his line, the ball eventually landing on top of the netting. Roberts, my man-of-the-match, was substituted to great applause with a quarter of an hour to go, and Tate got an equally loud reception when he was replaced by Saville with five minutes remaining, the victory now certain and survival looking a lot more secure. There was still time for Robinson to cut inside and force Knight to tip his shot over the bar, before the referee blew to end a thoroughly entertaining match.

The fight to retain that Football League place was to continue until the last kick of the season. On the final afternoon, Carlisle had to beat Plymouth, otherwise they would be relegated to the Conference. Scarborough had already finished their match, having drawn with Peterborough, and Carlisle were level 1-1 with Plymouth as that game entered injury time. Carlisle had suffered big problems only a few weeks earlier, for after selling Tony Caig to Blackpool, they had seen their loan-choice goalkeeper Knight recalled by Derby, and they needed special dispensation from the league to get goalkeeper Jimmy Glass on loan from Swindon **after** the transfer deadline had passed. As the fourth of the extra four minutes injury time drew to a close, Carlisle won a corner. Everybody went up for it, including goalkeeper Glass, and after a scramble Glass was there to score the goal that saved Carlisle and relegated Scarborough. Had that story been written down in a magazine, people would have dismissed it as being unbelievable!

Back in the Conference, Scarborough had their best ever run in the FA Cup in the 2003-4 season, reaching the Fourth Round and a home tie against Chelsea. This evoked memories of a League Cup encounter in 1989, when Scarborough drew 1-1 at Stamford Bridge and won the second leg 3-2, despite being at one time two goals down. Their 'reward' for this victory was a trip to Oldham, where they were thrashed 7-0 in a game in which Frankie Bunn scored six of the Oldham goals.

| Chelsea (h), FA Cup Fourth Round 2004 | Chelsea (a), Football League Cup Second Round 1989 | Chelsea (h), Football League Cup Second Round 1989 |

Matlock Town, 1975 FA Trophy Final

Stafford Rangers, 1976 FA Trophy Final

Dagenham, 1977 FA Trophy Final

Wolverhampton Wanderers (h), first league game 1987

Scarborough v Blackpool ticket

Enfield (a), FA Trophy quarterfinal 1982

Carlisle v Plymouth 1998-99 – The 'Glass goal' game

Leicester City (h), Football League Cup Second Round 1996

Preston North End (h), FA Cup Second Round 1975

SECOND DIVISION TROPHY
FINAL 1998-99

FLEETWOOD FREEPORT

v

WARRINGTON TOWN

At
The Anchor Ground, Darwen
(by kind permission of Darwen Football Club)

Thursday 8th April 1999
Kick Off 7.30pm

96. Fleetwood Freeport v Warrington Town

Played at **The Anchor Ground, Darwen** on 8th April 1999

North West Counties Second Division Cup Final

Fleetwood Freeport (1)2 [Johnstone penalty, Maindes]
Warrington Town (0)1 [Whitehead]

Attendance 350

For the second consecutive season, a Fylde side were involved in the North West Counties Second Division Cup Final. On the previous occasion, the final was between Squires Gate and Warrington side Tetley Walker at Skelmersdale, whereas this year's final was between Fleetwood and Warrington Town, at Darwen. Once again, Craig came with me and we had little trouble finding the ground, which was close to the 'Crown Paints' buildings I used to visit when working for a computer software house in the early 1980's. The game promised to be very close, with Fleetwood lying second and Warrington fourth in the league table, but the pitch looked to be in very poor condition, even to the extent of a slope towards the far corner. The majority of the crowd were supporting Fleetwood, and their noisy following was generating quite an atmosphere.

Fleetwood survived an early appeal for a penalty, before exerting most of the pressure. The ex-Tranmere player Mark Hughes looked very solid at the back, and Denis Walsh was causing Warrington a lot of problems on the wing. On eighteen minutes, Walsh beat the defence and was tripped in the box, leaving Keith Johnstone with the formality of slotting home the penalty to put Fleetwood ahead. There was a blow to Fleetwood, though, with Steve Murphy limping off immediately before the game restarted. His replacement, Paul Archbold, played on the right and was to enjoy an excellent evening.

Dave Nolan almost made it 2-0 with an overlap and shot that went into the side netting, whereas Barton's only troublesome moment at the other end came from a long range Ian Callaghan shot that was hit straight into his midriff. Walsh, who was already showing himself to be a class above any other player on the pitch, won one tackle on the edge of his own area and ran eighty yards before turning the ball inside to give Maindes a shooting chance. Just before half time, Barton had to dive to make an excellent tip-round save from a Tague shot that was the closest Warrington had come to scoring in the half. The Fleetwood support took to taunting the Warrington goalkeeper Thompson as the half progressed - at first this all seemed light-hearted, but soon it became a little more sinister.

Warrington's Whitehead shot wide with the first attempt of the second half, but Walsh put Town under more pressure, and his cross was only cleared to the edge of the box. Mark Hughes came charging in and volleyed the ball goalwards, Thompson just managed to dive and keep the shot out, but he couldn't hold on to the ball and it ran loose for Maindes to turn into the net via the unfortunate goalkeeper. There was some controversy about the goal, with a Fleetwood fan running on the pitch and Warrington claimed that he had interfered with Thompson, but the fan didn't come on until the ball was in the net. The Warrington fans, though, were unhappy, and claimed that this was just a continuation of the intimidation, which included Thompson's gloves being stolen by the Fleetwood fans at half time.

Whatever the arguments, nobody could deny that Fleetwood were full value for their lead, and they threatened to extend it over the next period. Thompson went down well to save one shot, and Walsh was once more causing severe problems on the right. The Fleetwood fans even started taunting Warrington by chanting "are you Blackpool in disguise?" Johnstone ought to have scored a third on seventy minutes, glancing a header just wide, as Fleetwood were content to let Warrington have as much of the ball as they wanted, then hit them on the break at lightning speed. Johnstone was again close from one such break, firing just wide, but on seventy-three minutes a Warrington player at last found room on the right and crossed for Whitehead to turn the ball into an empty net.

Warrington, despite being outplayed throughout the game, now believed that they were back in the game, and the Fleetwood fans, who had been rowdy throughout, were not too happy about this. A group of around a dozen or so of them went round to the Warrington end to stand behind the small group of Warrington fans, clearly hoping to provoke trouble, but thankfully the Warrington supporters didn't rise to the bait and eventually the Fleetwood support returned to its own end. Fleetwood weathered the Warrington pressure, and towards the end it was once again the Fylde coast side looking the more likely to score, with Houghton heading wide when Archbold was unmarked and much better placed immediately behind him. The whistle blew on an emphatic Fleetwood victory, and Dave Butler raced towards the Fleetwood fans to embrace them for their support. When the trophy was presented, each player raised it to the fans, with Walsh and Hughes getting the loudest cheers – and Butler getting multiple cheers as he kept going back to get the trophy and raise it over and over again!

A Darwen programme from their game against Blackpool
Mechanics in 1999

97. **Port Vale** v Queens Park Rangers

Played at **Vale Park** on 1st May 1999

Football League Division One

Port Vale (1)2 [Gardner, Griffiths]
Queens Park Rangers 0

Attendance 9,851

With Blackpool now all-but safe, (a draw at Wycombe actually confirmed that they couldn't be relegated) I chose the date of that last away game at Wycombe to go and see Port Vale. Technically this was not a new ground, as I had seen Stafford play there in the 1973 FA Trophy semi-final, but it would be the first occasion I had seen the home side involved in a match there.

Port Vale's greatest moment came in 1954, when they reached the FA Cup semi-final, defeating holders Blackpool along the way, before losing 2-1 to West Bromwich in the semi-final. Nearly forty years later, Albion again defeated Vale, this time at Wembley in the Second Division play-off final, but the Potteries side did achieve success in the stadium when Stockport were defeated 2-1 in the Autoglass Trophy Final that same year. Eight years later, Brentford also fell 2-1 in the same final, although this one was held at the Millennium Stadium in Cardiff. Wembley was also the stage for the Anglo-Italian Cup Final appearance against Genoa in 1996.

We used the day to visit relatives in Staffordshire, so while Barbara took the others to see Maureen and Steve, Craig and I went up to Vale Park for the crucial relegation clash against Queens Park Rangers. The two clubs were both on 44 points, the same as Bury, who occupied one of the relegation spots – and after today, Vale's only other game was at Bury in a week's time. One disappointment as far as I was concerned was that Tony Butler was absent through injury for Vale, and with him missing Iain decided not to go to the game with us. The traffic leading up to the ground was very bad, and Barbara finally dropped us off not far from her Uncle Alan's, leaving us with a ten minute walk from there. We went in the family stand, which was fairly empty at the time, but even so there were no programmes on sale – I had to ask a steward, who got me a couple from the next section.

Just before kick-off there was a minute's silence in memory of Sir Alf Ramsey, who had died during the week after a long illness. The only sound during the silence came from a police helicopter circling the ground, and of a young boy shouting to his dad to 'come and look at the helicopter'. The ground looked almost full, with the Rangers end at capacity and just odd sections of empty seats at the Vale end – the final crowd was the second biggest league attendance all season. Rangers opened brightly, and ought to have gone in front after eight minutes. A terrible back pass was easily reached by Rangers' Slade, who took the ball round Musselwhite. As he was at a tight angle, he pulled the ball back to one of the other Rangers forwards, whose shot was blocked desperately.

Musselwhite then produced a superb save just before the quarter hour mark, diving to tip over a bicycle-kick shot from Slade that looked a certain goal. There were a few occasions when a trainer was needed on the pitch, including one unusual instance when a Rangers player was hit in the face by the ball and the trainer raced on while play was still going on. The referee finally gave a bounce-up to restart the game. Rangers were proving to be very fast and effective on the break, yet it was Vale who took the lead after twenty-two minutes. A free kick reached Tankard at the far post, and he headed across goal. The ball fell to Gardner on the six-yard line, and despite appearing to get the ball stuck between his legs he managed to force it over the line and into the net. The Vale delight was even more evident a few moments later, with a 'Goal Flash' on the electronic scoreboard telling everybody that Gillingham had taken the lead against Vale's archrivals Stoke City. By the end of the afternoon, three more such flashes had told the tale of a humiliating 4-0 defeat for the Potters.

The score board then settled back to giving the score from today's game – but initially put it at 0-0, reminding me of the similarly 'forgetful' scoreboard at nearby Stoke when Blackpool were there. Vale ought to have gone 2-0 ahead shortly before half time, Foyle back-heeling to Tankard, whose low cross found Griffiths only a few yards out, but he tried to chest the ball over the line and it skimmed across him and went wide instead.

Rangers pressed strongly for the opening twenty minutes of the second half, and it took some last ditch defending and blocking from Vale to keep them out, but the killer goal came from Vale after sixty-six minutes. Griffiths headed a cross emphatically home at the near post to atone for his first-half miss. Griffiths then celebrated right in front of the Rangers supporters, who responded by trying to get at him in their fury.

Jeanne almost pulled a goal back from the restart, shooting into the side netting, but few Rangers fans noticed it as they were now involved in a running skirmish with the police. One Rangers fan raced across the pitch to try and get at the Vale fans, and mounted police had to come pitch-side to calm the trouble. Miklosko in the Rangers goal was called upon a couple of times to stop Vale going 3-0 up, one shot being a stinger from Alan Lee, but the 2-0 result was almost certainly enough to keep Vale up. As we were leaving the ground, Vale fans suddenly leapt in the air as they heard that West Bromwich had gone 1-0 ahead of Bury in the closing minutes of their delayed match – which meant that unless Vale lost by 11 clear goals at Bury, they couldn't possibly go down. There was a heavy police presence as we walked back through the town, but I didn't spot any trouble despite the rather menacing atmosphere that was around at times.

Blackpool (h), 1954 FA Cup
Fifth Round

West Bromwich Albion, 1954
FA Cup Semi-Final

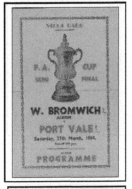

West Bromwich Albion, 1954
FA Cup Semi-Final – pirate

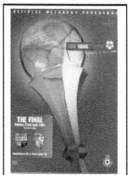

West Bromwich Albion, Second
Division Play-Off Final 1993

Stockport County, Autoglass
Trophy Final 1993

Brentford, LDV Trophy Final
2001

Genoa, Anglo-Italian Cup Final
1996

Aston Villa (h), FA Cup Fifth
Round 1960

Stoke City (a), Auto Windscreen
Semi-Final 1993

Preston North End (a), 1989
Second Division Play-Off S/F

Port Vale v Queens Park
Rangers ticket

Preston North End (h), 1989
Second Division Play-Off S/F

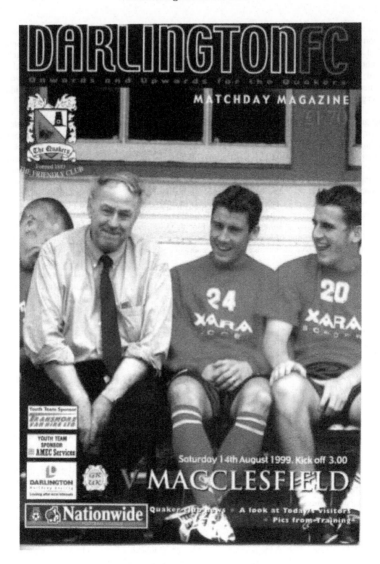

98. **Darlington** v Macclesfield Town

Played at **Feethams** on 14th August 1999

Football League Division Three

Darlington (0)3 [Gabbiadini 2, Duffield]
Macclesfield Town 0

Attendance 5,117

With Craig scheduled to play football most Saturdays throughout the 1999-2000 season, the opportunity for visiting new grounds was going to be limited. When the football fixtures had come out, I had originally pencilled in several potential new grounds – for example, Blackpool's matches at Cambridge, Wycombe, Reading and the new Wigan ground, Tranmere's game at Huddersfield, and Third Division matches between Darlington and Macclesfield and Hartlepool and newcomers Cheltenham. However, when Craig's fixtures were published, I had to cancel my plans for most of these games as I would be unable to get to them after Craig's morning match.

One game that was unaffected was Darlington's match with Macclesfield, and we set off for that one on my sister Pat's 52nd birthday, arriving at the ground around ninety minutes before kick-off. Darlington had spent most of their career in the lower reaches of the league, even losing their place for a short while when relegated to the Conference, but they did make unsuccessful Wembley appearances in the play-off finals of both 1996 and 2000. The 1999-2000 season also saw them create history by playing in the FA Cup Third Round at Aston Villa after being knocked out of the competition in the Second Round. This was because Manchester United refused to take part in the competition, choosing to play in a tournament in Brazil instead, and so their reserved Third Round place went to a ballot amongst the clubs defeated in Round Two. Darlington won the ballot, but unfortunately were beaten again in the competition at Villa Park, and this time there was to be no reprieve! They reached the Fifth Round in 1958, defeating Chelsea after a replay, only to crash out 6-1 at mighty Wolves. Darlington reached the League Cup quarterfinals in 1968, going out eventually *5-4* at Derby.

The Feethams ground adjoined the Darlington Cricket Club, and you had to walk through the cricket part to get to the turnstiles. We bought some fish and chips from "Scotty's Fish and Chip Bar" with the intention of eating them while watching some of the cricket, which was starting at 2 p.m., before going into the ground. Unfortunately, we were partially frustrated in our attempts to watch the cricket due to persistent rain, which began to fall as the game started. We managed to see five overs, with the batting side reaching 15-1 and having two catches dropped, before the rain intensified and sent the players scuttling into the pavilion. While we were waiting to go in, Craig was invited to join the Junior Quakers Club until I told the lady that we were only day visitors from Blackpool.

Entry to the ground was very cheap - £5 for myself and £3 for Craig. Even in the new stand it was only £7 and £4. The new club chairman, George Reynolds, was walking round the ground to huge cheers, accompanied by television cameras. I read in the programme that he had taken control of the club during the close season, when it looked on the verge of collapse, and his first initiative had been to drastically cut admission charges – the move paid off, with a bumper crowd of more than 5,000 inside Feethams. In fact, as the season progressed, Darlington had to make most of their fixtures all-ticket to accommodate the crowds they were now attracting.

The Macclesfield side included Ryan 'Rodney' Price, while the much-travelled ex-top division star Marco Gabbiadini led the Darlington line. After early Darlington pressure, Gabbiadini almost gave the home side the lead on ten minutes when he chased a through ball and chipped it over Price but also just over the bar. Chances were at a premium, and it was half an hour before the next sight of goal, Price getting down well to save a low Nogan shot after Gabbiadini had laid the ball back to him. At the other end, Barker headed just wide following a deep cross. Macclesfield had been the better side after the opening five minutes, but just before half-time Gabbiadini was baulked in the penalty area. Surprisingly, despite protests the referee waved play on. Gabbiadini had also been the victim of heavy treatment outside the penalty area, with the referee on one occasion showing excellent common sense by allowing play to continue while Darlington had the ball, then cautioning the offender a good two minutes later when the ball eventually went out of play. At half time, though, the score stood at a disappointing 0-0.

Darlington manager David Hodgson, the ex-Liverpool player, seemed to have woken his team up at half time, for within thirty seconds Price had to make a fine save from a Gabbiadini header, but the revival didn't last too long and soon it was all Macclesfield pressure. Baker scooped one chance over the bar, but I was surprised at how quiet their supporters were. There were a few hundred of them packed in the old stand, yet they barely raised a chant all afternoon. Neither, in truth, did the home supporters – perhaps it was because the game was so dull, but even so Blackpool fans would have been singing long before the game had even started. As Macclesfield remained on top, Collett had to dive to turn an edge-of-box shot for a corner, then he scrambled well to his near post from the flag kick to block a header from Wood. The ex-Chester player Priest almost gave Macclesfield the lead ten minutes from time when he blasted a shot inches over the bar from the edge of the box.

Without doubt, this had been a very poor quality match, yet it still managed to produce a brilliant finale. With eight minutes remaining, Gabbiadini started a move by freeing a winger, then was on hand to collect the ball as it ran loose following the cross and hit it low into Price's left hand corner. The middle-aged chap I was stood next to, who sounded more Potteries than Northeast, just yelled "Marco, Marco" as the goal went in. Gabbiadini deserved the goal, for he had shone out as the one player of true class, and less than two minutes later he found the other corner of Price's net to make it 2-0. Darlington were now on a high, and Gabbiadini was looking for his hat-trick. Darlington scored a third in injury time, but not through Marco. On this occasion ex-Blackpool player Duffield hit his shot low and under Price as the visiting defence lost interest in the game, and when the final whistle blew I could hardly believe I had seen a 3-0 game.

Chairman Reynolds was stood behind the goal, shaking the hands of Darlington supporters as they celebrated a maximum six-out-of-six point start to the league, after earlier dancing a jig in the main stand. He was certainly a happy chairman! As we left the ground, I saw a little of the cricket, with the score still only on 38-3 due to the rain interruptions before we set off back to the car.

| Plymouth Argyle, 1996 Third Division Play-Off Final | Derby County (a), Football League Cup quarterfinal 1968 | Peterborough United, 2000 Third Division Play-Off Final |

Hereford United (h), Play-Off Semi-Final 1996

Hereford United (a), Play-Off Semi-Final 1996

Millwall (h), Football League Cup Fourth Round 1967-68

Chelsea (a), FA Cup Fourth Round, 1958

Chelsea (h), FA Cup Fourth Round Replay, 1958

Aston Villa (a), FA Cup Third Round 'reprieve game' 1999

Wolverhampton Wanderers (a), FA Cup Fifth Round, 1958

Darlington v Macclesfield ticket

Wolverhampton (a), FA Cup Fifth Round, 1958 - pirate

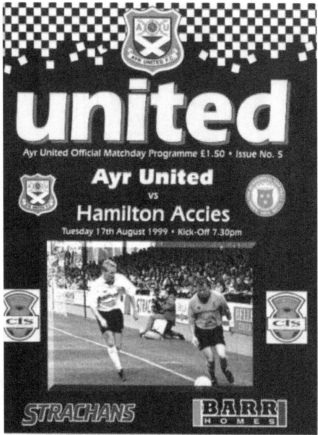

99. Ayr United v Hamilton Academical

Played at **Somerset Park** on 17th August 1999

CIS Insurance Cup Round Two

Ayr United (0)2 [Reynolds, Bone]
Hamilton Academical (0)1 [D. Henderson]

Attendance 1,789

I decided it was time to go and see some Scottish sides, such as Ayr United and Falkirk, play. I had 'supported' these sides for over thirty years, and apart from a friendly at Blackpool involving Falkirk, I had never seen them in action. Ayr United had never been one of the major sides in Scottish football, but they had achieved some minor successes. The 2001-2002 season was their finest ever, reaching the Scottish Cup semi-final and the Scottish League Cup Final, and although they lost to Celtic and Rangers respectively, they were far from disgraced. They also lost in the first two League Challenge Finals in 1990-91 and 1991-92.

My first opportunity came when I saw Ayr were due to play Hamilton at home during my fortnight off work at the end of August. So on the Tuesday afternoon, I set off for Ayr with Craig at around half two. It took us about four hours to get there, making one short stop off on the A74M. In the main, it was a reasonable journey, with the worst part being the twenty-five miles after leaving the motorway and heading for Kilmarnock. The final leg, from Kilmarnock to Ayr, was dual carriageway again, and we arrived at the ground an hour before kick-off.

We parked just past the racecourse, home of the Scottish Grand National, in a car park on Craigie Road. Ours was the only car there apart from that belonging to a police officer, who confirmed that we were okay to park there. We had a quick walk round the ground and bought programmes and a draw ticket outside – Craig was surprised when I received two Scottish pound notes in my change, as he had only ever seen pound coins before. It had been raining persistently throughout the day, and when the programme seller told us that there were no fish and chip shops around but that there was food inside the ground, I decided we'd go inside rather than walk around looking for something else. It was a shame in a way, for only a few hundred yards before we arrived at the ground we had passed a McDonalds.

The gates didn't open until about forty-five minutes before kick-off, and we went straight into the family stand, which cost us £12 in total. We had to go through a few doors, along some passages, and up several steps of stairs before we got to the stand. Even though we were the only ones in it, as there were only around a dozen people in the entire ground at that time, it wasn't easy to find a good seat. Many of the seats were reserved, but almost all had the view obscured in part by either the thick black stanchion or metal railings at the front of the stand. We finally found a couple of seats that gave us a reasonable view after first buying a hot dog and steak pie from the snacks outlet. We were so hungry we went back and got two more steak pies before the match began – and after it had started I noticed a sign for 'fish and chips' on the terracing opposite to where we sat!

The crowd seemed to be reasonably sized, with the Ayr end quite full and the stand well occupied, but there were barely fifty Hamilton fans who had bothered to make the relatively short journey. We noticed that a lot of people had CIS card-teamsheets with them, which gave the details of the actual players, but I didn't find out where they got them. I looked at half time, and also waited around for a few minutes at the end of the match to see if any had been left behind in the stand, but without any luck!

Ayr included in their side the halfback pairing of Craig and Wilson, and I was thinking that it would be nice if they were both to score. Ayr almost took the lead after two minutes, following a quickly taken free kick. The ball broke to Junior Bent lookalike Mickey Reynolds in the box, and he forced the ball past Reid but saw it go past the post. Reid made a fine save three minutes later as Ayr put on the early pressure and then he performed even better to get down and stop a low Reynolds shot from inside the box, although really Reynolds ought to have scored from the position he was in. Reynolds looked lively whenever he had the ball, and it was clear that he was a crowd favourite as his was the only name that had been chanted by the home fans. Second Division Hamilton were not out of it, and they troubled their First Division opposition on more than one occasion with their attacks. They had changed from their normal red-and-white hoops to wear light-blue and light-green hooped shirts, which produced quite a garish-looking effect.

As the half wore on, the referee seemed to take a larger part in affairs, and his constant whistling broke up any continuity that there was. McCormick for Accies fired a shot straight at Gill as the visitors began to trouble the hosts with increasing regularity, and the home crowd were becoming decidedly restless. Reynolds did get the ball past Reid in a scramble, but couldn't force it past the defender who had come back to cover on the line, and then he caused a few scares for the home fans when he raced for a through ball and ended up motionless after crashing into a camera-man. Fortunately, he was soon back in the action, seemingly none the worse for his ordeal.

At the back I noticed that Wilson was showing plenty of control on the ball, and on more than one occasion he turned and beat his opponent before delivering a controlled cross-field pass to an Ayr attacker. Ayr were playing some nice football in the build-up, but their final cross, pass or shot was often woefully off target, and the half-time whistle was met by a chorus of boos from the disgruntled home fans.

It was clear that Ayr needed to improve to avoid slipping to their third home defeat in a week, and they began the second half in a more positive frame of mind. It was annoying for Craig and I that much of the play was on the near side of the pitch, and was mainly obscured by the black railings at the front of the stand. With Ayr attacking the far goal, I had more of a chance to see Ayr's Craig play, and I noticed that he was playing the same role my Craig played for Kirkham, in that he was the lone player at the back operating in a sweeper role. As Ayr turned on the pressure, Reid made another excellent save to stop a close-range effort with ten minutes gone into the half, and Lyons created a chance for himself, but blasted the shot well over the bar as the woeful finishing of the first period continued into the second. Mid-way through the second forty-five minutes, Ayr made some substitutions, and I was surprised that Wilson was one of the players who left the pitch. The fans must have felt similarly, as they gave him an excellent reception. Ayr remained well on top, but after a goalbound shot by Davies had been blocked they fell victims to the sucker punch on the break. Hamilton quickly switched play to the other end, and from a cross Henderson hammered the ball into the ground and saw it bounce up and over Gill and nestle in the back of the net.

With only twenty minutes remaining, it left me in a slight dilemma. I wanted to see Ayr win on my first visit to see them, but I also wanted to be away from the ground as soon as possible, with a long journey in front of us. The cup format meant that all games were decided on the night, so if Ayr were to equalise, there was also the prospect of extra time and penalties to consider. I soon decided that I would rather see Ayr score and get home later if that was what had to be. Duffy almost equalised with a close range header, but Reid again performed miracles and turned the ball over the bar. It seemed that the 'keeper was going to be unbeatable, but with five minutes left Ayr at last got their reward with a marvellous equaliser. Reynolds received the ball way out on the left, and he set off for goal. He cut into the box, and from the left edge he fired in a low shot that arrowed towards the corner of the net, past the outstretched hand of the diving Reid, going into the net just inside the post. It was a goal that made the whole journey worthwhile, but when I asked Craig what he thought of it, he said he hadn't seen it! He had been sitting forward, feeling a little miserable as Hamilton were winning, and so he'd not been watching when it went in! A man near to us hadn't seen it either, for he'd left just moments before the goal. He was back seconds after the cheering had died down, with a somewhat-sheepish look on his face!

Hamilton almost went ahead again immediately, when a deflected shot by substitute Moore almost went over the head of Gill. Gill had dived for the original effort, but the goalkeeper recovered sufficiently to beat the ball away. Ayr, though, were pressing strongly for the winner, and in injury time, from their umpteenth corner of the evening, Bone finally headed the ball home after it ricocheted around the box. The nightmare thought of extra time and penalties was banished for good. At long last, the home fans even began to sing, and there was still time enough for Reynolds to almost get a third goal with a snap shot that Reid saved well. The cup sponsors, CIS, named Reid man-of-the-match and although he thoroughly deserved his award, Reynolds mustn't have been too far behind him. The full time whistle sounded moments afterwards, and there was a feeling of relief amongst the home support – they were realistic enough to realise that the drama of the last five minutes didn't compensate for the inadequacies of the previous eighty-five. We had little trouble getting away, and were finally back home shortly after one on the Wednesday morning.

Rangers, Scottish League Cup Final, 2002

Hibernian, Scottish League Cup Semi-Final, 2002

Celtic, Scottish Cup Semi-Final, 2002

Rangers, Scottish Cup Semi-Final, 2000

Rangers, Scottish Cup Semi-Final, 1973

Celtic, Scottish League Cup Semi-Final, 1969

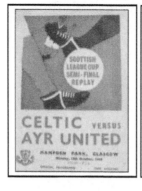

Celtic, Scottish League Cup Semi-Final replay, 1969

Nottingham Forest (h), Anglo-Scottish Semi-Final, 1976

Clyde (h), Centenary Cup Semi-Final, 1990

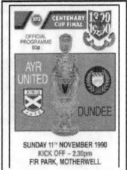

Kilmarnock (h), Ayrshire Cup Final, 1989	Kilmarnock (a), Ayrshire Cup Final, 1998	Dundee, Centenary Cup Final 1990

Dundee (h), Scottish League Cup Semi-Final 1980	Ayr v Blackpool ticket from 2001 and a draw ticket	Motherwell, Scottish League Cup Semi-Final 1950-51

100. Queen of the South v Stenhousemuir

Played at **Palmerston Park** on 11th September 1999

Scottish League Division Two

Queen of the South 0
Stenhousemuir (1)3 [Hamilton, Graham 2]

Attendance 928

The next game I was going to see was just over the Scottish border in Dumfries, to see Queen of the South against Clyde, but Craig didn't want to go after playing a particularly gruelling morning football match. The game finished in a 1-1 draw, both goals coming late on, so I didn't feel I had missed much. A week later, I had the option of trying again to go to Queen of the South v Stenhousemuir, or travelling to see Mansfield play Leyton Orient. I decided to leave it until Craig had played his morning match, but again he didn't fancy a long journey after he had finished as he had taken a couple of knocks during the game. As it would be a rush to get to Mansfield in time, I decided to go on my own to Dumfries. I also fancied the prospect of watching Stenhousemuir rather than Leyton Orient. Queen of the South hadn't achieved a great deal in their Scottish football history, with a Scottish Cup semi-final appearance in 1950 and Scottish League Cup semi-finals in 1951 and 1961 all they really had to show for their endeavours. They did contest two League Challenge Cup finals, though, losing 1-0 to Falkirk in 1997-98 before defeating Brechin 2-0 in the 2002-2003 season.

As I headed north towards Scotland, I listened to Liverpool losing yet again at home to Manchester United. It took me a shade over two hours to get to the ground, and as I arrived it began to rain quite heavily – a shame really, because it had been a nice day throughout the major part of the journey. In fact, it had been so sunny over the last few days at home that Lancashire had to leave the field in their County Championship game against Kent due to the low sun reflecting off some of the Old Trafford buildings and blinding the batsmen! I went behind the goal inside the ground, but immediately noticed the new stand to my left, which once again served to put Bloomfield Road to shame. The stadium announcer said that there may be a delay in the kick-off, as Stenhousemuir had been late arriving, but in fact the game began on time, and Stenhousemuir were even out on the pitch before the home team. Both sides contained player-managers in the number four shirts – George Rowe for Queen's and Graeme Armstrong for the visitors. Armstrong was apparently the British outfield record holder, having played in well over 1,000 matches during his career.

In a bright opening, Stenhousemuir goalkeeper Lindsay Hamilton got down well to save from Charlie Adams, while at the other end the visitors forced a few early corners. From the last of these, on twelve minutes, Ross Hamilton was totally unmarked at the near post and he headed powerfully into an empty net from just a couple of yards out. As the half progressed, the rain fell very heavily, resulting in a greasy pitch that made life difficult for the players. The cloud was so low at times that it almost obscured the hills surrounding the ground, although it did clear closer to half time. Queen of the South were generally on top, and Caldwell had two shots blocked in seconds, before Findlay forced Hamilton to make a good save on the half hour. Further Queen's pressure saw the ball ricocheting around the box without going into the net, as the elusive equaliser failed to come. Stenhousemuir were still dangerous on the break, and Banks bobbled a golden chance wide after Hamilton teed him up inside the box, before the half ended with Hillcoat in the home goal making a fine diving save low at his post from a Graham header following another corner. I went to the toilets at half time, and found that here they were perhaps worse than those at Blackpool – on a par with those at Macclesfield which I 'visited' the previous December.

The second half began with Hamilton almost scoring a second as Stenhousemuir began it as they ended the first, the youngster shooting narrowly over, but two minutes later it was 2-0. From a free kick on the left, centre half Graham had a free header and he placed it firmly into the back of the home net. Queen's rallied a little, but on sixty-three minutes their susceptibility to dead-ball kicks was shown once again as Graham again rose unchallenged to head home the third from a corner. The 'Doonhamers' fans weren't at all happy with what they were seeing, and broke out into a half-hearted round of booing – I was surprised in a way how remarkably patient they had been until then.

Hillcoat saved excellently from the 'Warriors' Watters to prevent a fourth, and at the other end Hamilton had an easier save to make as Queen's tried to mount a response. The action was still mainly at the home end, though, and Hillcoat tipped a McKinnon shot for a corner. This time, the home defence managed to deal with the crossed ball. On eighty-seven minutes, Queen's should at least have earned the consolation of a goal, but the incident summed up their afternoon. Cleeland found himself with a free header on the edge of the six-yard box, but with the whole goal to aim at he headed the ball downwards and somehow managed to hit it against Hamilton's legs, where it was cleared away to safety. Stenhousemuir immediately raced to the other end, won a corner, and once again won the header – this time the ball thumped the bar and came out. There was still time for another near miss in the home goalmouth before the final whistle blew to signal a very satisfactory away victory for Stenhousemuir that lifted them to second place in the league table.

105

Rangers, Scottish Cup Semi-Final, 1950

Rangers (h), Scottish Cup quarterfinal 1976

Rangers, Scottish League Cup Semi-Final, 1960

Manchester United (h), Lockerbie Disaster game 1989

Hibernian, Scottish League Cup Semi-Final 1950-51

Brechin City, Bells Final 2002

European Tournament featuring Queens in 1936

Preston North End (h), Floodlight Opening in 1958

First ever Queen's programme, 1933 v Beith in Reserves League

ghtning Source UK Ltd.
lton Keynes UK
OW05f1926221216
0694UK00008B/365/P